Voices
From My Past

A Memoir

Fred Cogley
with Des Berry

IRISH SPORTS PUBLISHING

Published by Irish Sports Publishing (ISP)
Unit 11, Woodview Court
Tandy's Lane
Lucan, Co Dublin
Ireland
www.irishbooksandauthors.com

First published 2012

A CIP record for this book is available from the British Library

ISBN 978-0-9563598-9-6

Printed in Ireland with Print Procedure Ltd
Typesetting, Cover Design: Jessica Maile
Photographs: Fred Cogley
Back cover image: Joe McCarthy
Front cover image: Getty Images

CONTENTS

FRED COGLEY

Fred Cogley was born in Dublin in 1934. He inherited a love of sport and journalism from his father, Mitchel, who was Sports Editor in the *Irish Independent* from 1944 to 1975. His grandfather, Fred, was also an Irish journalist, who married a young French lady in Santiago, Chile. They returned to Ireland and, while she helped to establish the Gate Theatre in Dublin, they both supported the Republican movement. In the 1920s they spent some time in the Curragh Camp and Mountjoy.

As a schoolboy in Dublin's St Mary's College, Rathmines, young Fred enjoyed a successful sporting career, gaining representative honours in rugby and cricket.

While still a schoolboy, he made his 'public' debut in 1950 as an occasional contributor to Sports Stadium, Radio Eireann's weekly sports programme, fronted by Eamonn Andrews.

A year after leaving school, in 1953, he joined the Sports Department of *The Irish Times* as a sub-editor then, in 1956, he moved to the *Evening Herald*, where he was a sub-editor and sports columnist.

Meanwhile, in 1955 he joined Harry Thuillier and Leo Nealon in introducing a new-style sports magazine programme to Irish radio, and, in 1961, he was invited to take up a position as Irish Sports Correspondent with the newly established *Sunday Telegraph*, a position he held for over 30 years.

With the arrival of TV to Ireland in 1962, he was offered a part-time contract as sports organiser/presenter/commentator and, 10 years later, when Michael O'Hehir resigned, Fred was appointed as Head of Sport, Radio and Television.

It is as a sports commentator that he is more widely known, having worked at all of Ireland's games in the home countries rugby Championship and rugby World Cups over a 40-year period.

Fred married Madeleine White in 1958, and subsequently brought four children into the world – David, Niall, Michelle and Denise. And, nowadays, he enjoys the company of seven grandchildren – Clodagh, Daragh, Roisin, Katie, Elaine, Eva and Jena.

A life-long teetotaller and member of the Pioneer Association, he maintains a keen interest in all sports and remains an enthusiastic, but regularly frustrated, golfer.

— — — — • • • • • — — — —

Back cover image of Fred Cogley:
"The earliest days of RTE... Our first, weekly magazine sports programme went on air in 1964, and this photograph was taken by Joe McCarthy in Cork, to prove that the TV signal was satisfactory at the other end of the country!"

ACKNOWLEDGMENTS

First and foremost, I must express my gratitude to Des Berry, who managed to succeed where so many had previously failed – he encouraged me to chronicle a selection of my experiences as a sports journalist and broadcaster. Like so many 'senior' former-somethings, I readily agreed to reminisce with stories of yesteryear and voices from my past. It was his idea to compile these into a book; while I would baulk at the prospect of undertaking such a daunting task. But he persisted and, through his diligence, this tome is now ready for your attention.

To Liam Hayes and Kevin MacDermot and their publishing team at ISP, I offer my sincere appreciation for the advice and consideration they have shown in the preparation and actual completion of *Voices From My Past*.

My wife, Madeleine, and the rest of our family have had to put up with me rummaging through parcels of photos, safely stored in hidden nooks and forgotten crannies. For the disruptions, my apologies and thanks for your continued patience.

I have been so fortunate to have so many dear friends and colleagues who have shared so much of my life and have made it such a joyful experience. In particular, I must refer to every member of the RTE Sports staff and those who contributed to it over the 50 years of my involvement in broadcasting, without whom it would not have been half the fun.

There is more, much more, that I have omitted but I sincerely hope that this will bring a smile and revive other enjoyable memories of voices from YOUR past.

Fred Cogley, 2012

PREFACE

The longer one lives, the more we enjoy recalling the characters who peopled our youth. Get a few older seniors swapping stories of times past and a colourful tapestry unfolds, humorous, nostalgic, sad and hilarious.

A long-time colleague, Sean Diffley, and I sat in the luxurious new Croke Park press box regaling each other with stories of the 'good old days' when we shared afternoons in the ancient East Stand in Lansdowne Road, frozen to the marrow at Internationals, or sun-drenched in the March-April springs of two early round matches in the Leinster Senior Cup.

There was much to recall. With no mobile phones and no computers, the story of the first game was aimed for the evening papers and the *Herald* and *The Mail* would sometimes furnish a 'runner' to take the first-half account and return later for the 'intro' and a short version of the second half. Occasionally, the runner would get lost or forget to come back or get diverted to something more important, whereupon there would be a race down the stairs, around the pitch in the hope that the phone in the Wanderers bar was operable.

Diffo and I had been unaware that a young journalist nearby had overheard part of our ramblings and found it interesting enough to probe further – "What was so-and-so like? What did you do at grounds where there was no phone and no press box?" In truth, it was a different world; so much has changed. The media has expanded dramatically and, in the process, there have been so many gains to compensate for the losses.

I don't think there is as much humanity in the media world. There once was room and time for the 'characters', some outrageous, some unfortunate, some remarkable and some extremely talented.

Later that young journalist, Des Berry, put it to me that he'd love to see a book incorporating my experiences gained over 60 years in radio, television and newspapers. One or two others whose ears I may have deafened, like Neil O'Donovan, encouraged me to test Des's enthusiasm. And the fruits of his labour in putting some shape on my off-the-cuff wanderings, is here presented.

I've enjoyed paying tribute to so many 'big names' of yesteryear, whose company I was privileged to share, if only for all too short a time. They deserve to be remembered with affection and I hope you enjoy this book as a tribute to some quite remarkable human beings.

Fred Cogley, 2012

Chapter I

ALI, OR NOT ALI?

Muhammad Ali came to Dublin in the summer of 1972 to face a relatively unknown journeyman professional Al 'Blue' Lewis in a non-title bout over what turned out to be eleven, lack-lustre rounds at Croke Park. It was part of a thirteen-fight schedule that took in six countries, designed to make coin following Ali's three-year suspension from boxing for refusing to be drafted into the US Army. He needed money in between losing a unanimous decision to Smokin' Joe Frazier in what came to be known as 'The Fight of the Century' at Madison Square Garden in March, 1971, and gaining revenge, also unanimously, back in New York in January, 1974. The 'Blue' Lewis bout was nothing more definitive than an exhibition match on August 1. It was as much about a promotion as a punch-up.

We all know the public persona of 'The Louisville Lip'. He was, and is, an amazing showman and one of the best, the best-known and most admired sportsmen of the 20th century. No one can take that away from him. There was a buzz of anticipation at RTE when news came through of his agreement to carry out an interview with Michael O'Hehir. I was detailed to collect Ali from the Kilternan Hotel, his base for the final preparations for the 'Blue' Lewis fight. There was a chauffeur-driven limousine hired for the rendezvous. I accompanied the driver. He was almost as excited as I was to meet the iconic Ali.

We drove in through the entrance gates of the hotel. In the near distance, we noticed what appeared to be two security-type men making their way down the avenue. On closer inspection, it was actually Muhammad Ali with another man, not known to us, who seemed to be some sort of sidekick. We stopped. I got out and walked over to Ali. There was no entourage – just the most famous man in the world and this other gentleman, who seemed to be taking notes.

I later learned this was one Drew 'Bundini' Brown, who was Ali's confidante, ally and part-time poetry collaborator from 1963 to 1981. He was, in fact, given credit for creating Ali's most famous two-liner:

"Float like a butterfly, sting like a bee.

Your hands can't hit what your eyes can't see."

I introduced myself to Ali and explained who I was.

"Hello, Mr Ali. I am Fred Cogley, from RTE. I am here to take you to your interview."

He half-dismissed me. This was fair enough, if he was engaged with his 'friend' in some sort of private or business discussion.

"Okay, just wait 'til I'm ready," were his opening words to me.

I turned on my heels and returned to stand sentinel at the car. Eventually, he walked over. I opened the door. He got in. His friend sat beside him in the back seat. I slipped into the passenger seat in the front. Back then, it was a 15-minute drive to RTE from the hotel. The traffic wasn't what it is now.

All the while, Muhammad kept coming out with things like ....

"As I walked out one autumn day ... na, na, na ... I don't like that. As I walked out one autumn night, I got a terrible fright!"

"Pearls, Champ! Pearls! Damn pearls!" his friend reacted.

All the way to RTE, Ali would recite a list of rhyming two-liners to the same over-the-top reaction from his friend, clearly the modern day equivalent of a 'Yes Man'.

"I can't wait to bruise this Al 'Blue' Lewis."

"Pearls, Champ! Pearls!"

This conversation was not for show. It was real. Serious. It wasn't meant to be humorous. The driver looked at me. I looked back at him with one singular thought in my mind.

"We've got two lunatics in the back seat."

There was absolutely no communication or chit-chat with Ali. He was in his own world, immune to our presence. It was as though there was an invisible shield between our guests and their hosts. We did not exist. And so the banter continued until we arrived at RTE.

"We are here now, gentlemen. There will be a few people to greet you. Michael O'Hehir will do your interview. He is our top sports broadcaster."

"I don't want to know anything about it," growled Ali.

"Fair enough," I said.

I opened the car door. Suddenly, a light was switched to 'on'. This heretofore rather sullen character instantly transformed into another persona. He waved to the public. He warmed up like an electric heater. It was as though he had undergone an instant personality transplant. The public image was diametrically opposed to the private man.

He was introduced to Michael O'Hehir.

"I've heard all about you. You're a famous broadcaster, aren't you?"

"Why, I don't know about that," responded Michael, immediately seduced by the charisma.

Muhammad was first-rate. He did a magnificent interview. The showman was on. The tape of that interview was lost, destroyed – whatever you want to call it – sometime after that because some wise person upstairs in RTE had it wiped. That was typical of the organisation and the disorder of the time. Sport was not exactly a priority. The budget was tight. Video-tape recording was an expensive process back then.

I collected Muhammad after the interview. He got back into the car. His friend was back at his side.

"Those were pearls, man!"

The shutters came down. Ali morphed back into the reserved, quiet, dismissive, uncommunicative individual he had been on the way to the interview. The message was clear. The show was over.

"Don't bother me! I have poetry to compose man."

"Pearls, Champ! Pearls!"

That was the experience of the driver and myself. When we left him back to the hotel, the driver turned to me.

"Could you ever have believed he could have those two sides to him?"

"No. But, I do now."

While Muhammad Ali was the greatest heavyweight of all time, and probably the most famous sportsman in history, he was also exceptional for the fact that, in my 60 years as a sports journalist and broadcaster, he was one of a select few out of the many 'greats' that I met along the road whose 'carry-on' was such an anti-climax. It left me feeling so cold.

Never meet your heroes, they say. It was certainly true on that occasion. Don't believe everything you see. Don't believe everything you hear. Sometimes it is only one half of the whole story.

Chapter 2

MADAME DESIREE 'TOTO' BANNARD-COGLEY

I was born in Dublin on June 27, 1934. I grew up in the Dublin 6 area of Rathmines, Harold's Cross and Rathgar. A flat on Kenilworth Road is the first home I remember. My mother's mother, a Mrs Costigan, died in 1937. She was, well, 'grand'. I have no memory of her as a child. I called her 'my old grandmother', as distinct from 'my young grandmother', from my Dad's side of the river.

She was an amazing, interesting woman. She was a dainty, French lady, very chic with loose, wispy, fair hair. I never remember it fading to grey. She had that natural, Gallic way of throwing on a beret and a scarf that would make her ready for any social occasion, grand or small. Her name was Madame Desiree 'Toto' Bannard-Cogley. She was the daughter of a Wexford-born mother, who married a Frenchman and lived in Paris where a certain appreciation or desire for the finer ingredients of life was nurtured.

I only really became aware of Toto when she returned from living in London. Her husband, my grandfather Fred Cogley, was a journalist. He worked for *The Freeman's Journal* and the *Irish Independent*. They had a fantastically exotic life, which was founded on a love story for the ages.

Toto was born in Paris. She went to 'The Conservatoire' there. She was quite bohemian and single-minded in her attitude. Her mother had great ideas about Toto marrying into the wealth and status of Parisian high society. She was groomed for that life from the cot.

My grandmother was one of the first women to attend The Sorbonne where some of the men displayed their dislike for this decision by throwing books and pens at her. It would appear these chauvinistic men clung more closely to the 'Fratcrnité,' loosely translated to 'brotherhood,' part of the French national motto 'Liberté (freedom), Egalité (equality), Fraternité'. She would have revelled in that sort of confrontation. Toto was a rebel. She came to Ireland on holidays, to Wexford where her mother had come from many years before. It was there she met and fell in love with the wonderfully-named Fred Cogley, a Wexford man and journalist. In later years, Toto often told me – when the time had come to pass – if I was down walking on the beach at Rosslare Strand, behind Kelly's Hotel, I would see their ghosts strolling along the seafront. It was where they used to go to while away the time.

Toto's mother didn't fancy the liaison with Fred at all. He came from the Wexford she had left behind years earlier. Clearly, this was a step back in time and a step down in status. He wasn't quite the rich, affluent man she had been planning for her daughter. Toto was interested in art, music and the theatre. Fred was a journalist and part-time pianist on the side. He used to compose music. He actually wrote the lyrics for a version of the song 'Kevin Barry' to the traditional air.

They were destined to be married.

However, Toto's mother decided this merging of minds was getting out of hand. She could see what was happening and she summoned her daughter back to Paris where she tried to marry her off to someone more suitable. Toto wasn't having any of this but her mother, in order to break up the relationship and prevent Toto from fleeing to Ireland, sent her on a cruise for her next holiday.

When Toto jumped ship at one of the ports along the route, she switched to a boat bound for South America. She ended up in Santiago, the capital city of Chile. In the meantime, she had sent a message to Ireland for Fred to get himself out to Santiago. He went without question or hesitation. They were reunited and were married there. Two years later, in 1910, my dad, Mitchel, was born in Santiago. It is one of the great love stories of any time. And to think all this happened back in the early 1900s!

Fred and Toto Cogley returned to Paris for a short while, but it was not a happy time in their lives. Toto and her mother did not get on. There was constant friction, so they came back to Ireland during World War I. Mr and Mrs Cogley walked right smack into the middle of an Irish stand-off with The British Empire. A rebellion was brewing. Because she was who she was – a revolutionary at heart – she got heavily involved in Republican fund-raising. She also developed a reputation as a singer and nurtured a deep and everlasting love of theatre.

My grandfather, Fred, wasn't involved with sport in the way that my Dad would grow to be. He was a news journalist. He was submerged into the world of politics. The struggle for Independence was a central force in his life. He wrote and carried out public relations work for the Republican movement. He was a man with semi-socialist leanings that would have been frowned on so much by the political establishment of the time.

Toto formed her own theatre club. It became a focal point for the Dublin literati back then. Painters, writers and entertainers used to frequent the club. Of course, they were all broke, or the next worst thing to it, so they would contribute to the entertainment value on whatever night they attended. She developed a very impressive membership list. When Michael Mac Liammoir – the actor, dramatist and impresario – and Hilton Edwards came to Dublin in 1927, they wanted to start a theatre of their own. They had no contacts, no nothing.

Somehow they managed to meet up with my grandmother Toto who, of course, had a long list of members. She found them very exciting as they – apparently in return – found her a source of great amusement and assistance. She became the audience builder, if you like, for the Gate Theatre. In fact, she was a founder Director of the Gate Theatre Club, as it was initially named, in 1928. To mark her contribution, she was honoured by being presented with the first membership card – Number 1.

Toto and Fred lived in an unpretentious flat on St Stephen's Green. The pair of them got very involved in the establishment of the Irish Free State. They were part of the lead-up negotiations. They used to store guns up in their attic for their 'neighbours'. The Black and Tans would make the odd appearance. They weren't very welcome. She, of course, being part-French

7

and part-Irish, had little time for the British. I remember her talking about walking up and down St Stephen's Green in the evening, calming down Eamon de Valera over the latest issue. They were right in the middle of that milieu in those days.

When the Treaty was agreed, Toto took her place on the de Valera side with Fred, who continued to be something of a public relations hound for the Republicans. He ended up in the Curragh Camp and she ended up in Mountjoy Jail for their political beliefs.

After the Irish Civil War, Fred lost any sympathy for the Republicans. When Eamon de Valera and the Fianna Fail party entered into government he saw the transition as reneging on the principles of the cause he had invested himself in.

From there, Fred made the decision to travel to England where he worked out the rest of his life and career writing for newspapers in London. Of course, Toto went with him after spending some time under lock and key. Again, she set up a small cabaret club, this time in London. Fred died from cancer in 1938. There was a swirl of suspicion around Toto as an Irish Republican residing in London. Soon after, Toto decided to return home to Dublin at the beginning of World War II. So, she came back not as an agitator, but as a shaker and mover of theatres.

On the home front, my mother, Muriel, dreaded the thought of Toto, her mother-in-law and French firebrand, living with us. When we moved to a garden flat on Effra Road, my mother didn't want a spare room for fear of Toto making it her permanent home. She was not so much intimidated as in awe of my culturally elevated grandmother. But, needs won out. Toto moved in. And what an impression she made.

I was moved into my parents' bedroom. She lived with us only for a short while. It wasn't long before she started photography as a hobby. She drove my mother mad because the bathroom was full of prints drying, hanging from the ceiling. No one could get into the bloody bathroom.

I often wondered why Mum and Dad didn't move to a bigger home because Mitchel was doing well even though he had inherited a lack of interest in money from his mother. They were a right pair. He would be just as likely to 'invest' in a bet on the 2.30 at Wincanton in Kilmartin's bookmakers on

Middle Abbey Street as put it in the kitty for a rainy day – more likely, even.

He could have been one of the two punters stood outside Kilmartin's one day when Mrs Kilmartin pulled up in a spectacular limousine, dressed chin-to-toe in a beautiful fur coat. She swept past the two 'eejits' at the door.

One looked at the other: "Ah, Jaysus, you have to admit, she's a credit to us."

Toto then started up what was known as Dublin's Little Theatre movement, through places like The Studio Theatre Club in Mount Street, in the late 1940s. Before that, she had created clubs styled as the French cabaret clubs, one of which was simply named The Cabaret Club on Harcourt Street and another in South Anne Lane, called The Leprechaun. Through these and other 'little theatres' many aspiring actors would later find a way into The Abbey or the Gate. Many had learned their trade with my grandmother. This was the basis for her existence. The theatre was her life.

Something of this gene passed on down the line to myself, manifested by my involvement in the formation of The Lantern Theatre Club in the mid-1950s, which arose out of the St Mary's College past students Musical and Dramatic Society. Alas, the flourishing of The Lantern had little to do with my good self even though I was in the opening production, 'Happy As Larry'. The demands of a semi-professional life in the arena of theatre quickly lost its attraction. Six nights a week certainly wasn't fun. It was hard work. Too hard.

Over time, the pressure from trying to combine a hectic work and social life left me exhausted. It drained my passion. I wouldn't say I was depressed. I was running on empty. Something had to give way. I decided on a visit to our family doctor, Joe Miller, who had a practice in Drimnagh. He quickly spotted the problem. He reckoned I could only do so much. I was stretched too thin. He was very straight-forward, down-to-earth. He advised me to stick to my work as a man about to make the leap of faith into marriage.

He had one question for me.

"Which gives you your income?"

"Well, my work in journalism, of course."

"Drop the drama then!"

I had seen acting as something fun and enjoyable – an outside interest to take me away from the pressure of work. My grandmother was a professional. She wanted me to fill a spot in one of her plays. It was intense and interesting but it wasn't fun at all. It was far too serious. There and then, the advice from Dr Miller gave me all the encouragement I needed to make a stand. I decided this wasn't for me. I had to bow out. It was not easy telling Toto about my decision. I gently retreated to the fun of amateur dramatics. Full stop.

Basically, it was far too great a commitment to get involved, even in a semi-professional way. It wasn't going to be my life. I was hard-pressed enough to get my journalistic career moving by writing columns and working as a sub-editor for the *Evening Herald*, after my initial stint in *The Irish Times*.

Toto continued to live out her passion for drama and performing until her death, carrying the love of theatre with her to the grave. She even named her poodle dog 'Props'. In fact, I recall one of my clearest early memories was of Toto telling me:

"Just because the dog has licked the plate doesn't mean it is clean."

I couldn't understand this. It was commonplace for her to put her plate on the floor for Props to lick it clean. I thought it was overdoing the hygiene to clean it manually as well. There was no need to do a job twice when it had been so well done the first time by Props.

Toto was an extraordinarily independent person, ebullient, lively, taking life as it came to her, not seeming to worry about the woes of tomorrow. You could say she had a laissez-faire attitude to life. I dread to think what would have happened if the many people to whom she owed money came knocking on 'our' door for it.

God love her, it would never have been an amount that would have ruined the Irish economy. It was pennies here and half-pennies there. This minor debt problem never seemed to bother her. Some people have images of their grandmothers as benevolent, aging women who only bent over to place money into their pockets. Toto was not one to pass on coins because she didn't have any money to begin with.

• • • • •

Her other son, my uncle Fergus, had been in the British Army during World

War II. He came back to Dublin from London. He was not in the best of shape. The War had taken its toll on him. He looked after the stage and lighting for Toto in The Studio Theatre Club.

To the best of my knowledge, she never salvaged anything out of the relationship with her mother. Her father was a peripheral figure to us. He was a coachman to horse and carriage in the Paris of the 1880s, according to her birth certificate.

For me, a career in journalism, and later in broadcasting, eventually married the two sets of genes between the journalism of my grandfather and father, and the theatrical nature of my grandmother, Toto. The performance element of television, and the love of sport handed down by my father, Mitchel, found a home in print, then on radio and, ultimately, television.

From my earliest days, the mystique of radio, particularly sports commentaries, had fascinated me. The excitement generated by Michael O'Hehir, the fluency of Eamonn Andrews, the style of Dr Ronnie Thornton, the new-world accent of Stewart McPherson, on BBC's Light Programme, along with the adaptability of Raymond Glendenning, the resonance of Rex Alston and the sheer mastery of English cricket by John Arlott all captured and held my attention.

None held it more beguilingly, though, than Madame Desiree 'Toto' Bannard-Cogley – a fascinating character. In her latter years, she was lucky enough to find a small home in a large house owned by the Keating family at the corner of Waterloo Road and Morehampton Road.

There may have been an artistic link there. Sean Keating, the romantic-realist painter, was known for his dramatic creations of images from The War of Independence. This would have provided common ground between them. His son, Justin, was a Labour politician, who served as the Minister for Industry and Commerce to Liam Cosgrave's Fine Gael-Labour coalition government in the mid-1970s.

Towards the end of her life, Toto lost almost all her sight as she moved into her 80s. Even so, in typically feisty form, she would occasionally go to the Gate Theatre, in the early 1960s, to hear and feel all the echoes of her past from the most sustained love of her life. It must have felt like going home.

What a pity she didn't keep a diary.

Chapter 3

MITCHEL COGLEY

Although Toto was deeply immersed in the political scene, it was the theatre all along that was her driving force. In a way, she and Fred were in on the start of so many things. They were there for the start of the State, if you like. And they were there at the start of the Gate Theatre, which was a true and lasting love.

Toto was an inspiration behind the Little Theatre movement of the 1950s and 1960s. She founded The Studio Theatre Club, which was a step-up in professional attitude compared to what had gone before at her various Cabaret Clubs. This was real theatre in microcosm. The Pike Theatre followed. It was more sophisticated, run by Alan Simpson and Carolyn Swift. It all evolved out of Toto's philosophy at a very interesting time in Irish Theatre.

She certainly wasn't a business person, as she would have readily agreed. If anything, the trail of minor debts followed her like the pigeons followed her breadcrumbs on St Stephen's Green. She had the capacity to gather people around her who were happy to work with her in lieu of payment – that may never have transpired.

The Lantern Theatre was another offshoot. Not only was Toto involved at the beginning of many movements and ventures, so too was her son, Mitchel, my father. He was involved in the start-up of *The Irish Press* in the 1930s and went on to be Sports Editor of the *Irish Independent*. I was part of the broadening of Radio Eireann at the time of censorship in the 1950s and in on the ground floor of the establishment of Radio Telifis Eireann in the 1960s and its growth thereafter.

Having seen my ambitions realised, my son, Niall, was a successor as Head of Sport at RTE before going on to experiment at the start of something totally new in Irish television – Setanta Sports – a dedicated sports channel. There has been a tree-lined, family association with the new and the novel and the establishment of different ways of doing things, mostly connected with some form of entertainment.

·····

The biggest influence on my life were my parents, Mitchel and Muriel. I was their only child. We were tightly knit. You often hear how an only child can be spoiled. What you don't hear is that you can get into a lot of trouble because there is no one else around to blame it on when windows are broken or items mysteriously go missing. But Mum had always encouraged me to develop friendships and I have been fortunate to have had so many life-long friends.

My dad, Mitchel, finished with school in Synge Street at the age of 16. He was something of a free agent, as the political activities of his parents, my grandparents, Fred and Toto, often landed them in prison. In those times, he was cared for by friends of the family for spells. This was not unusual in that traumatic period of political unrest. As a young boy he had a lively and catholic interest in sport and literature. He developed a wonderful flowing, writing style. This made his match reports and sports columns so readable. It must have been something he picked up from his father, Fred. He was very insightful, in terms of his pure appreciation of sport. He brought that to journalism. There was never anything snide or sharp or nasty in his pieces for his popular column 'Sporting Roundabout,' a weekly feature in the *Irish Independent* for over 30 years.

Mitchel had no interest at all in the politics of sport, which seems to have occupied so many people through recent years. There are those, it seems, who are in it to make a name for themselves. This was not what my father's generation was about at all. He had an understanding and respect for the players. If you didn't play well you weren't mentioned. He didn't get into the business of personal attacks. You were lauded when deserving of it. That was it. Simple. True. Honest.

He also had an ability to sum up, in a sentence, the entire kernel of a game, when it changed, how it changed, why it changed. He was always a very easy read. It was never over-complicated. There were many people, like the prolific Dave Guiney, who tried, many times, to get him to write his own memoirs. That would have been a real story, going back over the details of his parents' lives and the characters that littered his lifetime. What a tale he could have told about the people he met right through from the start to the finish of his career.

·····

In his days as the Sports Editor of the *Irish Independent*, the paper used to publish a regular feature. Any visiting sports celebrity, like American heavyweight boxer, Lee Savold, or Olympic sprinter, Harrison Dillard, or the record-breaking, Nazi-defying Jesse Owens would be taken to the *Irish Independent*.

Once there, my dad would meet them and bring them up onto the roof of the *Independent* building on Middle Abbey Street to look out over the whole of Dublin and have their photo taken with him. These became personal treasures though, sadly, most of them were lost over time. The number of famous sports men and women he met was remarkable.

The trips he went on filled him with a love of life and sport. He was in New York for the 1947 All-Ireland final in the Polo Grounds. That was a great thrill. He often recounted to us how some of the players were very nervous, even upset on the flight across the Atlantic Ocean. They had never flown before.

Their mood didn't improve when the pilot appeared in the main body of the plane to greet them and shake hands with some of the biggest names in the game from Cavan, like captain John Joe O'Reilly and Mick Higgins.

Panic spread. Eyes darted here and there. The shout went up:

"Who the hell is flying the bloody thing?"

• • • • •

On Mitchel's return from New York, he earned brownie points from my mum, Muriel, by bringing home the newest fashion accessories of the time, like the nylon stockings and the shiny plastic handbags that were such a rarity in Dublin. It was just two years after the end of World War II. There was still rationing in Ireland. I was the envy of all my school pals for the endless supply of Wrigley's chewing gum he had brought home.

I was also captivated by personal experiences generated by Mitchel's privileged position. For instance, he brought me out to Mosney when the former British and European Heavyweight champion, Lee Savold, an American by birth, was in camp for a fight. At 35, 'The Battling Bartender', as he was sometimes known, went six rounds with the legendary 'Brockton Blockbuster' Rocky Marciano, the only World Heavyweight champion to retire unbeaten, at the Convention Hall in Philadelphia in 1952. On the say-so of his manager, Bill Daly, Savold did not come out for the seventh round.

But he did come to Mosney. I was amazed to see this big, muscular giant in the flesh. He was so fast, so slick. He put on an exhibition during his training routine. Bill Daly offered the opportunity for three men to enter the ring for a round of boxing in which Savold would not throw one punch. If any of the three could land a shot on his headgear, they would earn a 'fiver'. That was a lot of money in the mid-1950s.

The first three men to the apron of the ring got in and whaled away. None of them could get near Savold as he blocked the punches or slipped them with ease. It was an incredible feat of reflex for a chap like myself to see close-up. He was a soft-spoken, gentle, deferential man.

• • • • •

Mitchel never got around to doing what I am doing – writing a memoir. Perhaps, putting my life and times down on paper acts as some measure of compensation for the stories, from his perspective, that have been lost forever.

Mitchel embraced other experiences, like helping my grandmother in the Gate Theatre where he was part of the chorus, or 'ensemble,' which, at times, backed up Michael Mac Liammoir and Hilton Edwards. I do know on one occasion, as part of a dramatic scene, Michael had spread this great cape wide in some grand gesture on a high, painstakingly erected staircase on stage. It all went well until my father trod on and tripped up in the cape. They all came tumbling down, the actors, the curtains, the cape. That was part of the tapestry of Mitchel's life. Unsurprisingly, it also marked the end of his on-stage career.

• • • • •

The influence of parents can be subtle. Dad held this pure interest in sport. The 'foreign games' ban was total anathema to him. He loved hurling. It was the greatest game as far as he was concerned. He played Gaelic football while he was at Synge Street. He played rugby because some of his friends were members at Clontarf. He never claimed any outstanding achievements, but there were numerous fun days.

On one occasion, he was playing soccer for *The Irish Press* on the old grounds in Harold's Cross, where the dog track is, in some Junior competition. He headed the winning goal. This didn't happen too often. He was so proud of it, refusing to take a shower afterwards, leaving the muddy mark on his forehead. He saw it as his trophy, proof that it had happened.

During the war years, he used to bring me around the grounds on his bicycle. Every Sunday, it was either up to Glenmalure Park – it was always called Milltown – Dalymount Park or Croke Park. For example, he would do a 'marking' for the newspaper for the first match at 'Croker'. At full-time, he would slip over to Dalymount to catch up with what was going on over there. Going to these places was what he did. Even then, it was part of my life, too.

Sometimes he would lean the bike up against a wall in the machine room at the *Irish Independent*, around by Prince's Street, from where the trucks would be driven to deliver the newspapers 'Nationwide', as Michael Ryan might say. He would leave the old two-wheeler there and wander off to some match, oftentimes with one of the famous photographers of that era, like Billy Merriman of the *Independent* or George Leitch of *The Irish Times*.

• • • • •

By 1950, the old world had disappeared. It was post-war. It was the end of one austere era, the start of another. There wasn't much of anything going on. There was a rather strange culture for the night workers, toiling right through the dark and on to sunrise. Times were hard. People took whatever chances they were given to break out or relax.

One late evening, Tim Kenealy came into the *Irish Independent* sports room, in Middle Abbey Street. My father, John D. Hickey (the esteemed Gaelic games writer) and a junior reporter were there on duty. It was a slow night. Everything had been quietly put to bed.

"Anyone in need of a few drinks?" piped Tim.

"Where would we get a drink at this hour? The pubs are closed."

"What about 'The Bona Fides'?"

This was the name given to public houses located outside the city limits. Back then it would have included The Morgue in Templeogue and The Goat in Goatstown. Every now and then, the Gardai would visit them after hours and request names and addresses. The pubs were allowed to accept customers who were 'travellers' or coming in from outside the immediate jurisdiction.

"How do we get there?"

"I'll organise a lift."

The three, my father, Kenealy and Hickey, left the junior reporter to hold the fort. A car pulled up outside the office. They piled in. The first stop was The Goat. They knocked on the door. They walked in. They had a drink or two, didn't like the atmosphere and moved on. The Morgue in Templeogue was next. They didn't like that either. They moved on again.

They were only in the door of the fourth place when Tim quietly turned to my father.

"Don't look, Mitch, but we are being followed!"

"How do you mean? Who would be interested in following us?"

"Well, listen, the last two places we were in, that little fella' over there came in behind us."

"What are you talking about, Tim?"

"Okay, wait and see! This is the fourth pub we've been in. Well, we'll move on again to the next pub. If he comes in after us, we'll confront him."

"Fair enough."

They took themselves out of the pub en route to the next place. A few minutes after they arrived, there were three knocks on the door. The secretive little man sidled into the bar and sat up at the counter.

"Right! That's it! I am going to sort this out good and proper," said Tim, who was a big man.

He walked to the counter. He tapped the mysterious man on the shoulder.

"I just want to query you."

"What's your problem?" said the stranger.

This was too much for Tim. He had seen enough. He lifted him up by the scruff of the neck and backed him up against the wall.

"You've been following us around. I want to know who the hell you are. What's your business? Why are you following us? Okay, now, no spoofing."

"Put me down. Put me down."

"What are you doing?"

"Please, please ... I'm not following you."

"You've been in all the four places we have."

"Please, please ... I'm not following you."

"Oh, so you expect us to believe it is just a coincidence, do you?"

"No, I'm, I'm, I'm…"

"Well?" barked Tim, raising his fist.

"I'm just your driver."

These were the sort of guys that made life so interesting for the rest of us.

• • • • •

In the mid-'50s, the Rackard brothers were heroes to me and, I suspect, my father. Mitchel's family came from a long line of seafarers in Wexford. My father took great pleasure in the rise of Wexford hurling to win the All-Irelands of 1954 against Galway and 1956 against Christy Ring's Cork.

I would have to go back to before my time to find the hour when the Wexford footballers were on top of the world. They were the only four-in-a-row county from 1915-1918 until Mick O'Dwyer's great Kerry side of the 1970s. The Slaneyside footballers were almost forgotten in the county after the widespread influence of the hurling team, back-boned by the Rackards Nicky, Bobby and Billy, in the 1950s. They made hurling number one in a county where football had theretofore been the foremost of the two GAA sports.

· · · · ·

When Mitchel sadly passed away in 1991, there were many warm words spoken in his absence. This is a tribute written by a good friend of his and mine, the esteemed Sean Diffley. It is an article I still turn to every now and then.

A TRIBUTE BY SEAN DIFFLEY – *Irish Independent*, November 11, 1991.

"Mitchel Cogley was the last of the old school, that happy band whose trade was tempered in the Golden Age of Sport, the innocent era that succeeded the late 19th Century birth in these islands of the cult of organised sport.

That Golden Age was the age before drugs and commercialism when gold medals and laurel wreaths were still preferred to the mere coins of the realm.

It began in the early nineteen-hundreds with its heroes ranging from Dempsey and Tunney, to Joe Louis, to Walter Hagen, who threw his British Open cheque to his caddy, to Cotton and Harry Bradshaw and Joe Carr, to Stanley Woods and Fangio.

Mitchel savoured it all, exuberantly, for almost six decades with his distinct jaunty enthusiasm about the nail-hard Mick Mackey; the solid men Joe Keohane and Dan O'Keeffe; the silken skills of Jimmy Langton and Christy Ring and the lordly Rackards. And of Tom Molony and Pat Taaffe; of Karl Mullen and Jack Kyle; of

John Joe Barry and Billy Morton and Jesse Owens.

ELECTRONIC AGE

Mitchel Cogley spanned those eras; from the Golden Age to the Electronic Age, 60 years of eager chronicling of the deeds of derring-do, riding about the world – as Hugh McIlvanney once wrote – on the public's enthusiasm 'having our privileged seats at great performances paid for by mature men's refusal to lose interest in the pleasures of the playground'.

Mitchel was the original fan with a typewriter; delighting in all sports, of every code and every kind, but careful to declare that of the lot, hurling and rugby were his favourites. Now he joins in that great playing field in the Sky, the old colleagues of the same ilk, Arthur and Paul McWeeney, W.P. Murphy, Arthur McGahon, Stanley Bergin, John D. Hickey.

Remarkably, Mitchel survived them all. That particular tote ticket lasted a long span before it was torn up. For those 60 years he had pounded out the prose, told his yarns, named his top dozen Irish sportsmen each year, a list that predated all those modern sponsored ones. He didn't write for effect but to dispense information for his fellow enthusiasts and, not infrequently, for sheer argument's sake.

But, he was never, as his friends knew well, just one dimensional. His interests were diverse. Once, aeons ago, he wanted to be an actor (and play full-back for Clontarf during the intermissions). But, as he often informed many an assembly, he eventually chose "the theatre of the absurd rather than the legitimate theatre".

Or, in the words of the old-time New York Sports Columnist, Jimmy Cannon, the friend of Hemmingway, Mitchel decided to work 'in the toy department ...'

His father was radical journalist with Wexford connections and his mother Madame Bannard-Cogley, was a noted personality in Dublin theatre, a friend of Yeats and Beckett. A brother, Fergus, became a professional actor.

It so happened that Cogley pere found it diplomatic, around the turn of the century, to absent himself temporarily from Dublin. So, it came to pass that Mitchel was born in Chile.

But, he grew up in Dublin and in his early years he helped out with the opening flourishes of the MacLiammoir-Edwards company at The Peacock and Gate.

Perhaps, Mitchel learned a lesson in theatreland, exchanging one form of penury for a slightly lesser one, vacating art with a capital 'A' with a very much lower case 'a'.

He joined The Irish Press in the early thirties where the Sports Editor, described once by Billy Morton as 'that gabby little Englishman', Joe Sherwood ruled the roost.

CROSSED RUBICON

The Cogley-Sherwood association lasted until Joe severed connections with The Irish Press by throwing a typewriter at the head of a terrified Christian Brother who had called to complain about schools GAA coverage. (The fact that Joe missed the Brother and the typewriter cannoned off the Editor, also had a bearing on his temporary departure to foreign parts.)

Around that time Mitchel crossed The Liffey and joined the Irish Independent and remained a gem in the crown of Middle Abbey Street for half a century before progressing to the euphemistically-named state of 'retirement', where he began his second coming as a busy and regular columnist, the epilogue of the distinguished career.

The stories related by and about Mitchel are legion. He was famously fluent in speech and in his writing. No one was more deadly with the dart. The flowery phrase could become deadly nightshade."

Chapter 4

MURIEL

My mother, Muriel, was the apple of my eye, as I was of hers. Muriel spent the latter part of her mother's life as both her carer and, at the same time, a full-time housewife to my father which, I gather, took some doing. She was a very glamorous woman. Apparently, her charming appearance brightened up shoppers in Rathmines and Harold's Cross.

With my mother occupied with her mother, I was too much of a handful as a growing, restless boy. I was farmed out to a nanny, Annie Walsh. She was a lovely lady and was prone to taking me on meandering walks around Rathmines. Annie would often come to a stop outside the front field of St Mary's College, on the Lower Rathmines Road, to stand and stare at the kids hopping and skipping in what seemed like endless enjoyment.

I used to look on enviously and imagine that I would one day be a part of this place when I grew to the faraway age of eight. I have Annie to thank for introducing me to St Mary's College even at that remove. Funny enough, my desire to be schooled there came to pass, but not without some delicate manoeuvrings.

The trams were a source of great fascination as they railed along Kenilworth Road, into Rathmines and on down to Lansdowne Road. In my innocence, as a seven-year-old, my great ambition was to place a rock or two on the tramline in the hope of overturning it. Thankfully, I never succeeded.

In 1941, we moved into a new flat, this time on Effra Road, down the back lane from Kenilworth Road. My parents needed more space for a growing son. The house was divided into two flats. The O'Hanlon family was upstairs and we lived on the ground floor. It had a back garden. My dad was not exactly up to getting his hands dirty in the soil. He wouldn't have known the difference between a weed and a flower. It quickly became used as a rugby pitch, a boxing ring and a long jump pit. I tore it up every chance I got.

I played cricket in the back lanes between Effra Road and Kenilworth Road with our neighbours, Stratton Sharp, from next door and the Livingstones, Ronnie and David, who frequented us every now and then. Stratton was a better batsman than a bowler, which suited both of us just fine. The centre part of the laneway was the wicket because it was nice and flat. It was the playground for many of our summer days and evenings.

There were also two garages facing each other at the end of Effra Road. We developed our three-and-in soccer skills between them. Another kid, Regis O'Keeffe, a few years older than us, used to run rings around us there.

I attended Primary School at Miss McGoldrick's on Brighton Road. It was there I experienced my first crush on a girl at the tender age of seven. Her name was Muriel Rowan. She had fair hair. She soon realised I was a fly-by-night and I wasn't going to be in her life for much longer. She quickly lost interest in me and settled on some brighter spark in the class. I have often wondered how her life turned out.

Around that time, I was invited to a birthday party on Leinster Road West for Ruth Newman, the daughter of a future *Irish Times* Editor Alec Newman, the successor to Bert Smyllie from 1954 to 1961 before he was abruptly fired because of stagnant sales of the newspapers and failed investments in Sunday and evening newspapers.

At that time, I was 'young enough to be honest' at the party. When all the cakes and sweets had been devoured, I didn't feel too well. I politely approached Mrs Newman, who noticed something was amiss.

"Would you like to use the toilet?" she asked.

"No. I think I will wait till I go home to get sick."

I did not have a great 'gra' for Irish at Primary School. In a funny way, this actually stood me in good stead in later years. My father was schooled at

Synge Street, but I had made up my mind that I wanted to go to that school with 'The Front Field' in Rathmines.

When I attended an interview at Synge Street with my father, I made a conscious decision that I wasn't going to make any impression, other than a bad one. A very nice Brother carried out the interview. He asked a few simple questions. I answered briefly. I soon saw an opening when he moved into the 'Irish' part of the interview.

"Cad is ainm duit?" he asked.

I looked blankly back at him.

This was my one chance. If I couldn't cut the mustard in Irish, the odds were I would not be admitted into the school and I would have to go somewhere else.

"Have you not been taught Irish?" he said.

"Well, I haven't really started yet," I fibbed, praying the Lord wouldn't mind too much.

"Maybe, you can come back next year when you have studied Irish."

I suppose you could say I was a 'successful failure'. I was subsequently accepted into St Mary's. Never underestimate the imagination of a seven-year-old! My father was a laid back sort of man and my mother had sown the seed of St Mary's in his mind. I was not going to his alma mater and that was alright with him.

The theatrical thread had not been totally lost on Mitchel and Muriel. I recall my father and my mother acting out one of the many scripts he had written. If he hadn't been a sports reporter he could have been involved in the theatre as a writer. This particular sketch – 'On The Bench' – was featured on The Late Late Show one night. They also used to perform it on their annual trips down to Lahinch for the South of Ireland Golf Championship. Mitchel was always working there. But they both saw it as a holiday opportunity, not that my mother would have known the difference between a golf ball and a rugby ball.

The sketch was the meeting of two people on a park bench in Dublin who had both been stood up by their respective partners. They fall into conversation on the bench and, eventually, pair off before making their exit stage left to much applause.

In the early '50s, I saw them playing it out in one of the clubs my grandmother, Toto had set up, The Leprechaun Club, in Anne's Lane, off Grafton Street, where I was brought regularly by my mother. She often gave Toto a hand with the club affairs, like making tea and supplying the occasional apple tart.

· · · · ·

Although Mum outlived Dad by five years, her health deteriorated severely in the latter part of her life. The generous and kind care of all those at The Royal Hospital in Donnybrook ensured she was able to enjoy the visits and attention of her first grandchildren in the autumn of her life. In their own ways, my parents had helped to brighten the rather dull days of the '40s, '50s and '60s. They often shared their gentle sense of humour, recounting stories, oftentimes told against themselves.

In 1959, Mum and Dad decided to move from Effra Road to Kenilworth Square, just around the corner, before downsizing to a nearby apartment beside Mount Argus Church. Dad, being Dad, decided he had 'work' to do when the day came to move. He scarpered off and left the real chores to my mother.

The furniture removal people arrived and went through the process of organising and extracting the bits and bobs. They drove our worldly goods around the corner and loaded them into the apartment on the first floor of a house on Kenilworth Square. It took the length of an afternoon to complete the process. At 5.30 in the evening, Dad returned to his new home. The move had been seamless – for him.

Two days later, Mitchel was waiting for a bus at the Rathgar crossroads. There was a small queue there. The traffic lights turned to red. A lorry slowed to a standstill just short of the lights.

This voice boomed out.

"Howya Mitch?"

My Dad looked around. The people at the bus stop pointed at the man in the lorry.

"Oh, hi there."

"You don't recognise me, do you, Mitch?"

"No. No. I don't think I do."

"I'm the fella that shifted your missus the other day!"

The people in the queue looked over at my father. Wisely, he didn't try to explain.

Chapter 5

FAIR ENOUGH

I was a student at St Mary's College junior and senior schools in Rathmines from 1942 to 1952. I was far more interested in sport than mathematics, geometry and geography, and so on and so forth. The academic angle held no interest for me. I always reckoned I would be involved in some way in sports journalism, presumably because I grew up seeing and hearing my father talk about a job he loved. As a schoolboy, I only ever thought of my interest in sport, playing games and reading the papers – the sports section, of course. Therefore, a broad education didn't mean anything to me. I presumed education fitted you out for a job. That was it.

If you were going to be a mechanic you did your apprenticeship. If you were going to be a doctor, you went to medical college. I couldn't see the connection between science and sport. I was interested in English. I did well enough in the language that it wouldn't stand in my way. I didn't spend too much time doing homework or silly things like that. Fortunately, at St Mary's, for me, it was rugby, it was basketball, it was athletics, it was cricket. It was everything I ever wanted to do and I had all the time in the world to do it. Or so it seemed.

How the years have sped by.

. . . . .

I first walked through the gates of St Mary's College in September, 1942. I was quite intimidated by my surroundings until I was introduced to Ray Joyce, who seemed to be an 'ancient' man-about-town. As it transpired, he was in the class above me. He must have been all of nine years of age.

He showed me around and made me feel at home. The boys in Junior 1, as the class was known, were very pleasant for the most part. It was a new experience for all of us, including Brendan Corcoran, Vincent O'Grady, Noel Farley and Paul Corrigan, who was the latest of 7,000 or so of the Corrigan clan to pass through those school gates.

We had our adventures in school. It was all very innocent. The most outrageous prank evolved in my later years. A string was tied onto a nail that was hammered into a water pipe. It was a lethal weapon in the wrong hands. In that class, we all had the wrong hands. And so it went. We waited for a teacher to notice the loose string. It was yanked. The nail exited the pipe and the water came spraying out, drenching the unfortunate teacher, much to our wicked delight.

If you unscrewed the seat of the desk in front of you midway through the class you could put your foot onto the rear of the desk, unknown to the boy sitting there. It would only take a minor tap to push the seat forward, sliding off its holder and leaving the victim sprawling on the floor. It was all hilarious unless, of course, you were the one on the floor.

It was also in the junior school that we first came into contact with Fr Francis Barry. He had a huge part to play in our sporting lives. He single-handedly introduced us to the magic of cricket. It instilled in me a love and understanding of the game that many people think is boring to watch and play. But, if you know the moves and strategies, like chess, it can be riveting. The drama and tension of a penalty shoot-out in football can be replicated and extended over a full day's play in a tight cricket match.

I was never a good batsman. I hadn't the patience to be a useful bat. My father used to say: "You might as well get out quickly for nothing rather than stay all day for next to nothing."

He didn't quite appreciate the very British subtleties of 'keeping your end up', as they used to say. However, I certainly enjoyed having the ball in my hand. I soon developed into quite a useful quick bowler.

Fr Barry did not require fine facilities or the proper instruments of the game like a smoothly hewn willow bat and a ball made out of cork-and-leather. He would have a wicket stump and a tennis ball and he used to bring a group of those interested to learn the basics of the game into the attic of the wash room in St Mary's. Hour after hour, we would while away the time. The left elbow was bent, the follow through was smooth, the bat brought close to the pad, playing down the line – all of the basics of the game. Later, in the back field, he set aside a couple of 'nets' where we put the lessons to the test. As I began to fall in love with the game, the names that littered international cricket started to make an impact on me.

Just after World War II, I listened to the voice of the marvellous John Arlott deliver commentaries on those fabulous Test matches for The Ashes between England and Australia and for that equally beguiling match-up between England and the West Indies. Don Bradman, Ray Lindwall, Keith Miller and Ernie Toshack were among the Aussie heroes. The West Indies had the famous Ramadhin and Valentine and 'The Three Ws' – Frank Worrell, Everton Weekes and Clyde Walcott; while England paraded stars like Len Hutton, Cyril Washbrook, The Comptons, Denis and Leslie, and my personal favourite, Alec Bedser.

· · · · ·

In 1976, Clyde Walcott, in the role of manager, led a West Indian team to a fixture against Ireland and proved himself to be a supreme diplomat as well as one of cricket's greatest players.

The day before the international match there was a welcoming dinner for the touring West Indians. A representative of the Irish Cricket Union stood up to make a speech and made an unintentional slight which could have been taken badly.

"I would like to take this opportunity to thank the ground staff. The weather hasn't been the best. But the wicket is in perfect working condition. It is a tribute to the diligence of the staff, all of whom 'worked like blacks' to get the pitch ready."

This comment was met with a stony silence. You could hear a vowel drop.

The speaker didn't intend any offence. It was just one of those remarkable oversights, born out of a different time. You might call it ignorance.

When Walcott got to his feet to reply, he made no reference to the comment passed by the previous speaker. He spoke immaculately all the way to the end of his speech whereupon he delivered a timely response.

"Every day is a proud day to play for your country and I can guarantee each and every one of the West Indian team will 'play like blacks' tomorrow."

He defused the situation with such class. The whole room erupted in laughter, all except the previous speaker who was quickly made aware of his slip up.

• • • • •

I had occasion to do the television commentary for an Ireland-West Indies international at the Leinster Cricket Ground in Rathmines. It was where I had played with St Mary's. In order to have an idea of identifying the players when they were fielding – it was okay when they are batting because the players were listed in order from the opening batsmen on – I approached Clyde.

He was a lovely man. He began pointing out the players, passing on their names and detailing where they might be in the field. There was a set of three players standing out on the pitch, having a bit of a chin-wag.

"Those three out there. On the left is Gordon Greenidge, in the middle is Viv Richards and the 'fair man' on the right is ..."

Immediately, I looked at him in an unknowing way.

"What do you mean fair?" I said.

"Oh, yes. We would classify the light browns as fair in the West Indies."

Oh, right. Fair enough.

Chapter 6

JACK KYLE

When France came over after the end of World War II to play Ireland in the Five Nations at Lansdowne Road in 1947, we, a naive cluster of teenagers, took a sympathetic view on how much they had gone through. We had this image of a team of emaciated, physical wrecks and how Ireland were going to steamroll them.

The next thing, these two giant second-row forwards – Robert Soro and Alban Moga – emerged like two hulking figures out of the dressing rooms. They were behemoths. It wasn't just their size that made them intimidating. They brought an attitude that matched. They made mincemeat out of the Irish forwards. It must have been the day we learned never to pity a French man.

We youthful spectators had a very good way of clearing space for ourselves, particularly at Lansdowne, which had a grass hill at the south end. There was no terracing there in the late 1940s. We used to meet as a group of boisterous youngsters. You could call it 'rough-housing'. When the hill started to fill up, we would stake out our area and push one another about the place. The adults steered clear of us. They gave us our space. If anyone invaded the area, the shoving would begin again. It was our version of a very territorial army.

Two weeks after the French match, I remember with relish how we beat England 22-0 at Lansdowne Road. Nim Hall was the English out-half dandy and was billed as the greatest thing since the invention of the motor car. He came with all the cocksure confidence of a champion and left crushed like a vine of grapes beneath stampeding Irish feet. Every time the English worked some space, Hall was nailed and milled by the Irish flanker, Don Hingerty, who was a very good wing forward from the UCD club. He was as fit as a flea and harder than a block of concrete. Poor Nim Hall didn't have the game of his life that day. Hingerty saw to that. That was my clearest early memory of seeing Ireland play at Lansdowne Road.

•••••

Jack Kyle was the Brian O'Driscoll of those days, maybe even more so. As great footballers, and as great sports people, we saw so little of them back then. We tended to know of them from what was written rather than what was seen. There was sparse radio coverage and certainly no television in the late 1940s. The legend of Jack Kyle grew rapidly.

The writing tended to be somewhat more flowery then than now. The descriptions of someone like Jack Kyle created a myth that he was almost a supernatural figure on the pitch, ghosting through defences that were powerless to stop him. There was an imaginary charisma about him as well, which was totally at variance with the sort of personality he was in the flesh. He was a marvellous individual, a shy man. The image propagated was of a super-human player when he was really a super-human person.

As a kid, watching Jack Kyle play live and about to win the Triple Crown and Grand Slam in 1948, it was as if he was the only one on the pitch. He usually tended to play well. There were those who said he didn't always bring his three-quarter line into the game. But that was probably because he was kicking for position. Don't forget, in those days, you could kick directly into touch from anywhere on the field and gain ground.

•••••

It took the brilliance and dedication of a band of remarkable rugby men to bridge the 61-year gap between Ireland's first and second Grand Slams. I was there for the first in Belfast in 1948 and, in my retirement, enjoyed every tackle, pass and kick at The Millennium Stadium in 2009, watching the coverage on television in the comfort of my own home. How I winced and wondered as Stephen Jones walloped that penalty towards the Irish posts. The Welsh had made a habit out of tearing up the most romantic of Irish scripts when it came to the oval ball game. The kick that could have broken hearts dropped short. At last, it was our time to wade in the glory. What a moment it was when Brian O'Driscoll took time out to accept the congratulations from Jack Kyle amid all the bedlam that engulfed the stadium in Cardiff. Two heroes bonded by time and the simple gesture of one handshake.

What an occasion it was in The Principality, and what a contrast to the Ravenhill of 1948. Northern Ireland was still recovering from the war years, 1939-1945. But, on March 13, 1948, there was only one thing on our minds – Ireland versus Wales. The Triple Crown. That's right! The Triple Crown. The Grand Slam was a relatively new and less enthralling notion back then.

I made it there as a 14-year-old schoolboy. I travelled up on the Enterprise Train with a few buddies – Tom Graham, Ken Sparrow, both since sadly deceased, and Tony 'Rocky' Woodhouse. There was a lot of security about. The train was stopped several times.

Once we made it across the border, the train was searched by Northern Ireland customs officials. Some of the brave hearts, or simple souls, depending on your perspective, were quite willing to take on these officials – verbally – which wasn't a very clever approach. I had visions of us ending up in the clink or, worse still, missing the game.

One of the smart-alecs in our carriage, who must have been convinced it was funny, had a bag of sandwiches hidden underneath his seat. As the customs officers came through requesting passengers to declare goods, a big eight-foot tall 'messer' with a few drinks on board, of course, stood up and leaned towards one of the officials.

"You missed the bomb," he said.

"What are you talking about?"

"It's under there," he said, pointing at the bag under the seat.

"Show it to me! Pick it up!"

Yer man bent his long back down to carefully pick up the bag. He turned towards the customs officer with all the slow-motion speed of a snail and suddenly thrust the bag, opened out, towards the official.

"Gotcha! Gotcha!" he squealed.

All the lads were convulsing in laughter. We were that giddy about the match. So childish. The customs officer was utterly disgusted. He shot back a stare of simply profound meaning.

"Would you grow up!" he said, as he wheeled away from the group of guffawing lads on their way to what would, for so long, be the greatest day in the history of Irish rugby. In those tense times, it was never wise to test the patience of the officers of the law. We were lucky the entire train wasn't evacuated. Some joke that would have been!

It poured rain as we arrived at Donegall Square. My first impression was of the trolley buses. We didn't have them in Dublin. We had trams. These were trams with rubber wheels that could enable the driver to weave in and out of traffic. They moved in eerie silence except for the click-clack of the overhead wires.

I remember being so impressed by the bus service for the supporters taking people out to Ravenhill. We were driven there surprisingly efficiently. It was well-organised. We walked the last segment of the journey and picked out our spot at the ground – jokingly referred to as terraces. In fact, they were banks of black cinder carpeting the unenclosed areas, but certainly good enough for our quartet of 'boyos'.

It was a God-awful day. The rain had been bucketing down. But it also turned into the greatest day for 61 years. We ended up just behind the dead-ball line where Barney Mullan got the first Irish try. I can still see it so well. I have that vision of him speeding towards us, screaming my head off, knowing he was going to make it. He plunged over right in front of us – no more than ten yards away. It was the closest I would ever get to a Triple Crown try.

I didn't see much of prop Jack 'JC' Daly's clinching try at the far end. It was on the same side, but moving away from us. I just remember a group of players going towards the far end of the ground and the crowd erupting with wild excitement to confirm the Triple Crown was ours.

Strange, it wasn't the Grand Slam that was the be-all back then. It wasn't in vogue in those days and had no profile to compare with the Triple Crown, even though France had been beaten in the opening Test match of the Championship at Stade Yves du Manoir in Paris on New Year's Day for what was the first-leg of the Grand Slam, with tries from wing Barney Mullan, centre Paddy Reid and flanker Jim McCarthy. The French were almost dismissed even though they had given us 'what for' at Lansdowne Road the previous year when their wing Jean Lassegue sprinted for two tries. These 'upstarts' were quickly shown the error of their ways the following January.

Despite this, the Triple Crown was the thing to win. There was nothing to compare with beating your nearest and dearest neighbours, England, Scotland and Wales. For many years, you could win The Championship, but it didn't mean all that much. The same went for the Grand Slam. It was all about the Triple Crown.

I guess this was partly due to that fact that the French had been excluded from the Championship for alleged breaches of rugby's amateur standards in 1931. They were to return to the Five Nations in 1939. Sadly, the World War wrecked that plan. They made their return to the competition in 1947. Strange as it now seems, it took the rugby public some time to see France as worthy opposition. Imagine that!

· · · · ·

The great Welsh winger, Ken Jones, started out as an Olympic sprinter. He took part in the 1948 Games in London, where he won a silver medal for Great Britain in the relay beside John Archer, John Gregory and Alastair McCorquodale. He found his true vocation, however, as a quicksilver wing for Wales, earning 44 caps over ten years from 1947 to 1957.

Some bright spark – it could have been myself – got the idea to arrange an interview with Jones and Ireland's Jack Kyle straight after what would turn out to be Jones' last Five Nations match at Lansdowne Road in March, 1956. Kyle and Jones agreed to the interview after the game. We couldn't go to them live because it was too expensive to keep the commentary line open, so they kindly agreed to come to us in the studio on Henry Street for Junior Sports Magazine – a programme created by Harry Thuillier which was first broadcast in 1955.

I commandeered a school friend of mine, Eddie Mooney, to borrow his father's car. Not everyone had such a luxury in those days. He parked the car at the back of the Havelock Square end. I met the two players outside the pavilion. We were under severe time pressure. I am not even sure if the two lads had had a shower. We rushed out the back exit of Lansdowne Road. They carried their gear over their shoulders. We found the car, which wasn't too difficult because there weren't many of them. We drove into town, over the River Liffey, down O'Connell Street, screeching to a stop around the corner on Henry Street.

We sprang onto the pavement, flew in the side door of the General Post Office, which doubled as the entrance to Radio Eireann. The lift was broken. Of course! We hightailed it up three storeys to the station, which was nothing more than an attic at the top of the building. The lads still carried their gear over their shoulders and I followed them as best I could with the wind leaving my sails.

The two of them sat in with Harry Thuillier and did a wonderful interview. They made it sound so easy and relaxing after what can only be described as a scramble to get there. They were the biggest names in international rugby and, yet, they were happy to cooperate. Can you imagine the players of today being allowed to flee the nest so readily? They were special men.

Chapter 7

THAT'S CRICKET

Cricket was very nearly the national game in Ireland before the establishment of the Gaelic Athletic Association in 1884 at Hayes Hotel in the Tipperary town of Thurles. There are still popular pockets of cricket around the country where you wouldn't necessarily expect to find them.

I reckon that, as a fast bowler, if I were to have pursued a developing career in any sport, I would have had a chance of making it very close to the top level in cricket. I hadn't that faith in myself when it came to rugby.

My interest in cricket was developed by Fr Frank Barry. He was a remarkable person. He introduced generations of boys at St Mary's to cricket. He established nets in the 'back field', as we used to call it, more or less on concrete. We would train there even out of season. I was impressed by the commentaries I would hear on the radio extolling the virtues of Australians Keith Miller and Ray Lindwall and England's Alec Bedser.

I looked up to them without ever having seen them because there was no television in those days. I imagined them as elegant, tall, quicksilver bowlers, hurtling their way towards the crease in order to remove any impediment, otherwise known as a batsman, in their way.

I fashioned myself on the fast bowling of Lindwall, Bedser and Miller and, later, England's Brian Statham. I would have developed my own bowling technique from playing in the back lane around Effra Road with my good childhood friend and next door neighbour, Stratton Sharp.

At St Mary's, we used to practise at the Leinster Cricket Club in Observatory Lane off the Rathmines Road. We were all astonished when Fr Barry somehow managed to import the wonderfully talented West Indian, Learie Constantine, a legendary all-rounder born around the turn of the twentieth century. He went on to become the first black man to sit in the House of Lords.

Constantine was one of the great cricketers of his era before the emergence of Gary Sobers, a West Indian with a front-foot attitude in his game as an immaculate stroke-maker and slashing bowler. He really was an eye-opener into the world of cricket.

St Mary's purchased the park in Kenilworth Square as an outlet for the energies of their students. Fr Barry spent all his time either coaching us or lovingly doing the detailed tending to the surface necessary to establish a good enough wicket to receive the ball.

When the uninformed, or uninterested, among us look at cricket, they see inaction and a dull spectacle working almost in slow motion. Yet, once you know the moves, the tactics, the strategies, it suddenly turns into a fascinating battle of wills, riveting to watch.

Of course, it can, at times, be boring to view when the tension doesn't build, when the pieces on the board that is the field don't fit seamlessly together. Mostly, there is something worth seeing at work, whether it is a duel between a bowler and batsman or a captain's tactical approach in moving his fielders around to find a way through the defence of a batsman. It is fascinating.

I must say my greatest claim to fame in my schools cricket career was taking all ten wickets in an innings against St Conleth's College in the Leinster Schools' Senior Cup of 1952. I do remember they weren't the strongest opposition I ever faced, and they were intimidated by the pace of the ball I was firing down at them. The drama built with every wicket I took. The tension soared as I moved past the five-wicket haul and on towards the snooker equivalent of a 147 or the darts Holy Grail of a nine-dart finish. I walked away with all ten wickets for the only time in my cricket career. It would be the pinnacle of my time in the game. I was 18 years of age.

We made it to the Leinster Schools' final that year, where we were surprisingly beaten by St Andrew's College. We made the basic mistake of going for my fast bowling on a slow wicket when St Andrew's had a couple of really able batsmen, like Ian Lewis, who was the father of the retired Ireland international rugby referee and former Irish cricketer, Alan. Ian was a beautiful right-handed batsman. If we could have dislodged him, it would have been the winning of the game. I can still clearly remember having him plum leg before wicket (LBW) early in his innings.

Ian was about to walk, but the umpire didn't see it our way.

"Not out," went the ruling.

And with it went our chance of victory. Ian moved on to score a high total. He later played for Ireland twenty times, from 1955 to 1973. He was a lovely, fluent batter. He had that timing and rhythm for the ball that made him such a natural. He passed those genes down to Alan, who also became a regular opener for Ireland.

When we brought on our spinner in the Schools' Cup final, which we should have done so much earlier, it was too late to save the day. It was down to me, really. I should have relinquished the bowling earlier. But, I was blinded by my determination to see it through or see their batsmen out.

As a schoolboy, when you are told you should let someone else take over the bowling, you feel it is a reflection on your failure to remove batsmen. In fact, it is usually down to the wicket and what type of ball it will best welcome. A change of bowler is similar to modern-day rugby replacements. The replaced player can feel like it is a slap in the face. In fact, it has everything to do with impact and other game management considerations.

On the night before the final, Tony 'Rocky' Woodhouse and myself made our way to a 'hop' at St Mary's past-pupils' tennis club on Mount Tallant Avenue. We didn't dance. We didn't drink. We made our excuses and left early. It had no effect on my bowling. As is the way, when the match was swinging in St Andrew's direction, it was made known to Fr Barry that I was not tucked up in bed before nine the previous evening.

"Sure, no wonder, that fella' was out at a dance last night," came the news to Fr Barry.

My future wife, Madeleine, was at the final with a crew of girls supporting St Mary's. The word was out. The story grew legs and wings. We had been gallivanting. It would have explained my lack of success with the ball. According to 'Madge', Fr Barry's eyes burned holes in the backs of the girls who were seen as leading us astray. He blamed the women for tempting us out to the dance.

Proper order, too.

• • • • •

Cricket suited my temperament. I enjoyed sitting in the clubhouse drinking tea, interspersed with a touch of action when we were the fielding side, spearheaded by the odd hostile over as a bowler. Generally, the pace of cricket suits the Irish temperament. We're quite laid back.

At a more elevated level, the strategies involved and the different opportunities for different talents and strengths of men appealed to all shapes and sizes. You didn't have to be a big, strong man to have a role. There was room for everyone. I was tallish at six foot, lean, stringy to the eye and quite fast over the ground. I played for St Mary's, Leinster Schools and The Schools of Ireland at cricket, the latter playing against The Gentlemen of Ireland and The Leprechauns, a cricketing version of rugby's Barbarians.

When I moved on to the Railway Union club for senior cricket, I played with the Irish wicket-keeper Dick Millar. To that point, I was used to the keeper standing back because, if the batsman got a touch to my fast ball, it would fizz on through for four runs. But, he would stand right up behind the wicket, looking to apply pressure by crowding the batsman. This made me feel uncomfortable. I felt he wasn't in position to take the fizzer.

The decision not to go on, not to train, was taken because I was working at nights in *The Irish Times*. I didn't have the self-motivation, the dedication to train on my own. And so my active playing career came to an end. I think I could have been a good enough bowler to play County Cricket in England. It was not exactly a well-worn path. Eddie Ingram played for Middlesex in the 1930s. There were very few who made it from my era. Professionalism was still not fully accepted over there and it wasn't well-paid. It was not considered a career opportunity from Ireland. It never really became a personal regret. My pleasure and interest from sports journalism quickly took over.

Still, it was a great honour to play against Ireland Internationals like Jimmy Boucher, Graeme Pollock – he was a super player – Louis Jacobson, N.C. Mahony and Stanley Bergin.

• • • • •

Some years later, I was sent by the *Evening Herald* to report on a cricket match between Carlisle, the Jewish club, and Leinster. I went in to check the Leinster team before the start of the first innings.

This guy from *The Irish Press* arrived.

"Have you got the teams?" he asked.

"Not yet. I am just checking the Leinster team," I replied.

"Will I get the Carlisle team?"

"Yes. That would be great."

"Do you know who would give it to me?"

"Well, I am sure Louis Jacobson will point you in the right direction."

I could hear the conversation between the journalist and Jacobson. It went something like this.

"Isaacson, Jacobson... Thank you for that. Oh, what was the second last name again?"

"Solomon."

"Oh yes. That's fine. Would you be able to give me the Christian names?"

"We don't have Christian names!"

"What do you mean? Everyone has a Christian name."

"Not us. We're Jewish my friend."

• • • • •

Cricket is like chess. When you saw Garry Kasparov and Anatoly Karpov playing in the World Championships in 1984 and 1985, it was similar to waiting for paint to dry. It is only when you know the moves that it becomes so enthralling. Cricket is the same. It has players as the pieces. They are both matches of patience, tactics and intelligence. It is difficult for people who don't play the game to understand the bravery needed to stand up to fast bowling where a round missile is fired down at your head and hands. Broken fingers are par for the course in the sport.

Playing the game, I learned about the gulf that exists between the ordinary player and the professional sports person. One afternoon, I was in the slips, fielding behind a batsman. The fast bowler at the far end slammed the ball down. The ball hit the edge of the bat, generating twice as much speed as it shot out three yards to my right.

The ball was two-feet off the ground. I dived to my right. I instinctively caught the ball. I rolled over three or four times. The rest of the lads swarmed around me.

"Fantastic catch! Well done, Fred."

That is what they saw.

What I saw was the ball bowled down and touching the edge of the bat. As it did so, it changed from a ball into a large orange. It then changed in appearance into a sort of small balloon. As it went across me, I just put my hand out to stop it. It hit my hand. My hand closed around it. In that instant, my concentration was so focused, that I could see everything almost in slow motion.

It then made sense to me when batsmen, like Mike Atherton, would say, "I started to see the ball big", and golfers, like Padraig Harrington, say, "The hole looked so big I couldn't miss". For players to get to that level, it must take an incredible amount of practise and focus.

The top international players in cricket are able to concentrate so well that they are capable of reducing the speed of what is happening down to almost a slow-motion effect. Fast bowlers fire down the ball at close to 100 miles an hour. The batsman is able to move into position, able to control the bat onto the ball in such a way that he can bat it back to the bowler, direct it between two fielders or decide 'this is a ball I am going to hit'.

I asked the great golfer, Christy O'Connor, once, "What is the biggest difference between a good amateur and a good professional?" He said, "The ability to concentrate."

It is like you are in a car and you hit a patch of ice. Everything slows down. The moment is drawn out like a lifetime. No wonder people insist that their lives flash before them in this instance of crisis.

Chapter 8

YOU BLOODY QUACK!

My first memory of Leinster Schools' Senior Cup rugby was as a spectator at the 1947 final between St Mary's and Belvedere. Charlie O'Flanagan was one of that famous family of Kevin and Mick, who held the distinction of being the only Irish brothers to both be capped at rugby and soccer.

Kevin was a very talented sportsman. He was capped by Ireland at football, played for the Arsenal, and was capped once by Ireland at rugby – on the wing against Australia in 1947. I recall hearing a BBC commentator relaying how, in relation to a goal scored by Kevin, it was the only occasion he had seen, in a senior competitive match, where the defending side congratulated an attacker from the opposition.

It was a free kick from inside the circle around half-way. He placed the ball. He stubbed his toe into the ground, in the manner of a rugby player taking a penalty. He started his run-up from the centre spot and let fly. The ball was still rising as it whooshed into the top corner of the net. Those were the days of the heavy leather ball. It was a phenomenal kick.

"Of all the matches that I have played and watched, it is the one kick that stands out in my mind," said the reporter, in one of those 'Memories are Made of This' type of programmes.

Kevin played with London-Irish. He went on to be the Honorary Medical Officer for the Irish Olympic Council and then got involved in the

International Olympic Committee. He devoted a huge amount of time to sport over the years. When Kevin, by then a qualified doctor, returned from Arsenal to play for Bohemians, there was a very great admirer of O'Flanagan standing on the terracing in front of the old stand, right on the edge of the pitch at Dalymount Park.

Kevin took the ball and set off on a typically bustling dribble down the wing. You could hear his biggest fan every time he took another touch on the ball or beat a defender. He was growing hysterical at this wonder run.

Kevin beat one defender.

"Good man, Doc."

Kevin beat a second defender.

"Keep it goin', Doc!"

Kevin veered infield.

"You're doin' great, Doc!"

Kevin was within shooting range. The crowd roared him on.

"Shoot, Doc! Shoot, Doc!"

Kevin unleashed a piledriver that sailed over the crossbar. It drew a groan from the crowd, followed by a disappointed silence.

Then a voice rang out.

"You bloody quack!" screamed our friend.

That shows the fickleness of those who hold you up as a hero one minute and hold you in contempt the next.

His brother, Mick, played rugby for Lansdowne and soccer for Bohemians. He was also a dual sport international, lining out once against Scotland in the centre for his only cap in the year of the Grand Slam 1948. It was, if you like, a double-double achievement that was remarkable back then. Nowadays, it would be impossible, given the restrictions imposed by professionalism.

•••••

The youngest O'Flanagan brother, Charlie, was also a naturally talented sportsman. He just didn't have the commitment that was required, even in those days: I mean, you had to take an occasional training session seriously. Still, he was captain of the St Mary's team for the 1947 Leinster Schools' Senior Cup final, which they lost. But the abiding memory for me was a penalty shot at goal Charlie had that could have turned the game in St Mary's favour.

He kicked it from near the halfway line under what was then the old wooden, single-storey West Stand at Lansdowne Road. There was a worn patch of ground right where the kick was taken from. In those days, the ball would have been like a lump of mud. He kicked it beautifully. It sailed towards glory only to smack off the middle of the crossbar. Instead of bouncing over, it came back into play. It was a hell of a kick for a young lad, and a symbol of the fine line between success and failure in sport.

• • • • •

Fr Walter Kennedy was the rugby coach at St Mary's College school. He had steered the Senior and Junior Cup teams through their campaigns for years. He did almost all of it himself. The Under-12s and Under-13s were left in the hands of 'The Prefects', the trainee priests of the time.

Like any self-respecting out-half, I preferred to avoid any undue or unnecessary contact with the opposition. Whenever the going got tough, you could rely on the No. 10 to get going – away from the action in sprightly fashion. I was a good back, put it that way. I was the kicker and very conscious of being there in the first and final minutes of a game.

I enjoyed playing at out-half. My idol would have been Jackie Kyle. I was a left-footed fly-half and Kyle favoured his left as well. There the similarities ended, I'm afraid. As a youngster, you grew up with the ambition to play like he did. It was, of course, an innocent dream that never came to pass. I did get a Leinster cap at Schools level and I got a few games with the 'firsts' when I joined the St Mary's club. But, my need to earn a few bob as a freelance journalist was too great to resist and so ended my playing career in rugby for St Mary's and at cricket for Railway Union.

• • • • •

Then, as now, the Schools' Cup matches were the highlight of the sporting calendar for schoolboys. I had sort of settled in as the out-half of my group at

St Mary's as we went through the grades from U-12 to the Senior Cup. I was an above-average kicker. The trusty left foot returned a fair few points from penalties, keeping us in the 1949 Junior Cup for one round anyway. We drew with Belvedere and were narrowly beaten in the replay. Our scrum-half, Paul Moore, was injured in the drawn game. Our next best option was too young to be sent in to be savaged by the opposing wolves. So, Denis McArdle was given the job of wearing the number nine jersey. He wasn't all that fussed by the honour.

On one occasion, I remember the ball coming back rather scrappily from the scrum. Denis was much more interested in football than rugby. He knew that if he bent down to pick it up and pass it, he was likely to get clobbered by the closing Belvedere back row. Instead, he reasoned the quickest way to get the ball from A to B, him to me, was to kick it. It was the first time I had ever seen a scrum-half 'lash' it out to the out-half. I wasn't expecting it, or the entire Belvo back row which quickly engulfed me. The only surprise about the result was that there were only a few points in it at the end.

I played two years in the Leinster Schools' Senior Cup. In my first year, 1951, we beat Roscrea after a replay in the first round, in spite of a very nervous start – particularly by our smaller pack of forwards. Our burly second row, Brian Whelan, was given the job of trying to prevent Roscrea's 'Tiny' Kavanagh from dominating at the lineout. Tiny was another one of those 'eight foot' tall giants, or thereabouts. At the very first lineout, the referee walked over to Brian and tapped him on the shoulder.

"You better get down from there, son. Wait until the ball is thrown in before you climb up on his back. Penalty Roscrea!"

I also remember my dad was in the old Press Box at Donnybrook that day. There was a lineout near the halfway line. Tiny won the ball with ease and walked straight through and over our scrum-half, Billy Meagan. I was next. I remember thinking 'I can't duck out of this one. I've got to take Tiny down even if my life is about to end.' I recall closing my eyes and accepting it was my fate to be mashed by this 'Tiny' monster. The reality was not as bad as I had imagined. He had been too well fed on the bread in Roscrea and he came to ground like a deflating parachute to prove a kernel of truth from the old adage – the bigger they are, the harder they fall.

My dad must have been relieved, although Mum would not have been impressed. I think Mitchel had advised Muriel not to attend any of my matches having once heard her impart to me her wisdom on how best to handle myself on the pitch: "If the other fella is bigger than you and he wants the ball, give it to him."

In the second round we faced mighty Blackrock College and very nearly sprang a surprise. It was another case of 'might have, could have, but didn't'. We were well in the game, just a point behind late into the second-half, when I launched a long-range drop at goal. It was right on target, sailing for the posts at the Wesley end of Donnybrook. A gust of wind caught the ball and it rebounded back off the top of the upright. Almost immediately, as if the 'Rock Boys realised it was their day, they produced one of those ''Rock' movements that swing from side to side. Billy Meagan and I crashed into one another around the halfway line as we tried to cover back. We were both banjaxed. They got a solid footing inside our half. They had a big fella, Dave McCarthy, in the centre. We had nailed him every single time except this once. And that was enough for him.

Their out-half, Frank Casey, ran a line across me. I had to take him. Jim Byrne, our crash-tackling centre, didn't come up quickly enough and McCarthy was able to take the ball on the float. He was such a big guy. He got around on the outside. There was no way of stopping him once he was in the open. They went on to win it from there. If my drop at goal had gone over, they would not have got back upfield and into the position to strike for the winning try. It was a pity. While we seldom managed to beat 'Rock, I don't think we would have got much further, even if we had won that afternoon.

• • • • •

In terms of representative status, I was picked to play for Leinster Schools once. It was against Munster at Donnybrook. They had Brian Wain at wing forward. He was out of the same mould as Alan Quinlan. He was a tearaway, as hard as they come. In the first five minutes, he obliterated our scrum-half, Gerry Nestor from Castleknock. After the third hit, Gerry whispered in my ear.

"I'm not taking that guy on again. It's over to you. I'm getting rid of the ball as quick as I can."

"That's alright with me," I said.

Three minutes and two bangs later, I was whispering into the ear of the first centre.

"He's all yours."

I don't think I have ever seen a Leinster back division move the ball quicker across the three-quarter line and to less effect. Wain had put the fear of God into us and was the key figure in that rare defeat of Leinster Schools.

· · · · ·

Thereafter, the connection with the past pupils took in the St Mary's College club, which was to be found on a farm beside where Templeogue College is now, across the way from the current St Mary's grounds on Templeville Road. It was called Kimmage Grove. Because of the exposure to the Dublin mountains, it was more commonly referred to as 'Kimmage Grave'.

The great Ireland full-back, George Norton, had been a member of St Mary's, but he couldn't make the first team because his brother, Austin, stood in the way. There was another outstanding player there, Terry Coveney, who was a marvellous, beautifully balanced centre. They would have been Leinster and Ireland standard. However, there were few war-time internationals. The main entertainment came from a few 'set-tos' against Services sides now and again.

Austin and Terry could have made an impact but there was always the feeling, rightly or wrongly, that St Mary's was too far out of Dublin. It wasn't one of the core clubs like Lansdowne, Wanderers and Old Belvedere. It certainly wasn't a fashionable club. There was always a chip-on-the-shoulder attitude that Leinster selectors never came out far enough to see a St Mary's match. If you were playing Wanderers or Lansdowne at headquarters – fair enough. George went on to earn eleven Ireland caps when he moved to Bective Rangers because he couldn't displace his brother Austin at St Mary's. Personally, I might have made the St Mary's club firsts on a regular basis, although there were several good players, like Johnny Hughes, ahead of me. Realistically, that is as far as I would have gone.

•••••

It was Christmas time at Donnybrook. There was an annual fixture between the rival tenants, Bective Rangers and Old Wesley. The well-known Wesley full-back, Tom Trinder, was coming towards the end of his career in the mid-1950s. He was standing on his own 22-metre line. Wesley won the ball and moved it into the centres. By some chance, the new Bective three-quarter, straight out of school, brought off an intercept. He hared away from the first line of defence.

Trinder was totally exposed. He was all alone and, with the pace of old nothing more than a memory, he contemplated how to bring down this young buck. The teenager could have gone around, over or through him. Trinder was rooted to the spot, waiting to be humiliated, as this nippy young fella travelled towards him.

The centre suddenly looked around for support, trying to decide what he would do. The range of options seemed to confuse him. As he came face-to-face with the motionless Trinder, he stopped and threw the ball to him out of sheer panic. You had one man waiting to be humbled and another instantly hit by confusion. It was one of those crazy moments, enjoyed by most in the true spirit of Christmas.

Another Bective story I enjoyed concerned the inimitable Mick Cuddy, a towering prop forward and one of the most enthusiastic supporters of Bective teams at all levels of the game. Without ever diminishing his interest in the club, Mick went on to help in the development of Leinster and Irish Rugby. Ultimately, he was honoured with the Presidency of the IRFU. He helped in creating the common-sense attitude that saw the introduction of professionalism.

The one distinction he alone can claim, as far as I know, occurred during one of those Bective-Wesley derbies. Twice the referee had to speak to the Bective touch judge to contain himself. At the third outburst of abuse, the referee was left with no option but to dismiss the touch judge. Thus, Mick became the only fella in the history of the game to be sent off while running the line.

Chapter 9

BEVERSTON

As an only child, my friends became very important to me as a source of confidence and reference. Ken Sparrow was my first pal. I met him in my first year at St Mary's. That friendship stayed solid right through those years. We were neighbours. He lived on Leinster Road, which I passed every morning. He was a brainy one. He was moved ahead of us in school and on to bigger and better things in the business world. He could have turned his mind to anything. Thereafter, whenever we met, we picked up the conversation as if we had just put it down. There was that invisible connection between us.

He went on to do engineering at University College Dublin. He left the rest of us trailing in his wake, going on to have a successful business career at Irish Ropes. Later, he was honoured with the Presidency of St Mary's College RFC. He only served for a few weeks before succumbing to a brain haemorrhage in what was a tragedy.

In those days, there was no danger in allowing seven- or eight-year-olds to amble freely to school. You picked up friends along the footpath. Pat Fitzpatrick, who is a Holy Ghost Father out in Canada, and Tony Woodhouse were two others. Along with Ken, this was the beginning of the formation of a core group, which affectionately came to be known as 'The Gang'. We were soon joined by Tom Graham, who quickly became my best buddy. We all played on the same teams, ran the streets and fields together.

Tom entered St Mary's when we were in Third Class. One of Tom's very attractive sisters, Olive, never really committed to The Gang. Nonetheless, she maintained contact over the years. She emigrated to the United States in her early 20s and quickly settled there, got married and had a family. On retiring from her job, Olive took the opportunity to travel the world and had one of those weird one-in-a-million, coincidental experiences.

She could have chosen anywhere from Hawaii to Hammersmith. In the end, she decided to make a long-awaited visit to The Land of the Rising Sun. Olive had always wanted to experience Japan. She had always been charmed by Tokyo. So, off she went with a workmate on the holiday of a lifetime.

One day, they were walking along a street in the city when, suddenly, out of nowhere, it seemed, a church rose up in front of them. They wandered into the holy building to whisper a few prayers. Inside, there were signs written in English. They found this surprising. English-speaking confessions were advertised.

"I think I might pop in. We have a long flight coming up and this might be a message from The Lord to settle my affairs before we take off," Olive joked to her friend.

"Really?"

"Why not?"

"Away you go, so."

Olive tinkled the little bell hanging temptingly outside the confessional box. She waited patiently. A short while later, one of the priests emerged from the rear of the church to welcome them. He directed Olive to one of the booths where her confession would be heard by another priest, already in the process of hearing confessions.

Olive pulled back the curtain. She knelt down.

"Bless me, Father, for I have sinned."

The voice from the far side of the darkness sonorously returned.

"I would leave it at that if I were you, Olive!"

She froze like instant ice. She stepped out at the same time as 'The Voice'.

"Do you not remember me?" he said.

It was a former college boyfriend of Olive's who had followed a subsequent path into the priesthood. A great cacophony of laughter rang out. Needless to say, he gave her Absolution without another word.

·····

Anyway, Olive was instrumental in the expansion of The Gang because it was largely through her that we met Stephanie O'Reilly and others from nearby girls' school, Loreto on The Green. We morphed into a mixed group with Ken and Pat Fitz and Tony, otherwise known as 'Rocky,' and myself interacting with Stephanie and Oonagh Lawlor.

We called Tony 'Rocky' because he was as hard as nails on the pitch, although he wasn't as brave away from it. I know because I got my eye split open in a Junior rugby match one day. I was sent to hospital and Rocky was detailed to accompany me on the way.

The nurse checked me out.

"Now, would you be able to stand up to take the injection? It would be okay to sit down if you feel a little queasy," she said.

"It should be okay," I said.

The colour drained from Rocky's face. The hard man, who was supposed to be looking after me, promptly took my seat.

"Oh, do you mind if I sit down," he said, going weak at the sight of the needle.

Meanwhile, our expanding gang would meet after school at various 'secret' locations around the city until, one evening, Stephanie brought along a friend, Patricia – or Pat – Purcell. She immediately fitted into our circle of friends. She lived in a beautiful, idyllic dream house, 'Beverston', adjacent to St Mary's College.

In contrast, I was coming from a flat on Effra Road. This was like heaven. It was an enormous house with a giant chestnut tree in the front garden. It backed onto the military barracks in Portobello. It had a back garden that was 60-70 yards long, including an apple-laden orchard.

We were all coming under parental pressure. Our mothers didn't like the idea of their children hanging around the crossroads after school. They wanted to know where we were and who we were with, which was reasonable enough. Pat Purcell's mother welcomed the friends of her daughter, including the rowdy boys from St Mary's, into the ivy-clad Beverston. It was many years later Pat Fitz's mother realised Pat Purcell was a girl, not one of the boys, as she had presumed.

We stood, sat, walked, ran around the front garden, playing all sorts of games, including mixed tip-rugby. It was much better than the fifteen-a-side version. Well, it was for the lads. I'm not sure the girls enjoyed it all that much.

In the summer house at the back of Beverston, we played an endless list of hit tunes from the '40s and '50s. We spent our time singing songs, like My Heart Cries for You, and She Wore Red Feathers, by the American, Guy Mitchell. There was great excitement when he travelled over to sing at the Theatre Royal on Hawkins Street for two nights in June, 1954.

There was also Mario Lanza. He was the first operatic singer who crossed the musical divide to become a pop star. We would all reach in vain for his notes to Be My Love and The Loveliest Night of the Year by screeching as distinct from singing. Before them, I know John McCormack had even greater success and was probably the most revered Irish showman of all time. He had something that made all the difference in the world. He was one of us.

The members of The Gang all did their thing, too. When we met we could all relax away from whatever job kept us occupied for 40 hours-a-week. Those were very nice and innocent days. I still remember the times we met under that huge chestnut tree in the garden in Beverston. The Gang agreed to convene there every June 29. We kept to our word for a while until Beverston was later sold on out of necessity and the tree was felled.

· · · · ·

Speedway was all the rage in the early 1950s. It was a novelty sport. It was held at Shelbourne Park where a bunch of exotic American racers, like Nick Nicolaides, Don Hawley, Johnny Roccio and Manuel Trujillo – and my favourites from Australia led by Ronnie Moore – were based, before they headed to the United Kingdom for big-time competitions. We liked to visit the stadium where the motorbikes whizzed around the track, spraying shale. It got us thinking. Hence, we built a bicycle out of scrap metal and anything unwanted that we could find.

We mapped out a circuit at Beverston that travelled from the side of the house, up the passage, around the vegetable patch and orchard as far as the wall of the military barracks, across the top and straight down to a tight chicane, back along the side passage, out the gate into the large front garden.

We wrecked shoes, pants, hands, knees, all parts of our bodies and the bike. The object was to break the 'world record'. Without a H.R. Samuel watch, we counted out the time 1001, 1002, 1003 and on, from start to finish – if the cyclist made it that far.

One time, Rocky was out to smash 'our world record'. He got up a head of steam quickly. Now, there were no brakes on this bike. It was not built to the most reliable engineering standards. It was constructed for purpose. All was going to plan. The record was in danger. He negotiated the chicane into the narrow passageway towards the gate at the side of the house. But Don Purcell had nonchalantly closed the gate. It must have been his record on the line.

Rocky was left with nowhere to go. He couldn't jump off because it was so narrow. He couldn't jam on the brakes because he didn't have any at his disposal. He slammed straight into the gate. There was a terrible clatter. Fortunately, nothing too heinous happened. Rocky didn't even need a tetanus injection, which would have tested his resolve to the limit. Maybe, that is why we called him Rocky, because he survived it. We hastily retired inside the house.

I don't know what would have become of us, or where we would have ended up, if we had not found each other. There was no alcohol. None of us drank. Mrs Purcell used to come into the kitchen and make fresh scones. We used to scoff the lot. She also used to smoke. We were at that curious age. Occasionally, the boys liked to smoke surreptitiously with a little assistance from Mrs Purcell. She was a lovely lady. We all have warm memories of her and her patient husband, Mr Purcell.

They were happy days.

•••••

The gang, as such, lived on and lives on to this day, even if in ever dwindling numbers. In fact, our latest reunion happened out in San Diego in the summer of 2010. Pat Purcell wasn't well enough to travel back to Ireland. A group of 'survivors' headed out. We had a lovely holiday out there, gently reminiscing about times gone by. Every time we assemble there is a sadness because there is usually someone that is, how shall we say, not visible any more. Alas, the big chestnut tree has gone too, ripped from the ground for one reason or another.

Even the beautiful Beverston has given way to time. It was knocked down for development. For The Purcell's, it became a millstone for them. It was such a big house. The early deaths of Mr and Mrs Purcell placed great pressure and demands on the siblings Eileen, Peigy, Kitty, Pat and Don. Kitty married John Bowden, another entrant into our family of friends, with whom we still share so many memories from those years. You could say we had the time of our lives.

Chapter 10

LITTLE DID WE KNOW

I first met Madeleine White in 1950. She went to school at Loreto Beaufort, in Rathfarnham. I had spotted her at 10 o'clock Mass every now and then. That is not to say we only went every now and then. One of my friends, Gerry Reynolds, used to cycle up home from school. He had a pal, Des White, a brother, as it turned out, of Madeleine's. They lived on Shanid Road, up off Harold's Cross. I insinuated my way in by convincing Des to do the introductions. I was 16 years old.

My first date with this girl was to suggest she might want to join the Percy Lawn Tennis club in Donnybrook, which would later become the St Mary's Lawn Tennis club. Her mum, Lil, and dad, Owen, thought that was a nice idea, a reasonable suggestion. Madeleine's mother's family, The Mowlds, had a wool shop on Stephen Street in town. There is a record going back to thirteen or fourteen generations of Mowlds born and bred in Dublin. They were real Dubliners from the rarest auld times with a warm welcome and a 'cuppa' for any and all casual visitors.

It was not without its trial, that first date. As we hopped on the bus, I realised, to my great shame, that I hadn't any money. I must have had my head lodged in the clouds. It never occurred to me that I might need to pay my way until we were on the bus. Fortunately, Madeleine produced the pennies. Little did we know, she would still be looking after me all these years down the road. Arithmetic has never been a strong point with me, so Madge looks after the finances.

I showed Madeleine around the tennis club. I like to think she was very impressed with it, if not by me. It was the beginning of a friendship that led to marriage that led to a family. Here we are, all these years later, still together, still 'surviving', still leaving the finances in her capable hands.

• • • • •

One winter's day, Madeleine wore ocelot – this is a leopard-like wild cat found in Central and South America – ankle-high boots. There were very few cars on the streets of Dublin at that time. The usual mode of transport was either on a bicycle or on a bus. There were professional photographers who would snatch snaps of couples walking down O'Connell Street or one of the city centre walkways. They would hand out a ticket. If you wished, you could go to the photograph company and pay for the photo that had been taken. That was a feature of city life in the 1950s, long before instant and digital cameras had flooded the market. These photographers were the forerunners of the modern paparazzi. In addition to working the streets, as it were, they would appear at all the Dress Dances in vogue over the winter months.

• • • • •

My first car was a 1948 Austin 8. I bought it in 1958, the year I was married to Madeleine. At first, it was a source of great pride. That didn't last long. It had a not-too-secure running board – this was the step to the side you used on your way into the car – which was rusted to hell. I got it for IR£80. And I was robbed.

The day I bought it I drove it down to show Madeleine's aunts and uncles in town. They all came out from the two shops they owned on Stephen Street, just opposite where Break for the Border is now, and close to the St Stephen's Green Shopping Centre, to view this lump of red metal.

Back then, there wasn't another car in sight smack in the heart of the city centre. I offered a spin around the block to everyone and anyone. My new wife mentioned how I should have let her know I was going to buy a car for the equivalent of eight weeks' wages in the *Herald*. I had, er, forgotten to mention my intention.

I pulled the choke out to get it going. As luck would have it, the choke kept coming and coming. It was attached by a piece of string, which had broken. The disappointment was overwhelming. The beaming pride quickly drained from my face. I had bought a car held together by string.

I went back to the man who sold it to me. He had a garage in Westland Row underneath the bridge. It was a second-hand dump yard. I was ready for conflict.

"Ah, you're back."

"I am. It appears this car is being held together with string. Look at the choke!"

He peered in the window. He opened the door, stood on the running board and simply re-tied the string.

"There you go. It's fine now."

·····

Madeleine and I were married at St Joseph's in Terenure, in the same church as my parents, at 11am on September 25, in 1958. We emerged to a howling gale and quickly had photos snapped around the side of the church by Jackie Merriman, who subsequently became a news cameraman in RTE. His brother, Billy, was an innovative sports photographer at the *Irish Independent*. From there, we retired to The Shelbourne Hotel for our wedding breakfast. We had more photos taken. We returned there in 2008 to have another set of prints taken on our fiftieth anniversary. Of course, Madge didn't look a day older. I, on the other hand, have been less fortunate.

Anyway, we were on our way to Dublin airport at 3.30pm that afternoon. Madeleine missed out on a family party in her parents' house in Terenure. This was a regret at the time as her family had a love of, and talent for, music that was in keeping with my own interest, handed down by my grandmother, Toto.

We spent two nights in London where Madeleine led me on a merry dance through the shops on Oxford Street. Then we boarded a plane – an 'Elizabethan' which had wings on top of the aircraft and the engines underneath – for two wonderful weeks in Mallorca.

There, we visited the cell-room museum in Valldemossa, designed in deference to the Polish composer, Frederic Chopin, and his lover, Amandine Aurore Lucile Dupin (Baroness Dudevant). She was better known by her pseudonym, George Sand, and was known to dress as a man. They spent one winter on the island and were forced to leave in haste due to ill-health. They could not bring Chopin's treasured Pleyel piano on the journey. It was sold to a French couple and resides in the museum as the outstanding legacy of Chopin's time on the Balearic island.

My wife could not resist tinkling the keys of the piano. That was not the done thing. There was a clear hands-off policy. That's how wild she was.

In 1959, I had changed the Austin 8 for a solid British-made Morris Minor. It was slipped into gear fairly rapidly as I drove Madge to the front door of the Cascia House Nursing Home. She was about to give birth to our first child. As was the way back then, I quickly scarpered. Once she was in good hands, that was enough for me. Our first son, David, was born there on November 5, 1959. I still vividly recall going in to visit Madeleine and hearing a woman scream out in pain in an adjacent room.

"That's it. Right then! See you later love."

I vacated the premises in a flash for fear that I would feel weak at the knees or do a Rocky Woodhouse on it, if you like. That is how brave I was. To this day, I am reminded of what a reliable support I was. Not.

David was a very good athlete, a sprinter. He wore the Irish singlet at a competition in Denmark. He is now a consultant orthopaedic surgeon at Tullamore Hospital. He is married to Janet and they have three girls, Katie, Elaine and Eva.

In 1963, our second son, Niall, arrived on February 2. He was always very musical, like Madeleine's brother, his uncle Des White. He followed the family path into journalism. He became the Head of Sport at RTE after Tim O'Connor, later branching out to co-found Setanta Sports, Ireland's first dedicated sports channel. He was appointed as Director of Broadcasting at TV3 in late 2011. He is married to Gabrielle, living in Milltown in Dublin, with their two girls, Clodagh and Roisin, and our grandson, Daragh.

On May 19, 1967, our first daughter, Michelle, came into the world to join her brothers David and Niall. I couldn't make it to that event. I was away on Ireland's tour to Australia. While that tour had been one of my outstanding experiences covering rugby – it was the first time any northern hemisphere country won in the southern hemisphere – I have to admit that it ran very much a poor second for me, personally, that week.

Communications were nowhere near as prompt as they are today, but Tim O'Connor, back in the RTE offices, somehow managed to get the news to me and I had a small celebration Down Under. In fact, Madeleine was brought into the RTE studios as a matter of financial common sense. I was coming through on a studio line and it was cheaper than making a phone call to or from home, that would have cost the earth in those days.

Tim O'Connor brought Madeleine into the studio on Henry Street. I was later informed by my wife how embarrassed she felt to have to conduct such a personal conversation at the end of a microphone with the words between us boomed all over the studio. Michelle works in Financial Insurance, lives in Dublin, moving between there and Mountmellick, where her partner, Steve Reddan lives.

On April 24, 1970, Denise duly came along as our fourth child. She started out as a nurse and is now working in the pharmaceutical industry in London, where she lives with her husband, Rob, and daughter, Jena. Rob is a real English rugby follower, one of those 'Swing Low, Sweet Chariot' types. It is very hard to take and he finds us just as hard to take when the Ireland-England matches swing around in the Six Nations.

I did tell him at his wedding that he would be, "extraordinarily welcome to become an Irish rugby supporter". But he has no chance of getting Denise to become an English supporter.

Chapter II

MY FIRST BROADCAST

Since my days in school, I have always been fascinated by radio sports broadcasting. I can still vividly recall following the 1948 Olympics through the medium of BBC radio at our family home on Effra Road and the commentary of Dr Ronnie Thornton on Ireland's Triple Crown match against Wales in Swansea, back in 1949.

I have a great regard for the commentators of the time. All the BBC commentators' names were familiar to me. The great English cricket broadcaster, John Arlott, had been a police officer for twelve years. He had a lilting Hampshire accent that made him stand out. It was remarkably incongruous in a world where the posh Tory melody was all you expected to hear on BBC.

Back in those days, Ernie Toshack was a spin bowler on the Australian cricket side. He came in fairly high in the order of batting to act as a 'nightwatchman'. This is a word used to describe the tactic for nominating a mediocre batsman to play out time as, say, light faded, instead of putting in a recognised batsman who could be bowled out before he could settle in for a long haul the following day.

Anyway, Toshack was going to have to defend against Surrey pace man, Alec Bedser. The commentary kicked in as Bedser threw down to Toshack. It whistled by the off-stump with Toshack tentatively waving his bat at the ball.

"It was much like an old lady poking at a bee's nest with her umbrella," said Arlott, or words to that effect. I can still hear him oozing out that sentence. It painted an easily identifiable picture in the mind's eye. He had defined great commentary in one sentence.

There were resounding names in those years. Raymond Glendenning was an ever-present force for the BBC. He had a beautiful voice, wonderfully modulated. He was speaking to a British audience, of course. We, not being that shade of people, were very aware that when Glendenning spoke of an Irish sportsman losing he was trenchantly 'Irish'. If that same Irishman started winning, he would quickly become 'British'. Raymond broadcast on football, racing, boxing – he covered the whole shooting gallery in an era when the second World War had engulfed Great Britain. He was instantly recognisable through his horn-rimmed spectacles and immaculate handlebar moustache. He was prevented from joining the armed forces by a pre-War injury. The BBC was delighted to have someone who was well-versed in a wide range of sports.

Those were difficult times. On one occasion, the BBC was scheduled to broadcast a big soccer match in Manchester. The city was clouded in fog, or so the story goes. The commentator thought he was relieved of his duty. The BBC got back on to inform him that he had to carry out the broadcast of a match that did not take place because the British could not allow the Germans to know that there was a fog over Manchester.

And they think we make it up as we go along! Well, in this case, he did.

In Ireland, Jim Neilly swears it was he who came up with, "the referee is looking at his whistle and is about to blow his watch". Mick Dunne, God rest him, who was RTE's Gaelic games correspondent for many a year, was drafted in to work on television coverage of snooker, whereupon he came up with the following statement:

"For those of you watching in black and white, the red ball is behind the yellow."

If those voices were to ignite my interest in the mystique of radio and, later, television, there were quite a few Irish broadcasters who had to work in dreadful conditions, but still managed to hold the listener spellbound in the post-War era. Without television there were few films on sport that were in any way memorable, with one remarkable exception.

I have seen the film of the 1936 Olympics in Berlin, which was an incredible event for so many reasons. Hitler's favourite filmmaker, Leni Riefenstahl, was commissioned by the Nazi regime to make a documentary 'Olympia', which later won first prize at the Venice Film Festival in 1938. Even by today's standards, it was the most riveting spectacle, the stylish photography, the way it was relayed. There was the propaganda, of course, the infamous expectations of Hitler as he planned to show Aryan superiority over inferior nations and his typically aloof reaction to Jesse Owens' wins in the 100-metres, 200-metres, long jump and 4x400-metres relay finals. This was part of the background to my developing an interest in journalism, in broadcasting and in sport generally.

· · · · ·

I had been at the Radio Eireann studios once in 1948 as part of the St Mary's Elocution Choir. We were taught so well by Maura Cranny to form our words. A deaf man standing a mile away would have been able to lip-read all of us. We were all so keen to pronounce every syllable correctly.

Brendan Byrne led our choir. We were like nervous kittens – and with good reason – when we entered the studio. We were to perform the poem, The Wild West Wind. 'Byrner', as we called him, was the deep-voiced lead. Earlier in the week, in one of the rehearsals, the choir had been summoned to provide an interlude of entertainment at a parent-teacher meeting, or something similar to it. It became a sort of dress rehearsal for the forthcoming broadcast. As usual, Byrner was leading us verse-by-verse. But he got stuck like an old record player. Every time we came to the end of the first verse, he would lead us back into the start of the first verse again. It was like he was on a loop. He did it three times, and three times we followed like sheep. I have forgotten how we eventually finished the song, but the fear of a repeat performance on radio had us all quaking in our shoes.

The studio was to be found in the attic of the General Post Office (GPO). We were all standing around this microphone, which was placed on something resembling an anti-aircraft gun. A chap emerged to announce the opening of the station with this children's programme at 5.30pm. He was in full evening dress, bow-tie and tails – for the radio. Those were certainly different days. We needn't have worried. When the moment arrived, the nerveless Byrner never wavered. The Wild West Wind blew a gale that night.

• • • • •

Anyway, Eamonn Andrews was running a programme in Radio Eireann called Sports Stadium with a producer named Gus Ingoldsby on Friday evenings at 9pm. I wrote in to the programme letting them know there were a lot of schoolboys listening to it, but there was nothing in it for kids like myself to latch onto. I got no reply. Not surprisingly. As a rule, journalists, particularly sports journalists, were not noted for replying to unsolicited letters.

So, I wrote again a month or two later, cheekily mentioning my previous concerns. Eventually, I received a reply requesting that I submit a sample script. I did so. Some time later, I got a note from Gus Ingoldsby. It was an invitation for an audition, based on a copy of the script I had sent to the station. I went into the Radio Eireann Studios in the GPO on Henry Street, just around the corner from O'Connell Street. It was the first door on the left. I specifically didn't mention anything to my dad. He might have thought I should have been focusing more on school exams than writing to Radio Eireann. The fact that I had been there before with the choir definitely gave me a compass on where I should go. This vague familiarity also assisted in controlling my nervous tension.

It was funny. When it actually came to the broadcast itself, I had rehearsed it so much, so completely, that, although it was written out on three typed pages, when I finished the audition I realised I hadn't even turned the first page.

It would have been, how shall I put it, very 'elocutionised', projected in a very toffee-nosed accent. It would have made Maura Cranny proud, very proud indeed. It must have sounded reasonable because I got a note from Eamonn requesting that I come in on a Thursday for rehearsal to do a piece that Friday, live on air.

This was a great thrill. In I went. In those days, you had a rehearsal on the Thursday afternoon, another rehearsal on Friday morning, a dress rehearsal on Friday afternoon and, then, the live show on Friday night. I am not saying that was the best way of doing it. It was just the way it was done back then. Everything was tightly scripted and edited and timed. Everybody had a place in the machine and you daren't move outside it.

My broadcasting debut occurred in the winter of 1949-1950. The buzz I got as a 16-year-old, rubbing shoulders with veteran experts, further confirmed, in my mind, this was what I wanted to do with my life.

Joe Lynch was then a young member of the Radio Eireann Players (REP). No, this wasn't a football team, rather a Repertory Drama Group. He would later enjoy an industrious career as an actor, particularly as the character, Dinny, in the long-running series, Glenroe. He was designated to sit and read some of the scripts submitted by countrywide correspondents.

I was so nervous that first time. He seemed so calm.

I said to him: "How do you overcome your nerves?"

"Everybody is nervous."

"You're not. You look on top of it all."

"Well, that is because everyone shows it in a different way."

"How do you mean?"

"Some might feel sick. Others might have butterflies in their stomachs. Look at me!"

Joe's eyes tilted down to the back of his hands. He turned them over and opened them out flat. They were sweating quite heavily.

"Those are my nerves."

In comparison to the way things are done now, it was very simple in so far as it was very well rehearsed. Once again, when I went on air, I didn't turn a page. I had three sheets at my hands, but I never looked down at them. I was on autopilot. It was like touch-typing. You train yourself to do it without looking at it. If you put in the work, it almost becomes automatic.

Joe O'Dea, a brother of Jimmy, the great comedian, was another in the REP. He had a tremendously resonant voice. It boomed out from the radio. They used him to make the opening announcement or introduction to the Sports Stadium programme. The Radetzky March, by Johann Strauss, would signal the start. Joe would grandly announce "S-P-O-R-T-S S-T-A-D-I-U-M" and the music would swell in behind him.

I did four or five broadcasts on school sports for Sports Stadium over the next month or more. That was my foot-in-the-door, my introduction to a career that was to become my joy for 60 years.

• • • • •

It is all so different to today. When you look at the way programmes are managed and controlled and produced now it is so much more efficient. It is also far less formal. Alas, there has also been a downside because, with the informality, has come a mangling of the language and poor pronunciation, interminable waffle and no apparent editorial supervision.

When the television build-up, preview and review become more important than the game itself, there is a definite imbalance. In my opinion, the sophistication of coverage tends to go too far. A simple example: The amount of information that is coming across with captions – how far a player has run, how many times a player has kicked the ball, off his left foot, off his right foot – doesn't mean anything to anybody.

I would spend two days familiarising myself with the players, their numbers, the basics. On the day, in the preamble to the game, the viewer sees the names, numbers, the age, height and weight of each for approximately 30 seconds. It is a total waste of broadcast space. This is the sort of statistical crowding that becomes a mess in the minds of the viewers because they can't assimilate the information. There is way too much of it.

If it has taken the commentator two days' preparation to familiarise himself with the information, the viewer is not going to be able to process it in 30 seconds. This is an indication of where television is over-gilding the lily.

I don't disagree with a person's right to make a living through pushing new-found technology. I just think that aspects of the job can suffer in order to accommodate unnecessary baggage. It is as simple as that.

If you have 20 cameras at an event, they are very often there because it is a big game and directors are trying to show how important they are. There are some events, like at a golf tournament, where you have 18 holes. This can be justified. But, at a football match?

I have seen very good coverage of football matches with a minimum of three cameras. This is very tight. It requires a very good director to make that work. But, when you get into the 18 and 19 cameras, it really is too much. There is the theory that the more you put in the better it should be. That isn't always true. If you overcook something, it ain't good. If you undercook, it ain't good either. There is a point you reach where more is less. The law of diminishing returns kicks in.

Chapter 12

MICHAEL O'HEHIR

Michael O'Hehir was Ireland's outstanding broadcasting personality in the late 1940s. There was no better way to pass a Sunday afternoon anywhere from Malin Head to Mizen Head to Carnsore Point than by tuning in to Michael for whatever big match he was commentating on to laze away the afternoon.

Eamonn Andrews was another super broadcaster – beautiful voice, beautiful control. He could generate great excitement in a contrasting way to Michael, who was such a lively, free-spirited commentator. Eamonn was more controlled, able to paint a picture and build the atmosphere of the occasion as well as anyone. They were the men in Ireland I looked up to when I started out on what has become a long and rewarding road.

· · · · ·

There was the one about Michael O'Hehir's failed attempt to fuse RTE radio coverage one afternoon. In the days before we had the ease of communications we have now, there was a time when a telephone was a luxury in the home. And it wasn't all that long ago.

In the mid-1950s, television wasn't even in the ether. Michael and his sound engineer, Sean Ginnane, a great servant of Radio Eireann, were posted to do a Gaelic football match for the radio in the West of Ireland – I think it was a National League match between Mayo and Galway, say, in Westport, if memory serves me correctly. At the same time, Kerry were due to play a very inferior opponent at Fitzgerald Stadium in Killarney. It could have been Waterford.

Even Michael could not be in two places at one time. However, he did have the bright idea of doing more than just his match report. He wanted to arrange a system so that he could be kept abreast of what was happening in Killarney.

Michael had a friend who lived near Fitzgerald Stadium and who had a telephone. He dialled up this friend and requested a favour for a 'stringer', or some such reliable person, to knock on the man's door at half time during the Kerry game so that Michael could establish contact with him to get the latest on the game there. It all sounded so foolproof, in theory.

"Sure. Of course," responded Michael's friend.

The arrangement was that this kind man would make sure he was at home during the interval and after the match so that Michael could keep his listeners 'in the know'.

Anyway, the day came. Michael had arranged for one of his reporter 'pals' at the Kerry-Waterford match to act as the go-between. It was all set up. The reporter had the address and the instructions. It seemed straightforward enough.

At half time in Westport, Michael rapped the floorboards of the one-up, one-down chicken coop they were broadcasting from. Michael was stationed overhead to give him an elevated overview and Sean was in the basement or ground floor.

"Sean, will you ring that house in Kerry," asked Michael.

He immediately reached for the wind-up phone and put a bit of 'elbow grease' into it. He got through to the Post Office Exchange and they transferred Sean to the number in Kerry.

What do you know! The 'pal' answered the phone. The reporter was there beside him. It worked like a dream. Sean wasn't exactly a dyed-in-the-wool GAA man. He scribbled down the information, tapped on the floorboards overhead and handed a note up to Michael. He opened it and it read simply:

'Kerry 0-1 Waterford 1-8'.

This was a sensational development. Sean was impervious to the meaning of this. Michael was immediately suspicious.

"There must be a mistake. Are you sure this is true?"

"That is what he told me."

Nonetheless, as the local band was winding down their piece for the interval entertainment, Michael turned back to his microphone.

"We have a remarkable story developing in Killarney where Waterford lead Kerry 1-8 to 0-1. We will check that out. But that is the score we have to hand."

Michael immediately hammered on the floorboards.

"What do you want?" shouted Sean.

"Would you ever check that scoreline?"

Sean got back on to the Exchange. He was put through to the house. There was no pick-up. The 'pal' had done the favour. He had obviously popped out of the house until the final whistle.

"There's no one there, Michael."

"Well, get on to someone who can confirm that score."

"What about the gardai?"

"Yeah, good idea."

Sean got back onto the Exchange for the third time.

"Can you please put me through to the local Garda station in Killarney please?"

"Okay, sir."

The next thing, there is a voice on the phone.

"Hello, Killarney Garda station."

The garda on duty didn't have a clue who was winning the match. He was at work in the office.

"Hold on," he said. "We have a car in the area. I will patch you through to it."

A brief silence was broken by a sleepy voice.

"Hello! This is Garda Murphy here."

"Hello, Garda. I am sorry to trouble you. This is Sean Ginnane from Radio Eireann here. Could you tell me what is the half-time score in the match there in Killarney?"

"I could. It is Waterford 1-8 Kerry 0-1."

"Are you sure?" asked Sean.

"Of course I'm sure. Hasn't Michael O'Hehir just given it out on the radio!"

• • • • •

Any mention of the GAA and New York reminds me of a later incident when Radio Eireann upset the owner of Gaelic Park. John Kerry O'Donnell was displeased with some aspect of the coverage of games in New York. As a consequence, RTE and Michael O'Hehir were banned from broadcasting at the ground. The row remained unresolved. So, John Kerry organised a substitute known as 'Lefty Devine' to do the needful. RTE had to air Lefty's commentary in Ireland or do without.

Afterwards, the *Irish Independent* interviewed Michael to get his opinion on Lefty's broadcast. Michael was very gracious in reviewing the commentary, complimenting Devine for the solid job he had done at short notice.

The *Independent* ran a headline on top of the article. I have never forgotten it.

"O'Hehir is Human to Forgive Devine."

My father took credit for that one, believe it or not.

• • • • •

When I was in the *Evening Herald* in the late 1950s, early 1960s, I got very friendly with Michael in the sense that a youngster would be made feel important by being given the time of day by someone holding his exalted office. His commentary on horse-racing was so marvellous. It wasn't any surprise that the BBC would take him up or that he would be invited out to 'call races' in America.

At home, he did one of those sponsored programmes on a Monday morning. It was called the Vaseline Hair Tonic Programme. I was immediately fascinated. I had arrived from the stricter world of the Eamonn Andrews' production style, at a time when there was a slight release from the public service censorship days, where everything had to be scripted, timed and researched ad nauseum.

Michael came into his fifteen-minute programme with a box of matches. On the back of the box, there were three or four headlines scribbled down. That was his script. He would ad-lib the entire programme. At times, the strictness, the unwieldiness of the Radio Eireann administration would frustrate him.

Occasionally, he would get me to cover one of the sports he wouldn't have been recognised for and had little interest in. So, I would do pieces to air on golf, rugby or rowing because I had done this type of work for Sports Stadium. It was all part of the learning process for me.

When he would come home from his regular adventures in America, he would bring back all kinds of recordings of the latest Broadway shows. He would often include them in his programme.

One day, he played for us this great rendition of The Battle Hymn of the Republic. It was a classic, performed by The Mormon Tabernacle Choir. He decided it would be the perfect centre-piece for his next programme.

The powers-that-were took one look at the running order and turned it down, demanding Michael replace it with something more appropriate for the times they lived in.

"What's wrong with it?" said Michael.

"The sponsored programmes cannot have any religious themes or aspects to them. You know the rules."

"You can't do this."

"We can. The Battle Hymn of the Republic, sung by The Mormon Tabernacle Choir – get it out of the show!"

Michael was raging, but not to be defeated. He changed the running order to include "a new recording of John Brown's Body". No one in Radio Eireann copped that he had just changed the name of the 'Battle Hymn'. The rules were not broken. Well, not really. That is how pedantic, backward and downright silly it was back then and how stubborn Michael could be.

Anyway, Michael's preparation consisted of a note or two on the back of his box of matches. He was tremendous when let loose on the audience. He was always happier when he wasn't tied to a format. In contrast, when preparing for a match commentary or a big racing event, nothing was left to chance in his research.

He influenced me in a way that was largely observational. Now and then, he would give you advice, but he never seemed to want to presume he had so much experience and advice to impart. It was the nature of the man. He was quite a shy person in many ways. He didn't seem to have a broad group of buddies. The racing journalists, like Louis Gunning in *The Irish Press*, Mick Byrne in *The Irish Times*, Tony Sweeney in *The Daily Mirror* appeared to be his closest associates. One of my dearest friends, Tom MacGinty succeeded Michael as racing correspondent at the *Irish Independent* when Michael moved to RTE.

Those guys travelled around the country together. They had organised with the Post Office a way to get the results back to the newspapers. One of them would be detailed to do all the results. They were sent through a ticker-tape machine. Very often, they would be handwritten in the receiving office on a series of carbon copies.

The first copy was fine. However, if you were unlucky enough to receive the last copy, it could be smudged, difficult to read, basically barely legible. They would then be delivered to the various newspaper offices. Some youngster of a trainee, like me, would get to try to decipher the jaded handwritten Post Office carbons. What a contrast to today's technological age.

Photographers like Billy Merriman and his brother, Jackie, weren't able to shoot ten pictures in one second. Dermot O'Shea, the Pictures Editor in *The Irish Times*, recounted how Billy locked two cameras together with clips and screws – one on top of the other. He would look through the viewfinder when the horses would take-off at a fence, clicking the top camera, and snap them with the bottom camera on the way down, in case they fell or made a spectacular mistake. Of course, this is all carried out electronically now. They can do so much more. Yet, the work achieved in those archaic times still stands as a testament to the skills of the old-time 'snappers'.

Michael O'Hehir used to always say: "A bad match is no excuse for a bad broadcast," explaining that people had gone to the bother of tuning in to a game. It was his job to retain their interest. The listener wanted to be entertained. If the match was dull, you had to give it colour, bring it to life.

You would often hear people talk about how bad the match they were at had been, while those who stayed at home would be able to retort, 'God, it sounded great on the radio'.

There were those who would say Michael wasn't factual. He gave a false description. I think he was absolutely right. You have to add something to the event so that the listener is either better-informed or entertained at the end of the broadcast. It was one thing to have a listener turn on the radio; quite another to hold him hostage to it.

If you analyse and parse it, you find a basis for lifting sports broadcast to where it should be, towards the front of any form of entertainment. The fact that it is often viewed as 'The Toy Department' didn't make the Sports Department any easier to work in or less demanding. It was a job. It had to be done and done properly. There were aspects to it that were rewarding. There were aspects that were a chore.

Very often, people who are not interested in sport tend to dismiss it. But, be assured, the amount of effort that goes into producing a sports page, or a sports broadcast or a sports commentary, is every bit as intense as any other area of the media.

First and foremost, according to Michael, radio commentary was a broadcast. It had to be entertaining. It had to be informative. It had to be well-constructed, well-projected and it shouldn't travel too far in any one of those directions because you risked losing your audience. The skill of the commentator was to communicate a picture through his voice and to hold his listeners' attention.

Some of them were naturals. I don't think, for instance, Michael gave a great deal of thought to all of the aspects of the job. He was a genius. It came easily to him. He didn't have to dig too deep for the truth. It just happened.

Personally, he was the one who opened the doors for me to do my thing. He was certainly the most influential figure in my development as a broadcaster. It was a close working relationship rather than a personal one.

Don't get me wrong, not everything Michael did was perfect, or anything like it. He made his mistakes too. His style of broadcasting, his particular timbre of voice, was not receptive to everyone. Some thought it was very grating.

Michael would have been very sensitive to criticism, but that goes with the territory. From an audience of one million, if 90 per cent of the people are happy the broadcaster can be very satisfied. This still leaves 100,000 listeners who do not like what he or she is saying, for one reason or another.

By and large, commentators should be aware of the different demands of radio and television work. They are two separate entities. In radio, the commentary is everything. In television, the commentary is secondary to the pictures. If the picture is not showing what the commentator is communicating, the viewer has a problem.

Through radio, you rely totally on the broadcaster to generate the atmosphere, to tell you what is happening in an entertaining way. There is no point in sitting down at home, or turning the car radio on at the beach to be told you have tuned in to a bore.

You can't do that. It is an insult to the people who have gone to the trouble of tuning in. Micheal O Muircheartaigh is another example of a great commentator, totally different in style to Michael O'Hehir.

Michael O'Hehir was much more practical. He talked about what was happening on the field of play. It was slightly more informative. He had a much more commanding delivery.

Micheal O Muircheartaigh weaves in stories, works-in anecdotes about the players. He fills in the colour excellently. Perhaps, O'Hehir was the black and white to O Muircheartaigh's colour.

If you put O Muircheartaigh on television, however, it doesn't work as well. He doesn't feel as comfortable because he is too confined. When you say 'it is a high dropping ball into the square' or 'he is soaring towards the clouds for the ball', on radio, your imagination takes you there. When you see that on television, 'the high dropping ball' could be a mis-kick and the salmon-leap is a slight stretch to the clouds. The magic is lost. To laud that as a once-in-a-lifetime fetch – as a radio commentator might do with justification, but not necessarily accuracy – is all part of the drama. To say so on television is seen as a falsehood and an irritant to those who can see for themselves.

Michael O'Hehir used to do a simulcast of the All-Ireland finals on radio and television when Telifis Eireann opened in 1962. It cramped his radio style and it overdid the descriptive detail for television. It didn't work, precisely because they are different disciplines.

When he eventually made the exclusive move to television, he took with him a lot of the habits and sayings that were part and parcel of his radio repertoire, but they were never quite as effective on television. He was at his best on radio.

When you are a spectator in the ground, you don't want the fella beside you to meet you with an elbow and the constant interruption of: 'Did you see that? Will you look at that?' The television commentary should not be the guy sitting beside you in the stand.

Secondly, you should remember that, at any point of a televised match, the viewers are effectively looking down a tube. You only have that two-dimensional view. The spectator in the stand is getting the three-dimensional angle. If you are focused in on, say, a rugby scrum on the halfway line, a whole lot of things could be happening outside that limited scope.

For instance, the spectator at the ground can see that the out-half has moved to the blindside or the full-back has covered this move. All of these things are relevant to the overall picture and the overall development of the game. You have to be aware of what is going on at all times. The television commentator should be providing the third dimension that is relevant to what is being seen. He has to have the panoramic perspective. That is what many commentators do not quite appreciate today. It is more like a radio commentary toned down for television.

Michael O'Hehir also said that when a player gets injured, don't over-dramatise it. Firstly, you cannot diagnose at a distance. The only thing you can do is unnecessarily worry that person's mother, father, husband, wife, sister, brother into a state of distraction. An ill-chosen comment or criticism can cause distress. Caution is often a commentator's safest conveyance.

· · · · ·

Ultimately, Michael left his post as Head of Sport at RTE to become the General Manager at Leopardstown Racecourse in 1972. This didn't work out too well. He left there within a year. I always felt he left RTE before he should have. There was so much more to achieve. Okay, he had his problems with the hierarchy, but it was left to myself and my successor, Tim O'Connor, to develop and steer the sports ship.

People saw Michael O'Hehir as a commentator, pure and simple. That was the public perception of him, as, indeed, it may have been of me as well. Like myself, he was employed as a full-time administrator and a part-time commentator. He also laid the foundations for a very workable and viable sports department at RTE.

It was always a bone of contention that he could never get his way with the senior management within RTE, who didn't particularly enjoy employing a department head with a larger-than-life public personality. That did not sit easily with some. He never felt fully supported, which made it easier for him to walk away.

· · · · ·

Radio Eireann had inherited the laid-back English style of commentary in tone, if not in accent. Michael had come along and changed all that. He had brought an American twist to his delivery, which he would have tuned in to when he made trans-Atlantic flights to see horse racing's version of the Triple Crown in the United States, consisting of the Kentucky Derby at Churchill Downs in Louisville, the Belmont Stakes at Belmont Park in New York and the Preakness Stakes at Pimlico, in Baltimore, Maryland.

Michael was unusual, almost unique, in that he had the American perspective on how a broadcaster could communicate with his public. His style was more closely aligned with the electric excitement there than the understated English approach. He advised me to follow this path. For a while, I tended to almost copycat him. I suppose this was down to the influence Michael had over me as a young man trying to make my way. Looking back on some of my earlier work, it bordered on the hysterical. I learned over time to adopt Michael's advice to fit my own persona. The decibels were lowered. The tone was more measured. I found my own identity. Don't forget, we were very much in virgin territory on television at RTE in the 1960s. There was nobody who had been there and done that. It was all part of the learning process.

It was only later that Cliff Morgan and Bill McLaren brought that very Michael O'Hehir passion to BBC, a passion born out of a love of the game.

Peter O'Sullevan, in horse racing, never over-the-top, was tremendous at building excitement through a race, making his television debut in the 1960 Grand National. He was known as 'The Voice of Racing' to McLaren's 'Voice of Rugby'.

Chapter 13

MY IRISH TIMES

My formal association with sports journalism began in 1953, the year after I left St Mary's College. Having completed a shorthand and typing course in Miss O'Donnell's school on nearby Leinster Road, an opening came up as a trainee sub-editor in the sports department of *The Irish Times*. I was fortunate enough to get it.

I believe I was the last appointment made by the legendary editor, Bertie Smyllie, who died the following year. He was a doyen of the industry. He was the last great Orwellian-type figure in Irish newspapers. He really ruled the roost with an iron fist and enjoyed holding court across the road at The Pearl Bar, or off Westmoreland Street in some other hostelry.

One of my colleagues and great friends, Tom MacGinty, often recounted a story of his newspaper beginnings. Some years earlier, Tom's schooling in Belvedere stood to him at a job interview. Having put Tom at his ease, Smyllie got down to business. He wanted to know what Tom had to offer this venerable Anglo-Irish newspaper institution.

"What about your Leaving Certificate?"

"I'm afraid I failed it."

"You failed?" said the shocked editor. "You failed your Leaving Certificate examination?"

"Yes, sir. I failed Irish," shared Tom.

The mighty Smyllie burst into anger.

"Ridiculous. An absolute disgrace. This business of compulsory Irish is a scandal. We would be delighted to have you on board."

Of course, MacGinty didn't tell Smyllie he hadn't fared too well at English, Mathematics and a few others. It didn't matter. He was in.

It must be said the great Smyllie could not have chosen a better young journalist than Tom MacGinty. He later became the Chief Sports Sub-Editor at *The Irish Times* before moving to the *Irish Independent* to become one of the most respected racing correspondents in the country. How fortunate I was to learn the basics from Tom. He was an excellent mentor, if not quite an Irish scholar.

.....

The wage for that first job was around IR£3 a week. I was a junior probationer in the National Union of Journalists. There were six years of training before one became a senior, back then. It was a long apprenticeship and there was much to learn.

My first real responsibility, apart from making the tea, was compiling the hunting appointments. All the hunts around the country, from the Killinick Harriers in Wexford to the Galway Blazers, would pick up *The Irish Times* to confirm the details of when their hunt was going ahead.

Consider the puzzlement one day when *The Times* announced under the heading, Hunting Appointments: "Clonliffe Harriers – Meet Burgh Quay 11.30. Bring spikes".

There was a sub-editorial staff of three – Tom, Charlie McArdle and myself. Very quickly, and very fortunately, I was learning far more than a junior should learn because I was able to get into the nitty-gritty of the job, working at lay-out and page make-up. Within a year, I was able to lend a hand putting pages together on 'The Stone', as it was called back then in the days of hot metal.

Later, Ireland cricketer, Stanley Bergin, came in to join the sports staff. He moved over to us from the *Irish Independent* on the promise of an offer he couldn't refuse. He doubled up as a sub-editor and reporter. He was one of

Ireland's opening batsmen for several years, along with N.C. Mahony and Louis Jacobson. Stanley helped us while away the quiet hours between 10-11.30pm by playing office cricket in the corridor beside the editorial desk as the paper was 'put to bed'.

The wicket was one of those full-page diaries. We positioned that against the end wall. The ball was made up of recycled copy paper that had been binned, scrunched up into a ball and wrapped by sellotape and rubber bands. I would bowl. Stanley would bat.

For this purpose, he used a long a strip of wood used to keep the newspaper files in place. If you hit the window with a pull-to-leg, it was worth four runs. If you clattered it above a certain height, it was six runs. We were normally looked on with some disdain by some of the more senior members of the editorial staff who were locked away in the newsroom. The sports department, or the toy department as it was commonly known, lived up to its name in that case.

•••••

Paul McWeeney was our sports editor. Tony Goodridge, a South African by birth, was the next in line. He started out as an assistant manager at The Hibernian Hotel and somehow worked his way into journalism, later becoming the rugby writer for *The Daily Telegraph*.

Frank Johnstone, a very assiduous guy, was the soccer correspondent. Patrick Mehigan was the Gaelic games correspondent. He wrote under the name of 'Pato' in *The Irish Times*, but he published numerous annuals under the pseudonym 'Carbery'. His style was unusual. It was quite literary and poetic. He linked Irish ballads and songs into his stories. He was quite a good step dancer, too. In his 70s, it was not unusual for Pato to return from Croke Park doing a little jig as he entered the office in sprightly form. This was a man who loved what he did.

He was also one of the first to do sports commentary on the Irish radio. He actually did an interview with the great American boxer, Gene Tunney, the World Champion from 1926 to 1928, who was spotted at a match in Killarney. Pato asked Tunney to do an interview. He refused. But, not for long. Pato came at him a second time. He was armed with a plan.

"Mr Tunney would you mind doing a radio interview?" said Pato.

"Who is this interview for?"

"I forgot to mention the first time, it is actually coast-to-coast."

In other words, it was Dublin to Galway. Of course, Tunney was thinking more New York to Los Angeles. This struck a chord with Tunney.

"Oh, it's that big! Sure, I'll do it!"

The late Sean Kilfeather of *The Irish Times* edited a compendium of Pato's writings and mentioned this story in it. Pato was a lovely character, a real gentleman, as could be said of all the staff in there.

•••••

The Evening Mail was a law onto itself. They had the exclusive market for small advertisements in the Dublin area for years and years. Billy Kelly was the sports editor and George Gormley was his assistant. *The Irish Times* took over the *Mail* for a few years in the mid-1950s. The new editor, Alan Montgomery, came into the sports room to make an immediate impression. He had walked into a different world.

"Is this the sports department?" Alan asked.

Kelly and Gormley were holding the fort, as they had done for decades.

"Sshh! Mr Kelly is having his afternoon nap," said Gormley.

That is the way it was in those days in *The Evening Mail*. They had a way of doing things and nothing, not even a new boss, was going to change them. The arrival of the *Evening Press* blew them out of the water with cheap advertising rates and a national distribution. That was the end of snooze time and the *Mail*.

•••••

Mick Byrne was a flamboyant character and a successful gambler – so successful that, at one point in his life, he was able to hire a plane to fly him and the other racing hacks to meetings and back. Imagine. In those days. By the time I joined *The Irish Times* in 1953, Mick's lifestyle had taken a turn for the worse. He had gone from hiring aeroplanes to borrowing money to get by. No one knew more about racing than he did through his contacts with all the jockeys, trainers and owners. But that is no guarantee of staying afloat – financially. It was a salutary lesson for a young tyro to learn.

Journalism had a reputation for heavy drinking and wild living in those post-War years. The wages were very low. It was hard to find a job. The drinking culture was fostered in hard times. Journalists spent a lot of time in the pub, squeezing contacts, discussing the affairs of the day or just for the sake of a pint and, yet, not everyone felt the need to drink. Tom MacGinty was a non-drinker. Charlie McArdle drank very little. I came in as a 'Pioneer', a non-drinker from school. I would have to say that there was never any peer pressure one way or the other.

People have asked me since: "How did you stay off the drink in that job?" It was, in fact, much easier to say "I don't drink" in that sort of company. I don't think I would have had the will-power to limit myself to just 'one or two'. It was a big help to wear the Pioneer Pin. It was always respected and I was never asked to remove it from my suit jacket.

• • • • •

I learned all the disciplines of newspapers to do with page layout, to do with printing, to do with sub-editing. I was quickly capable of holding the fort if Tom had a chance of skiving off to meet his fiancée, Blathnaid O'Broin. Tom was happy to give me as much rope as I needed to take on some of the senior work. While I got valuable hands-on experience, Tom and Blathnaid prepared for their wedding.

It was in 1955 that *The Irish Times* published a 7am special cricket edition in order to have the latest news of The Ashes Test series in Australia in its morning edition. It was the year Frank 'Typhoon' Tyson and Brian Statham demolished the Aussies batting to enable England to dominate the series. Having enjoyed some success as a fast bowler at St Mary's College, I had a particular interest in Tyson's remarkable figures of seven wickets for 27 runs in a single innings of the third Test in Melbourne.

I can still remember the problems he caused us back in Dublin as we tried to tie-up the 'final edition' of the *Times*. Every time we were ready to 'let the page go' the teleprinter would rat-tat-tat again with a 'flash' of yet another wicket for Tyson. Eventually, the 'lino' – or print – staff and the machine room guys insisted we fold our tents for the morning. Obviously, today, the 'stop press' excitement is no more. The electronic media systems have taken over.

•••••

The Irish Times sports editor, Paul McWeeney, was a great character in his day, a useful squash player and always able to give as good as he got. He allowed the people on the staff to get on with the job. He just made sure the big events were properly covered. The only time I remember him coming into the office and asserting his authority was when MacGinty was asked to answer a complaint from the printing area about how some of the sports people were late in seeing the page away from the 'stone'. Consequently, certain papers could have nearly missed the trains that would bring them deep into the country.

The complaint climbed all the way to the editor, who, in turn, wanted to know who was responsible for this mistake. MacGinty was about to be sent up to be chewed out until Paul heard about this.

"No, no, no Tom, if there are any complaints about the sports department, it is to the sports editor they must come. I will deal with this."

The matter was settled and Paul, casual as ever, never referred to it again.

McWeeney just didn't seem to have a care in the world. He used to do a Sunday column for *The People*. His style of writing was very fluent, very easy and very correct for *The Irish Times*. But, he could churn out the biff, bang, wallop as well for *The People*.

Nine times out of ten, guys working either in the reporters' room or the subs' room would have a contact with Associated Press (AP), Press Association (PA) or Reuters. If any sort of story came in to the Westmoreland office, the last news outlet to get it would be *The Irish Times*. The stringers around the country would go bananas because stories they would send in would be rifled by someone in town and sent on to AP as a way of making a few extra quid, added value I suppose it would be called these days.

"Give me that! The AP deadline is in twenty minutes."

"What about our own deadline?"

"What about it? There's plenty of time."

Your main employer was the last one to get the information.

Paul also had a sixth sense if there was even a suggestion of a 'freebie' going anywhere. He would find it and pass the information on to the rest of the mob.

"I think we might have a word with the public relations officer or the honorary treasurer because there were some very interesting hand-outs at that thing," he would say.

It was all the more surprising then that Paul should have got the short straw when assigned accommodation at a British Open golf championship in Scotland one year. He was even less pleased when the well-organised Jack McGowan, who wrote on golf for the *Belfast Telegraph*, greeted him in the press room.

Paul had a slight impediment or hesitation to his speech. He had staggered into the press room on the first day, looking a little dishevelled.

"There you are, Paul. How ye doin'?" greeted Jack.

"I'm not ve-very well, Jack," replied Paul in his trademark stammer.

"What's your problem?"

"My problems be-be-began when I was de-de-deposited in my hotel 7,000 miles away from the golf course. It to-to-took so long to ge-ge-get here and there were no taxis."

"You should be in my place. I'm only down the road, two minutes from the first tee," issued Jack, unaware of Paul's annoyance.

"And the ph-ph-phones. I was two hours wa-wa-waiting for *The Irish Times* to come through last night. I mi-mi-missed my dinner."

"You should be in my place, Paul. There are phones everywhere. There was one right beside my bed. I had no trouble getting through to the *Telegraph*. There I was writing my copy last night. What do you know, I felt short-taken. I went into the john. You won't believe it, Paul; there was a phone in there too. I ended up dictating my copy to the *Telegraph*, sitting on the john. What do you think of that, Paul?"

"How ve-ve-very ap-ap-appropriate, Jack!"

•••••

For many years, Tony Goodridge was Paul's under-study, covering rugby, golf, hockey in the main. He had a sharp sense of humour. He was on his way into the office one morning. The main revolving door was on Westmoreland Street and, as he approached it, MacGinty was rushing out to a charity event in a flap, flying through the revolving door, almost falling out onto the street.

Tony was rather old-fashioned with a West-British voice.

"Oh, there you are Tom."

"How are you Tony?"

"You are looking quite dishevelled and in a bit of hurry."

"Oh yes, sorry Tony. I am rushing around to the St Vincent de Paul."

"Oh, really? I normally get mine at Kennedy and McSharry."

With the mention of the name of this high-quality genlemen's outfitters, the suggestion was that Tom's dress sense was not quite what it should have been.

When Frank Johnstone passed away, I realised that I was the sole survivor of that particular group from *The Irish Times* sports department. Frank was the soccer writer. Tom MacGinty was the one who guided me through the rudiments of journalism, the rules and regulations of reportage. As a trainee sub-editor, Tom, Charlie McArdle (the racing correspondent), the racing tipster, Niall Sheridan (who worked under the pseudonym of 'Birdcatcher'), and P.D. 'Pato' Mehigan (one of the literary greats of GAA) were wonderful companions and workmates. I am the only one left. Maybe, it is the natural order of things. It means I am now next in line in a one-man queue.

Chapter 14

HARRY THUILLIER

In 1952-53, Phil Green was appointed as Radio Eireann's first 'Sports Officer'. He tried to modernise it, introducing more time for an unscripted Sports Stadium. There was still a hangover from the 1940s when everything had to be scrutinised by the army surveillance people because nothing could go out that was considered by the censor to be of a sensitive nature ... like the weather forecast.

As far as I remember, it was the first time Irish radio went into a non-scripted format. By the early 1950s, the claustrophobic cover of censorship had been mostly peeled away, but there remained a civil service attitude to doing things properly and strictly within budget, which left little room for innovation. Radio Eireann didn't open until 1pm and closed at 3pm, returning to air from 5.30pm to 11.45pm.

It wasn't until 1955 that Junior Sports Magazine (JSM) was first broadcast. This was the creation of Harry Thuillier. Arising out of his exposure as a very personable presenter, with a nice light touch, Harry was asked to do sponsored programmes. In the late 1950s, early 1960s, he would become the most popular presenter of this type of programme. People like Larry Gogan, Denis Brennan, Joe Linnane and Gay Byrne would have all been in the market for the same work. The creation of JSM turned out to be a defining move in my career. It also formed the basis to forward the careers of several other broadcasters of the time, such as John Bowman and Jimmy Magee, to name two.

So many things in life happen as a matter of chance. I don't know that there is such a guide as destiny in our lives. I do know that I have been very lucky when I needed to be. I was walking across O'Connell Bridge one day from *The Irish Times* on my way to meet Dad in the *Irish Independent*. I happened upon Harry, whom I knew from his work on Sports Stadium. I hadn't seen him for three or four years. He was full of an idea he had for a junior sports programme on Radio Eireann. We had a short chat bemoaning the lack of openings there were in Radio Eireann. He spoke of this 'great idea' he had for teenage kids – Juniors.

His only problem was he had to persuade the Head of Children's Programming there, Seamus Kavanagh, to adopt the idea. He was to send in scripts and Seamus would have a look at them. But, Harry didn't have the time, the interest or the inclination to do the writing.

"Would you help me with the scripts," he said, out of the blue.

"Sure. I would be delighted to," I said.

"Now. I have to tell you the budget is tight, very tight."

"Oh, I don't want any money for it. But, could I contribute to the programme on air in some small way?"

"There shouldn't be a problem with that."

It was the opening I had been looking for. A new partnership had begun.

A few months later, we were invited into Henry Street to read the scripts that had been created to see how they would work. Harry, Leo Nealon, who was a very capable GAA commentator, and myself sat around a microphone and let fly with our various ideas on how to work the show.

The first broadcast went on air in 1955. The first piece was on Thuillier's experience as an Olympian at Helsinki in 1952. He gave me the headlines and I ghost-wrote the main body of the piece for him. JSM ran as a magazine programme with a weekly quiz from then to the mid-1960s, starting out on a Friday before switching to a Saturday afternoon in 1957. That was when we recruited a fresh-faced Jimmy Magee. Even then, he had a great memory for the facts and figures of a wide variety of sports. Sean Diffley was another to come into the fold, covering rugby and athletics. After that, the great Irish

Olympian, Paul Dolan, joined up, along with Dermot Kelly, who went on to become one of the main producers at RTE Sport.

Although we were frowned on, at times, by the more senior members of the small sports department in Radio Eireann, we also covered big sporting events because every kid had a hero, like Jackie Kyle or Christy Ring or Nicky Rackard, and we wanted to bring those heroes to our audience for a programme that remained under the umbrella of the Children's Department. Initially, it was due to run for six weeks. By the end, it had been on air for ten years.

It ran its course when RTE was founded. Under the leadership of Michael O'Hehir, RTE was being developed dramatically. Harry Thuillier had become one of the most prolific presenters of the 15-minute sponsored programmes. Junior Sports Magazine was subsumed into the output of a formal and integrated service.

It will be remembered with gratitude by so many who enjoyed the carefree approach of Harry, whose cheery personality hid a steely determination to extend the boundaries of broadcasting. JSM laid down a whole set of standards based upon 'on-the-day', on-the-spot sports reportage if it was at all possible.

If we couldn't be there, we would pretend that the voice was resonating from Thomond Park in Limerick or Nowlan Park in Kilkenny even though it was, in fact, recorded from just outside the front door on a noisy Henry Street in Dublin.

These were the various little tricks of the trade that were forced on us by the technical and travel limitations of the time. I recall doing a report sitting by an open window high above Henry Street. The impression given was that I was broadcasting from a hockey match in Limerick. The idea was to include an 'atmosphere' in the report, which was taped on an old L2 portable machine, then transferred to a disc machine and carried from there to the studio, ready for transmission.

It was not until we heard it on air that we realised the 'atmosphere', supposedly from Limerick, included the familiar Dublin sounds of voices calling "*Herald* and *Mail*", and the Moore Street banter of "five pence the three oranges" and "put the fish back, Mista".

Chapter 15

BILLY MORTON

I inherited my father's broad interest in all sports. Each one has their merits for those who play them. There is no such thing as one being better than the other. It depends on the personalities of the people involved. Some people like jazz, some like rock 'n' roll. It doesn't mean one is better than the other, merely different. It was a fairly catholic, all-embracing upbringing. If there was a ball there, you kicked it or threw it. If there was a cricket bat there, you let fly.

In the late 1940s, I was very fortunate to accompany my Dad to a range of sporting events. At this time, the immortal Billy Morton was bringing vitality and interest to athletics. He was a man of boundless energy and a very American can-do attitude.

Billy held a love of athletics close to his heart. He would not let anything or anyone get in his way of promoting it. In his prime, he had been a fine marathon runner, an Irish champion and record-holder at one time.

There is the story of how he was leading the 26-mile endurance test in a local or regional meet as he made his way back to Croke Park for what would have been a celebratory final lap of the track. Astonishingly, the wicker gate leading onto the track was locked. The organisers had forgotten that the runners were still out on the course. Billy had to wait for them to open the gate. He ended up with egg on his face in the form of a second-place finish.

I remember watching Bert Healion throwing the hammer in College Park. He was out on his own in Ireland during the War years, 1939-1945, throwing his lifetime best, 58.80 metres, to rank second in the world to Germany's Karl Storch in 1943 and staying in the top five throwers in the world for five consecutive years.

I also vividly recall Bert Healion letting the hammer slip out of his control at an athletics meeting at Glenmalure Park, the old Shamrock Rovers ground. There was no cage, no netting, no nothing. The wild shouts went out in a scene reminiscent of a golfer who shanked his drive. The hammer sailed unapologetically through the air to crash through the old unreserved stand. Luckily, there were no spectators there at the time, but those in attendance had used the area to rest their bikes and one or two were buckled by the force of the hammer crashing into them.

High-jumper Dicky O'Rafferty was a wonderful western-roller. He was quite remarkable in that he wasn't the tallest man in the world, and yet he could leap so far over his own height, regularly scaling six-feet, four inches. Dicky dominated this event in Ireland for the best part of 20 years and was the first Donore Harrier athlete to win a gold medal at the British AAA Championships in 1937.

Often, Billy would travel to Great Britain to entice big stars to come to Dublin. It was only when he got their agreement that he would then build a meeting around these elite athletes. The great Arthur Wint, the Jamaican 400 metres – or 440 yards as it was then – gold medallist and 800 metres silver medallist at the 1948 Olympics in London was a sight for unwounded eyes. I can still clearly see his majestic, gliding frame effortlessly moving over the ground down the back straight at College Park.

Billy had so much to do. There was the odd oversight, like the time he organised an athletics meeting at College Park and forgot to arrange for the gold, silver and bronze medals for the podium. Always a quick thinker, Billy proudly presented the winner with his personal idea of original prizes.

First Prize: A framed photo of Billy Morton.

Second Prize: A smaller framed photo of Billy Morton.

Third Prize: Just a plain photo of Billy Morton.

He was a modest man.

•••••

Billy invented the sports press conference in Ireland. He was the first to have the idea of a) making an announcement; b) getting the press to attend.

"Gentlemen of the press, you will be delighted to hear that we are going to have five World Champions at our next meeting at College Park," he would loudly announce.

"Which?"

"Which what?"

"Which World Champions?"

"I don't know, but we will have five of them there."

If pressed, he would throw out one or two names and then make the corrections as the confirmations or refusals came into him.

•••••

In the *Evening Herald*, there were often complaints from Billy Morton's competitors that whenever they sent in press releases they never received the same profile. There were accusations of bias and favouritism. This was not true. There were phone calls to the office. Unpleasant ones.

"It is a disgrace."

"What is a disgrace?"

"Why don't you give us the same space you give to Billy Morton?"

"Wait a minute. How many times have you sent in material?"

"We send something in once a month and we only get a single paragraph."

"Yeah, but Billy Morton sends in material every day."

That was Billy. He would drown us in copy, most of it rubbish. But when there was a hole to fill in the *Herald*, for lack of sports news, Billy's latest venture was always there. It was an example to others. Persistence pays off.

•••••

In the 1950s, Billy called a press conference to announce the development of Santry Stadium as an international athletics arena with a state-of-the-art, for those days, 'En Tout Cas' running track and that the best tennis players in the world, playing under 'The Jack Kramer Professional Tennis Circus', would come to Santry. They were the forerunners for the transformation of international tennis from the amateur to professional era. At the time, they were pariahs to the traditionalists.

"Billy, how in the name of God is Jack Kramer's Tennis Circus going to play in Santry? It is an athletics stadium. Will it be on grass?"

"It will not be on grass. It will be played on a hard court."

"What do you mean?"

"En Tout Cas laid the running track. They are the best tennis court makers in the world. They will put in the hard court."

"But Billy, all you have to do is mow the grass," said Tom Cryan of the *Irish Press*.

"Did you not hear, Tom? Grass is on the way out!"

That was the end of that. The tennis court was built. And The Jack Kramer Circus came to town.

• • • • •

In 1958, five men went under the magical four-minute barrier in a mile race at Santry Stadium. I was there because Gerry Merren, the sports editor of the *Evening Herald*, asked me to go out to do a short piece of no more than 100 words for one of the international agencies. I think it was Reuters. They had booked a telephone line with our Post & Telegraphs.

In the years leading up to the opening of Santry Stadium, Billy Morton organised a series of mile races in 1956-57 at Lansdowne Road where the competitors ran five laps to the mile. In that time, there was a great rivalry between Brian Hewson, the great English runner, and Ronnie Delany.

That was how Billy generated the revenue to build Santry Stadium. Lansdowne had been an athletics track before it was developed into the home of Irish rugby. In fact, the Dunlop family, who owned the grounds originally, had laid a cinder track there, but it had long been covered by the 1950s.

Santry had been opened earlier in the summer of 1958 when Albert

Thomas had set a world three-mile record. It received an immediate reputation for being a 'fast track'. The Delany mile with Herb Elliott, Merv Lincoln, Murray Halberg and Thomas was going to be the feature event.

Australian Herb Elliot was then described as the 'greatest miler in the world'. We all wanted to know if Delany, the reigning Olympic champion, could beat him. The place was jammed. The phone in the stadium rang just before the start of the race. I told the copy-taker at the other end to hang on and I could give him the 100 words when the race was finished, with the official first, second and third across the finish line.

The race started. It looked like a fast one because they dipped below the minute for the first quarter, went under two minutes for halfway. The world record then was 3.58.6. As the runners wheeled around into the last lap, the crowd was going bananas. You couldn't hear anything with the rising noise. As they whizzed by the finish line, I had to look twice, three times at my watch.

I couldn't believe it. It was definitely a new world record. So, the man at the other end of the phone said he would hold on for a few more minutes. I started to regurgitate the race. The next thing, the time was announced – 3.54.5. The world record had been smashed. Unbelievable.

Now, my 100 words suddenly exploded. The American desk came on. The Australian desk was on. They all wanted reviews and interviews. There I was, with a phone at my ear and a piece of paper in my hand. The runners were scattered here, there and everywhere. It was pandemonium.

I picked up bits of information from whoever I could until the dark started to creep in. I was finishing off. There were very few people left in the stadium. It was then a request came in for a comment from Delany. Of course, Ronnie was long gone.

"Everyone is gone," I said down the phone line.

"Well, we need something from Delany!"

"Hold on a minute. I think I see him."

"Oh great, I'll hold on."

"Yeah, it's Fred here. I just had a word with Delany."

"Fire away."

"After the race, Ronnie Delany, the 1,500 metres Olympic champion, was so impressed with the performance of Herb Elliot, he said: 'There is only one way of stopping Elliot. That is to tie his legs together'."

"Oh, great! Great quote!"

"Cheerio now," I said.

The following morning, *The Irish Press* led with Delany's comment which, of course, I made up out of thin air. I have never been able to tell Ronnie that one.

$$\bullet\ \bullet\ \bullet\ \bullet\ \bullet$$

The following is my father, Mitchel's, report in the *Irish Independent* on the race on August 7, 1958.

FIRST FOUR HOME BEAT EXISTING RECORD. FIVE IN ALL GET WITHIN FOUR MINUTES.
By Mitchel V. Cogley.

The four-minute barrier became a shambles at Santry Stadium, Dublin last night when it was crashed by no fewer than five runners in a field of eight with 20-years-old Herb Elliott of Australia leading the pack in this fantastic mile with a time of 3 minutes 54.5 seconds, the fastest mile ever run. This time not only shatters Elliott's own world record of 3-57.9 but also renders negligible any further consideration of the much-debated "paced" mile of 3-57.2 by Derek Ibbotson in July of last year.

In last night's mile, too, the previous world best was also beaten by Merv Lincoln, second in 3-55.9; and by Ireland's Ronnie Delany and Murray Halberg of New Zealand, third and fourth, respectively, in 3-57.5. In fifth place was another great little Australian, Albert Thomas, in 3-58.6. With a story of such magnitude one hardly knows where to start. The greatest of expectations were exceeded in a race that will go down through history.

"We may never see such a race again." These were the words I wrote when reporting Ibbotson's record run of 3-57.2, with Ronnie Delany second, Jungwirth of Yugoslavia, third, and Ken Woods of Britain, fourth, all inside the four minutes, at the White City, London on July 19 of last year. In little more than a year later I can only repeat – "We may never see such a race again."

Not that it was really a race, as such. The phenomenal Elliott was always in the closest touch with whoever hit the front – Thomas for two laps, then Halberg for a spell and Lincoln at the bell – and, when he let himself go to blaze the victory trail, nobody else mattered.

He streaked away in a majestic last lap that crushed all opposition, the very epitome of speed and power blended in the perfect athletic frame, so easy and so perfectly fresh a winner in such fantastic time that one can only wonder at his potential.

After the race he said to me: "Under such conditions as tonight the next mile target can only be 3.50." I asked him would he do that time himself.

And this most modest and unassuming of young men, a former pupil of St. Aquinas Christian Brothers College, Melbourne, merely smiled and said: "If I don't do it, somebody else will. It could even be your Ronnie Delany. I think he was short of real competition tonight."

Which brings us back to last night's mile. An unexpected starter was the ebullient little Australian, Albert Thomas, who last month put the new Santry track on the map with his world three-miles record.

And it was Thomas who set the pace with blistering laps of 58 seconds for the first quarter, 1 minute 58 seconds for the half mile. Closely in touch were Elliott, Lincoln, Halberg, with Delany, possibly thinking the pace could not be maintained, holding himself back in fifth place.

But the pace was not merely maintained; it was stepped up, with Lincoln taking over from Thomas to set the bell tolling at 2 minutes 59 seconds, Elliott poising himself for the kill just behind, with Halberg and Delany then too far behind to offer an effective challenge.

Nothing could live against Elliott's surge to the front. Lincoln chased him gamely without making any impression and the only real race was that between Delany and Halberg, passing out the gallant Thomas, for the third place which went to the Irishman by inches.

Elliott, incidentally, was timed for 1,500 metres at 3 mins 39.6 secs, which is one second inside the official world record held, by Istvan Pozsavoelgyi, the Hungarian.

Tonight Elliott will be in action again, this time in the two miles against Thomas and it will come as no surprise if both of these magnificent runners set up new world figures.

In the general flurry of excitement, an event in which ordinary circumstances would have aroused tremendous interest passed almost unnoticed in its final stages.

This was the high jump, which gave us some magnificent jumping, with all three visitors topping 6ft 6in, C. Porter of Australia, clearing 6ft 7 in, at his first attempt to equal the Irish record and then, in the excitement of the mile, failing in his attempt to beat the Irish record, which he now holds jointly with Floyd Jaeter, of USA.

The jumpers were so pleased with their efforts that they are all having another "go" tonight, when the Irish record may well soar to a new height.

GARDNER EQUALS RECORD

In the 120 yards hurdles, K. Gardner, second in the 100 yards, got among the records with a grand display of hurdling to win in 14.2 secs. and equal Eamon Kinsella's Irish and all-comers record.

In the local events, John Lawlor once again beat 200 feet in the hammer, while T. Dunne showed the way home in a field of four steeplechasers.

In addition to the mile, an Irish all-comers record was put up in the 100 yards when the Canadian resident Trinidadian, Mike Agostini, raced to a 9.5 second victory. He was happily greeted after the race by his first teacher, Rev. J.J. King, C.S.Sp., Granard, Co. Longford, who had Agostini as one of his pupils at St Mary's College, Port of Spain.

The capacity attendance of something over 20,000 applauded all the mile heroes to the echo, paying the greatest tribute they could to the magnificent Australians, Elliott and Lincoln, and giving a special "hand" to Delany, whose magnificent time of 3 mins, 57.5 seconds, is, of course, a native record.

As he and Halberg, the cheerful New Zealander, battled it out for third place some 25 yards behind the winner, it must have been at once heart-warming to beat the previous world mile record and yet galling to be fighting for the minor placing.

· · · · ·

That day in Santry, when Herb Elliott smashed the world mile record, was also a poignant moment for that great entrepreneur Billy Morton, the one-man athletics industry who made it all happen.

At the end of the evening, the place was silent as a prayer where, only hours earlier, history had been made as Elliott swept down the home straight well ahead of Australia's Merv Lincoln and our own Ronnie Delany.

I was strolling across the stadium, exhausted from the intensity of the work, when who did I come across? That's right. Billy Morton.

"Billy, you're made!" I congratulated him.

"I'm not so sure, young Cogley. Will the crowds come again if we can't guarantee more records like that?"

I couldn't see his reasoning then. Alas, Billy knew what he was talking about. Sadly, he was right. Santry never enjoyed a meeting quite like it again.

Chapter 16

THE RINGSEND REGATTA

By 1954, Ronnie Walsh was the presenter for Sports Stadium. Eamonn Andrews had left for England where he became a great figure in broadcasting. Ronnie asked me to be the rowing correspondent for Sports Stadium because I had been writing an occasional column on rowing for *The Irish Times* with the help of Wally Stephens in step with infrequent pieces on the sport for Radio Eireann.

"Sure," I said.

One day, I got a phone call in the office.

"Are you the fella that does the rowin' on the radio?"

"Yes. That's right."

"I wonder would you give us a mention in your next piece?"

"Well, yeah, who do you represent?"

"Ah, I represent the Ringsend Regatta. We are celebrating the 750th anniversary of the Regatta this year."

"That sounds very interesting."

"There will be fellas from all over comin' to it. The entire Dublin basin will be involved."

I took his information and told him I would be happy to include it on the radio. The following Friday I finished off my broadcast with a reference to the excitement surrounding the Ringsend Regatta in the Dublin basin.

There was an immediate reaction from the Irish Rowing Union, which was not best pleased that I had included 'Skiff Racing' in the bulletin. These were the big old rowing boats that were raced in homage to a time long since passed. It had nothing to do with the pared down scull racing version. They were two different pursuits. I hadn't made any attempt to differentiate between them. Little did I know how this honest mistake would turn out to be a blessing in disguise two years later.

· · · · ·

Nineteen-fifty-six was the year of the Olympics in Melbourne. It was also the year of the international women's hockey Conference in Australia. This was later to become the World Cup. The Irish were sending out a team and I happened to know two of the girls going out. I mentioned it to Harry Thuillier at our Junior Sports Magazine meeting. We agreed it would make a nice piece if I could get a recorder. The old L2 machine was about the size of a large piece of heavy luggage.

On the day, I headed out to Dun Laoghaire with the recorder and my future brother-in-law, Cyril White. We were soon in something of a panic. The bus was late. The boat was leaving at 8pm. We jumped from the moving bus with all the athletic prowess we could muster and took off on a foot race down the Marine Parade. The perspiration was pumping out of me. I realised we had no chance if we followed everyone else to the passenger departures area, so we skipped over the railway line in the hope of grabbing a few quick words with one of the girls. It was a no-go area. Alas, we could see we were too late. The ship was moving away from the pier.

Suddenly, this huge big docker loomed in front of us.

"What do you think you are doing here?"

"We were supposed to talk to someone on the boat. There's a team going to ..."

"Hold on a minute there! Are you that fella off the radio?"

"Yes, well yes, I am."

"Fred Cogley."

"That's right."

"What is it ye want?"

"We have been sent out to talk to the Irish ladies' hockey team, but they're gone."

I could sense my entire radio career sinking into oblivion.

"Wait a minute there! Paddy! Paddy! Bring her back," he roared.

"What is it?" came the reply from a man on the ship.

"Bring her back in," the docker screamed again at the top of his voice.

We couldn't believe it. The boat returned. The girls thought it was sinking. I shot up the gangplank. I did two or three interviews with the girls and returned to the dockside.

"Did ye get everything ye wanted?"

"Yes. We did. Thanks a million. You saved my life."

"Paddy, take it away!"

"What can I say, except thank you so much."

He put his huge hand on my shoulder – I still have the mark – nearly driving me into the pier.

"A few years ago, you did a very good turn for us on the Ringsend Regatta. It's a pleasure to return the compliment."

Unbelievable! It was just one of those marvellous things that happen over the course of a career.

Chapter 17

TONY O'REILLY

In the 1950s, we witnessed the emergence of a formidable character – Tony O'Reilly. He had all the appearance of a red-headed Jonah Lomu – the incomparable, towering All Black – as a six-foot two, 14-stone winger. This was gargantuan back then when most wing three-quarters were will o' the wisp types. Tony would have preferred to play in the centre. Playing for Ireland at that time, the opportunities to express himself were few and far between because of the emphasis placed on a kicking strategy.

We never really saw the best of him in an Ireland jersey. Quite simply, we didn't have the quality of players to bring out the best in him. Yet, as a winger in a three-quarter line of genuine skill and pace, he was lethal. When he had players, like the English centre Jeff Butterfield, to create space for him, he proved to be devastating for The British Lions (unofficially referred to as The British and Irish Lions on this side of the sea even prior to its official name change, in 2002) on tour to South Africa in 1955 and New Zealand in 1959. Overall, he racked up 37 tries in 36 appearances for The Lions terrorising southern hemisphere defences wherever he went.

In 1955, it would prompt Wales out-half Cliff Morgan, the stand-in captain for Irishman Robin Thompson in the third test against the Springboks, to proclaim of the 19-year-old: "It's funny. As captain you wanted the best out of everybody and I knew that Tony would play better on the left wing. I had great admiration for him since, even at that age, he had all the classic virtues – body turned slightly away from the tackler, knees and legs high as he runs, tremendous courage. The Irish tend to say: 'Ah, lucky fellow. Everything's lucky in Ireland'. But there was nothing lucky about Tony's life. He was already 25 years older upstairs in his mind than anybody I'd known."

I couldn't have explained it any better.

• • • • •

Tony was also a devoted supporter of the multi-national invitational rugby team, the Barbarians, who always play in Black and White hoops, with the players retaining the socks of their clubs. He also holds the distinction of making the most appearances for the 'Baa-Baas' (30) and scoring the most tries for them (38).

He was just a phenomenal sports person. At the time, apart from all his other attributes, even in Belvedere College as a schoolboy, he had that capacity or charisma to attract attention, whether it was at rugby or cricket.

Physically, he was a man masquerading as a boy. He was tall and strong. Whatever it was about him, he always happened to be at the centre of the defining moments of matches. For instance, he was playing on the right wing for Belvedere against Newbridge in his first year in the Leinster Schools' Senior Cup. It looked as though Belvo were on their way out of the Cup. Newbridge were winning narrowly and pressing for victory.

Newbridge held possession. They moved the ball quickly towards the wing where they looked like scoring or, at least, putting Belvedere in a perilous defensive position with time almost up. As the ball was whipped to the left winger, O'Reilly hurtled through for an intercept. From inside his own 22, he raced the length of the pitch for the match-winning try. It was the stuff of schoolboy dreams. It was his reality.

In the 1954 Senior Cup final, O'Reilly was captain of a talented Belvedere side, playing against Blackrock. His presence, his reputation, his x-factor appeal made Belvedere slight favourites to beat Blackrock. This time, Belvedere were on the move. They were directing the ball out to Tony in the middle of the field in Lansdowne Road. But Tom Cleary was a very lithe, athletic 'Rock centre. He ghosted onto an intercept near halfway just as the ball was about to get to O'Reilly. He had the legs to make the line in what was the match-sealing score for Blackrock.

You can imagine the disappointment of O'Reilly, the captain that year, as he made his way back to his own posts. As Cleary moved past, Tony, going in the opposite direction, offered his hand in congratulations to the boy who had just ended his Cup dream. For a schoolboy of 18 years of age, in those circumstances, at that moment, in an unobtrusive, unshowy gesture, it indicated something extra about O'Reilly. He went on from there to international fame and fortune. His achievements won recognition from Queen Elizabeth when he was knighted in the 2001 New Year's Honours to become Sir Anthony O'Reilly.

In 1955, his first year out of school, he won his first cap for Ireland. In the same year, he was chosen for The Lions on that tour to South Africa. Not only was he up to playing for The Lions, he broke try-scoring records for them. It was always the bizarre, extraordinary things that he did that made him stand out from the crowd.

One story goes that Tony was in The Shelbourne Hotel one day when he received news that his wife had given birth to triplets. He jumped into a taxi. The driver recognised his passenger.

"Ah, is it yourself O'Reilly?"

"It is. Can you get me to the hospital quickly? My wife has just given birth to triplets."

"Very well. And congratulations!"

"Thank you very much."

"You must have left the engine running that night," piped the taxi driver.

I have met Tony quite a few times. He has always been very gracious, particularly towards my dad, Mitchel. He was a great admirer of his writings with the *Independent*, which he would eventually go on to take over in later life.

When Tony went to London to work for Heinz in 1969, we did a television piece with him about his life up to then. The attention to detail he put into that was quite remarkable, not that he was obtrusive, not that he suggested we do it his way, nothing like that. He just wanted it to be right. I think that was probably the secret of his great success. Whatever he did, he just wanted it to be right. He was one of the great sportsmen.

His best rugby position, if he had the players inside him, which he didn't always have with Ireland, would have been left wing. Ireland seldom won the sort of possession up front, or had the backs inside to use the ball well enough, to bring O'Reilly into the action.

This is why his record with Ireland did not compare with that of The Lions. Ireland had honed a reputation as a kicking side, rather than a creative one. There were George Norton and Barney Mullen in the 1940s, into the 1950s, and Tommy Kiernan in the 1960s. We had so many penalty kickers. Even later, we had Ollie Campbell, Tony Ward, Ralph Keyes and, more recently, Ronan O'Gara and Jonathan Sexton.

It was Ireland's ability to scramble and put the opposition under pressure – the 'boot, bite and bo***ck tactic', if you like – more than sparkling back movements that kept them within striking distance. There were exceptions, of course, like Davy Hewitt, a fantastic three-quarter, and Kevin Flynn, a beautifully skilled player in the midfield, and the incomparable Jack Kyle.

There were relatively few occasions when an Irish backline moved with purpose. You could freeze to death on the wing and hardly ever get a chance to run with the ball. Tony wasn't used to being on the periphery of life. So anxious was he to get the ball, he would often wander offside in midfield trying to get to the opposition. This tendency to give away penalties, and consequently points, often drew boos of frustration from the crowd. These were the days before drift defences. If Jack Kyle was the outstanding personality of the 1940s, Tony O'Reilly filled that role in the 1950s, not for Ireland, but for The Lions.

Looking back over my shoulder from today's world of professionalism in sport, it is amusing to recall just how much has changed in attitudes, in administrative principles and in the whole approach towards the game. For example, in the rigid amateur days, the Rugby Union attempted to 'protect' their players from any whiff of controversy. Billy Jeffares was the Secretary of the Union in the early 1950s. The offices were in Westmoreland Street, opposite the old *Irish Times*. Tony O'Reilly was a contemporary of mine. He was at Belvedere while I was at St Mary's.

As an aspiring young broadcaster, I got permission from Harry Thuillier to request an interview with Tony for Junior Sports Magazine before he headed off with The Lions to tour South Africa in 1955. I contacted Tony to ask would he do an interview for the radio. He said sure. We had to go through the Union to get permission from them. So, I wrote off to Billy Jeffares to sanction the interview, expecting it to be just a formality.

It was standard procedure back then. Jeffares was the Secretary of the Irish Rugby Football Union. He had taken over from his father, Billy Senior. Punctilious is the word to best describe the attitude of officials in those days. The Secretary of the IRFU would read out the Ireland team selection at that time, having received it from The 'Big Five' selectors, comprising two from Ulster, two from Leinster and one from Munster. Connacht was left to see the joke.

Consequently, the Connacht players found it difficult to get recognition for their talent. They had to overcome a natural bias by sheer weight of numbers. The mathematics of the situation did not make sense for them, or any fair-thinking person.

Anyway, Jeffares Junior wrote the most extraordinary letter in return to my request for an interview with Tony, stating that the IRFU Committee needed to see a full list of the questions intended and – as near as possible – a summary of the answers. I couldn't believe this. But it had been considered normal practice for years back then. Player interviews were a rarity. In fairness, the IRFU took no action when the interview was aired without their imprimatur.

Not too long before that, some of my senior colleagues assured me that it had been the practice of the Irish team to be announced in alphabetical order. Billy's father, the Secretary before him, would read out the names in alphabetical order. If a journalist had the temerity to ask which position a player occupied in the forwards, for example.

"First up, first down," would come the reply.

That meant if you were first up to the scrum, you were the hooker or the prop. As far as he was concerned, he was there to supply the names. The journalists were not part of the establishment. They were seen as intruders into an amateur game.

It wasn't unusual, back then, for players to be billed for a pair of socks that weren't returned. They weren't allowed to keep their jerseys, much less swap them with opponents. It carried on into the 1970s when Tony Ward's popularity was not considered appropriate for a team sport. Individuality was frowned upon and, anyway, hadn't his picture appeared in a tabloid newspaper as he stood proudly in his underpants. Tut, tut.

•••••

I suppose Tony O'Reilly was perhaps the first real 'personality' in Irish rugby to suffer at the hands of officialdom. His larger-than-life persona, and his sporting ability, seemed to generate official hostility. As he became internationally successful in business, his rugby career stuttered. He was no longer an automatic choice in the early 1960s. Indeed, after 1963 he had faded out of the International scene altogether. He might have been gone, but he was not forgotten.

In the heart of the city of London, the Royal Artillery ground was often put at the disposal of visiting International sides for a limb-loosening run-out on the day before an International at Twickenham. So it was in 1970 that I joined several other journalists at the ground watching the Irish team complete their preparations.

There was one gap in the three-quarter line and we wondered who the selectors would call upon as a replacement. While we waited for the team bus to arrive we speculated. When it pulled into the ground, there was no sign of any new face as the players trooped into the changing room.

Suddenly, there was a commotion outside. This impressive, chauffeur-driven Rolls Royce swung in through the gates. The replacement had arrived. It was O'Reilly – back to play for Ireland for the first time since 1963. He was one of the few men to have won International caps in three different decades, the 1950s, 1960s and 1970s – just. Who else but Tony could have made an entrance like that?

Sadly, the return was short-lived. That International was his last for Ireland. He often recounts one incident from the game. When he was recovering on the pitch from a knock on the head, he heard a disgruntled Irish voice call out from the touchline.

"Why didn't you kick his bloody driver as well while you were at it?"

Chapter 18

RONNIE DELANY

Dad had been a night worker for most of his life. I started out that way too. Although I found great camaraderie among my colleagues, I also learned that the social constraints were difficult to deal with at *The Irish Times*. I was asleep when the rest of the world was awake; working when the rest of it was dozing. In 1956, I had the opportunity to move across to a day job at the *Evening Herald*. While I missed out on the fun we enjoyed at *The Times*, my new post brought with it special advantages.

The dominant sporting event that year was The Melbourne Olympics. It turned into Ronnie Delany's greatest moment. On the morning of December 1, I was listening to the radio, preparing to go into work. I was tuned in to the BBC at around 7.30am. RTE didn't open in the mornings back then. Rex Alston was the BBC commentator. I could feel the tension and excitement crackling through the radio. The 1,500 metres was in progress. As Ronnie came through in the final straight, I just leapt up and ran to the door. I charged out of my room, screaming. I woke up the whole house. They must have thought it was on fire.

"What? What's wrong?" shouted my father.

"Delany has won! Delany has won!"

There was no breakfast, no time to digest what had happened. It was straight out the door, onto the bike and a mad pedal to the office. The whole day went by in a whirr. The buzz and excitement in the Abbey Street office was incredible. It is the gift given to sports journalists that they can be a part of a great, glorious story blossoming like a flower before you. The excitement on that day was palpable. It was full steam ahead for as long as the working day lasted. All hell was breaking loose. Arthur McWeeney, Paul's brother, was the chief sports writer for the *Irish Independent*. He was the only Irish national paper representative out there. While he may not have enjoyed the best of health, Arthur rose to the occasion with a series of reports and features for the *Herald*, the *Independent* and the *Sunday Independent*. He churned it out non-stop. The material was delivered by telegram, sub-edited and replaced the agency material that had filled the first edition.

Ronnie Delany's gold medal in Melbourne was one of the highlights for any sports journalist. For me to be involved, even at such a remove, was an honour and privilege. The excitement and adrenaline was surging as we battled to get the latest editions out on the streets.

· · · · ·

From 1956, Ireland produced a stream of middle-distance runners from 800 metres upwards, the Noel Carrolls, the Eamonn Coghlans, the Ray Flynns, the Marcus O'Sullivans and, more recently, Sonia O'Sullivan.

That was all on the back of Ronnie Delany's glorious hour, or 3.42.01 to be more precise, at the Melbourne Olympics when he scorched clear of German silver medallist, Klaus Richtzenhain, and Australian great, John Landy, in bronze, bridging the gap back to 1932 in Los Angeles when Bob Tisdall (400 metres) and Pat O'Callaghan (hammer) last won Olympic gold for Ireland.

Which raises an interesting question – why haven't we produced more field event athletes since, such as hammer throwers? We had Dr Pat O'Callaghan, but that was before the outbreak of World War II when more important issues were being battled through and bombed out from 1939 to 1945. Irish shot-putters, discus and hammer throwers, who had been fairly prominent in Irish sporting history then-to-fore, faded away like light at the end of a summer evening. Even today, the quality has not emerged in the throwing disciplines. I wonder why?

Ronnie Delany's victory overshadowed the achievements of boxer Fred Tiedt – he won a silver medal at welterweight – and the rest of the Irish team in Melbourne. In some ways, it represented one of the most exciting newspaper days of my time 'on the desk'. Everyone wanted to know the 'whys and wherefores' of the race; the pictures, the reactions.

To meet this demand, the *Herald* was firing up the machines, changing pages 'on-the-run', getting the up-to-the-minute information out into the world. There are not many days like that in a career, even though there is a regular tension every time a paper goes to press. Arthur McWeeney's constant stream of copy was the authentic overview of a great occasion we were lucky enough to be able to relay to the men and women on the streets of Dublin.

•••••

Ronnie Delany spent a lot of his time training in America with his coach, Jumbo Elliot, at Villanova University, where he became one of five Olympic champions to work under Elliott.

Ronnie practised every detail of a race, right down to breasting the tape as a middle-distance runner. This was planted in his mind going into the Olympics. It was one of the strategies Jumbo employed to break down that sense of not being able to win gold. It was all part of the mental preparation. You only have to breast the tape when you are winning, or contending, to be first over the line.

The difference between winning and losing, or recognising the difference is so small. It is the fella who goes out thinking, 'I don't care what time this race is run in, I am going to win', who will be first. Ronnie had a very good competitive attitude. It stood to him.

I now know Ronnie very well socially and through various functions over the years. He was brought up in Sandymount and went to school at CUS, the Catholic University School on Leeson Street in the city centre. His wife, Joan, was part of our dramatic society, like her older sister, Ann, who was also involved in the St Mary's Musical and Dramatic Society, which later became The Lantern Theatre Club.

• • • • •

Ronnie Delany's indoor record all over America was just sensational. He was the original King of the Boards long before Eamonn Coghlan assumed the mantle of Chairman of the Boards. He won the hearts of New Yorkers by remaining unbeaten in Madison Square Garden, a venue made famous by the great Joe Louis and our old friend, Muhammad Ali.

To have Delany holding the American sports followers in the palm of his hand was wonderful. He refused point blank to be tempted into running for records because he knew that, when you establish a record, it is very hard to better it every time. If he had broken the four-minute mile indoors, any time he didn't do it would have been listed a failure or a disappointment.

Wisely, he set his sights on being unbeaten as a runner. He approached those as races not as time trials. He established an amazing run of success that made him a legend in America. He went on an incredible spree of winning 40 successive races indoors, from 1956 to 1959, although the indoor circuit didn't quite receive the adulation or limelight of the outdoors. He also held the World Mile Indoor Record from 1958 to 1962.

Delany could have had a much higher profile when he finished running. I thought official Ireland didn't make any real use of his talents. Perhaps, it was jealousy or, at best, lack of imagination. We were denied the use of a great worldwide influence. He could have been employed as a travelling ambassador abroad, opening doors of opportunity for our official representatives. However, the chance to bestow on Ronnie Delany the credit or recognition he deserved was lost. We had a very rare jewel but, as with other outstanding sports people, official Ireland did little to polish him.

It took another couple of generations for sport to be seen as a valuable promotional asset. Maybe, it was an inferiority complex because it very often happened that Irish competitors in different sports would get into winning positions only to throw away what seemed like a golden chance. It is a national trait that we are only properly beginning to move away from.

I marvel at Padraig Harrington. He has to fight so hard. You look at the five-wood he hit to the 17th hole in winning the 137th British Open at Royal Birkdale, in 2008. That was an incredible shot. It was his gold medal moment.

To have pulled that off, to me, showed that this guy really had the bottle to do it. He had gone through a series of runner-up finishes to attract the unfortunate reputation as a 'choker', but when his chance came he had the mental strength and the skill to sweep to victory. Padraig was another man who showed us we can overcome. Northern Ireland's Graeme McDowell and the immaculate Rory McIlroy have quickly followed in his footsteps. Even the incredibly talented Darren Clarke, at 42, delivered late in his playing career to claim the British Open at Royal St George's in 2011 as the oldest winner of the venerable Claret Jug since Argentina's Roberto de Vicenzo in 1967.

In general, lack of belief seems to lurk somewhere in the back of most of our minds. We think, deep down, that these foreigners must be better than we are. There must be one of them who will come up with something magical to take the prize out of our hands.

Dave O'Leary would be one who would probably say: 'What a load of rubbish, look what I did against Romania in Genoa?' He held his nerve under pressure at the World Cup in 1990. In general, I think we have too often looked for performance instead of achievement. Delany knew the difference. Padraig Harrington learned it.

It is harder to explain in the context of a team sport. When we hail the great rugby achievements of Munster and Leinster we have to remember how significant were the contributions of overseas players, like Rocky Elsom, Felipe Contepomi, John Langford, Jim Williams and Doug Howlett, and coaches Michael Cheika, Matt Williams, Alan Gaffney, Tony McGahan and Joe Schmidt. In more and more sports, it is clear the present generation recognises that victory is the only currency in competition. It is all about achievement. Performance is only for exhibition and personal satisfaction.

· · · · ·

Sadly, Ireland did not offer a lavish lifestyle in the 1950s. Those were the days of the *Herald* boot fund because many of the lads who actually sold the papers in all weathers wore no shoes. You think back to those times and you realise the level of poverty that existed in Dublin city and around the country.

It was frightening. In one instant, Delany lifted the spirit of a suffering nation and placed it on a podium for all the world to see. In one surging run, he had shown us all what could be achieved with the right combination of talent, dedication and belief.

There were shoeless children out working back then, at ten or eleven years of age, selling newspapers in their bare feet. That is how low it was. Belvedere College established a Boys' Club in the centre of Dublin for young kids who were disadvantaged. The main priority was shelter, clothing and food. Looking back now, it is difficult to fathom how there was a time like that. And it wasn't all that long ago.

The good old days were only the good old days for people who had jobs. There were so many people who had to go without. Families boarded in one room. We've all heard the phrase 'swinging on lamp posts'. I remember travelling through parts of the inner city, like Gardiner Street, Sheriff Street and William Street, and the little boys and girls would be swinging on old ropes tied around lamp posts.

In contrast, I would have been in town on my bike. I could leave it with other two-wheelers outside a shop and no one would go near them. In spite of the level of poverty, there was a respect for people on an individual basis and they were inclined to share what little they had with each other. That was then.

Chapter 19

HARK THE HERALD

Herb Elliot returned to Ireland after his monumental win at Santry Stadium in 1958 to run again at the track. It was never going to be the same. The day before the race I asked him if I could do an interview with him afterwards.

"Sure. But, I won't do it at Santry. There will be too much going on. Will you come back to the hotel in Clontarf?"

Mick O'Hehir gave me a recorder for the interview, which would air on The Vaseline Hair Tonic Programme. Rather than give me a tidy, portable recorder, he handed me a big desk reel-to-reel electric monstrosity.

I waited for Herb in the lounge. He walked in.

"I am just going up for a shower. I will be down in five minutes," he said.

"Great. I will be ready."

Michael had taken the plug off the recorder just in case it didn't fit into the socket. No problem. I got the recorder sorted and made my way over to a two-pin socket. I had three wires exposed from the recorder. I wasn't too sure which was which. I had two matchsticks. They could hold the wires in the plug. I inserted the first. Grand. I inserted the second.

BANG! An explosion. I was afraid I had blown the whole machine apart. I decided the best option to take was to plead uninjured innocence. I gingerly removed the wires from the wall, wrapped them around the recorder and placed the machine back on the table, saying nothing.

A few minutes later, the owner or manager, a woman, appeared in a state of remorse.

"I'm so sorry. I'm so sorry."

"What seems to be the problem?"

"All the fuses in the hotel have gone."

"You're joking."

"No. Everything is down. What am I going to do? I've sent for the electrician. Do you know something, I am going to go down to that ballroom. There is a fella there with one of these new fangled electric guitars and he doesn't know what he's at."

"Oh, you're right. You can't trust those musicians," I said.

Shortly, an electrician arrived on the scene.

"Are you okay here?" he said.

"What is the matter?"

"I've just fixed that problem with the fuses."

"Ah, seeing as though you are here, maybe you could help me. I've got this machine. There are three wires on it. I don't want to cause the hotel any more upset. Could you put them into the wall for an interview I am doing?"

He walked over to the socket that I had just demolished.

"Have you got a match?"

"Have I got a match? I have a box of them. Here you go."

I waited in trepidation. But he knew what he was doing, which wire was which and where it should go. It worked fine. Along came Herb.

"Are you okay? You look a bit flustered," he said.

"Oh sure, there was just a bit of a problem with the fuses in the hotel."

"I know. I was just in the shower and everything went black."

The interview was wrapped up quite quickly. I didn't have the heart to tell Herb or the owner who was responsible. I thanked both of them profusely for their kindness and scarpered out the door.

$$\cdots$$

As we prepared for our wedding day on September 25, 1958 – you see some men remember these things – I was glad to take any opportunity for extra shift work or writing a column to provide valuable additional income.

Madeleine White and I had been a pair since school days. We decided to 'tie the knot' when I had achieved the status of senior journalist. So it was that I tried to supplement my salary by reporting on Saturdays or turning over to help out with the *Sunday Independent* or working on the production of Junior Sports Magazine or helping Michael O'Hehir with his sponsored radio programme, The Vaseline Hair Tonic Show.

At one point, the *Herald* asked me to write a daily sports comment piece called, On The Sports Front, under the pseudonym, The Pilot, to balance out the success of Joe Sherwood's lively and controversial column, In The Soup, for the *Evening Press*. Joe was a retired sports journalist from the North of England, a very abrasive, very competitive, superb writer. He generated controversy which, in turn, attracted readership. For me to appear to compete was a tall order. But, it offered a line of promotion and it also taught me some valuable lessons in its season in the sun.

Having moved over from *The Irish Times*, I was employed as a sub-editor from 8.30am to 1pm. Then, I had to roll out the column in the afternoon and have it ready for print by 4.30pm.

One of the ways to generate interest was to climb onto a hobby horse of one kind or another. I wrote an article about foul or dirty play in sport. Rugby was an obvious target. I picked out a number of players from Wanderers who I had seen perpetrating nasty fouls more than once, suggesting they should be disciplined by the club. I received a few supportive letters. I published them to stir the pot. I wanted a response. But, not the one I got.

The editor, Leslie Nevison, came into the sports room one day and called me aside. As a newly arrived, fresh-faced senior journalist, just out of junior ranks, I was slightly in awe of the editor.

"You will have to present yourself at the boardroom."

"The boardroom?"

"Yes. The chairman wishes to speak to you."

"The chairman? Dear God! What have I done?"

I gathered he wasn't about to offer me a raise. At the appointed hour, I went up the stairs and walked into this musty room with a large table and chairs scattered here and there. The chairman was T.V. Murphy, a smallish man as I remember. He was waiting for me, upstanding and serious.

"Sit down," he said.

He walked over to the newspapers and started to fold back the *Evening Herald*s. He took issue with what I had to say about foul play in rugby and mentioned how the concentration on Wanderers Football Club had sullied the game.

"Two days later, you published two letters about the article supporting your view."

"Yes."

"I don't want this drivel to appear again in this paper or any paper published by this house."

"But ..."

"If we wanted gutter journalism, we would have brought Joe Sherwood from the *Evening Press*. That is not what this newspaper stands for."

"I understand."

"Now, I want to emphasise that the fact that I am a member of Wanderers has no influence over this, nor is it relevant that my son-in-law is captain of the Wanderers club at this time."

P.D. Young was the captain of Wanderers and England. Apparently, I had stood on a lot of toes.

Eventually, the pressure to produce fresh and interesting copy five days a week got too much for me, physically and mentally. It was just too great a burden for me to carry. I made my failing health known to the newspaper, and those in authority were very understanding.

Interestingly, I got a raise for ending the column. I had been promoted to senior journalist status to write the column – 10 guineas a week. You could carry a marriage and purchase a house on that income back then. When the work got to be too much, I retained my status as a senior and was paid IR£2, 12 shillings and six on top of my salary to do the column one day a week.

• • • • •

Here it is, my first column.

Monday, January 21, 1957.
ON THE SPORTS FRONT, by "PILOT".
IF YOU DON'T AGREE, SAY SO.

Hello there! Welcome to the first "Sports Front".

From now in, yours truly will be around here every day except Tuesday, with some notes and news and maybe a talking point or two to help you through an idle hour with the boys. Of course, if you don't agree with something I say in this here column – just write in and say so and we'll thrash it out in print.

Which brings up another point – letters. Maybe you have a bee in your bonnet about something or another and would like to get it out. Well, it's easy because all you have to do is drop a line to "Sports Front" and between us we'll give it an airing and see how it goes.

IT'S DELIBERATE

Now before we get down to real business, I'd like to warn you about my deliberate mistake. With each article, I'm going to include some error – it might be in a date or a score – at the beginning or at the end of, but keep an eye open for it. Of course, needless to say, there is no prize – ah, no – it's just good, clean fun!

I don't know exactly how strong your memories are, but from time to time we'll take a trip back over the files – not too far, say about 10 or 15 years – and recall some item that was then hitting the headlines. How many times do you think after a particular game, "I'll never forget that", and yet within a year, or even less, you've forgotten almost the entire match?

It's possible, too, that among us there's a man or woman who can remember an encounter of 50, 60, or even more years ago and if there is, we'd like to hear from them.

Too quickly and too often fine performances fade from the memory and it would do no harm to remind the younger sports followers of the great men of the past when, we are told, men were men and women were women – as if they could have been anything else!!

But to get back to the present and the very recent past. On Saturday, I went along to Anglesea Road to see Old Belvedere take on the Northern club N.I.F.C., expecting a lively tussle but how wrong I was! Some of the glamour was taken from it by the fact that Tony O'Reilly and Jack Kyle didn't turn out but this cannot excuse the sides from turning in such a spiritless 70 minutes – they only played 35 minutes each way.

For myself, I much prefer to see teams keeping the ball in the open, rather than the "no-quarter-given-or-asked" variety but I draw the line when it comes virtually to tip-and-run. I agree that not all our club matches are so unattractive but it must be said that a large percentage of them lack the ingredients that would draw the spectators.

GRUMBLING

Since the list of representative matches for next season was announced there has been quite a lot of grumbling from certain clubs because they feel that they will be deprived of their leading players for long spells. Well, all I can say is that it served them right. If they encouraged their teams to play bright rugby they would find far more spectators coming along and representative matches would not be needed to bring in the necessary cash.

And while I'm on the subject of improvements, the temptation to pour forth on one of my pet topics is too much for me. So here goes.

Why aren't there substitutes in soccer and rugby?

I really believe that both games could be improved if reserves were allowed for players who, through injury, could take no further part in the match.

How many games have been thoroughly spoiled for both players and spectators when a man has been taken from the field, leaving his side short-handed and unable to cope with a full-strength opposing team. In this respect, there can be little doubt that the GAA are streets ahead of the other bodies because they have seen the necessity of such a course in fairness to all concerned.

I know that sometimes it lends itself to abuse, but it must be remembered that the right to bring on subs is not reserved to one side. Nevertheless, I have never heard a serious complaint about a sub, nor have I heard a losing team attribute their defeat to the fact that the opposition had a "fresh man" for part of the game.

IT'S NOT FAIR.

When a player goes off the field in an important rugby or soccer match, the handicapped side can no longer employ the tactics they had planned, but rather they *rely on sheer determination to carry them through and more often than not they prove unequal to the task – who can blame them? But, surely it's not quite fair to a team, who have worked really hard building up, say, to a Cup campaign, to be deprived of success by an unfortunate accident.*

Should reserves be permitted injury-hit teams would be far less handicapped and the game would not be reduced to a farce, as so often happens. However, the attitude – "What did my great-grandfather will do me" – seems so deeply ingrained in a lot of the powers that be that I suppose they find it hard to see how a game can be improved. Nonetheless, they should get down to serious thinking. Has anyone any further suggestions?

DO YOU REMEMBER?

And now after that a bit of dissertation, let's take a look back. Ten years ago today, it was announced that the Dublin Corporation Planning Committee were considering a letter from a cross-channel firm, British Entertainments Ltd., London, who were seeking a site in Dublin for the establishment of a £250,000 sports stadium. The Corporation was recommended to investigate the matter further with the Board of Works.

That was ten years ago, but unless it's hidden far away I haven't seen a sign of what we most urgently need in Dublin – a central stadium. However, big bodies move slowly ... you never know, anything can happen!!

Also a decade ago this week, the Irish boxing team defeated Italy by five bouts to one.

Were you there? The home winners were F. McGrane (fly), D. Connell (bantam), T. Hyde (welter), M. McKeon (middle), and G. Colman (heavy), but it was Mick McKeon who stole the limelight as it was his victory that ensured Ireland's triumph.

Well, that ties it up for the time being, but don't forget those letters and we'll see how much we agree or disagree with one another. And finally, the deliberate mistake (see bottom of page).

Did you get it? If you didn't you can make amends on Wednesday when I'll be back with another "On the Sports Front".

• • • • •

Yes, that was it. 'The Pilot' had been launched. But was it bravery or foolishness to include a "deliberate" mistake? Sometimes the deliberate one can be lost among all the unintended ones!

As part of my column I sometimes included a 'Did You Know?' fact consisting of a strange or unusual sporting fact. One day, in a book, I came across 'The War Rules for Golf'. These were official rules for a time of war. You would imagine there would be occasions, like in an air raid, when you would be allowed to delay your shot without breaking the rules. It is permissible, in certain circumstances, in golf to move your ball away from an object, i.e. a water hazard, sometimes with a penalty, sometimes without one.

The War Rules were slightly different. For instance, in the event of a player's ball coming to rest against a landmine, the player is allowed to pick up and drop away from the hazard without a penalty. In the event of gunfire or artillery fire, it is permissible for players to take cover without sanction of penalty. Wonderful!

· · · · ·

It was during this period that my dad, Mitchel, Sean O'Shea and Maurice Mortell, two chaps from Caltex, had the idea between them of having awards for the top sports people in Ireland. It was held for the first time in 1958 and was a sort of follow on to Dad's popular weekly column in the *Irish Independent*. Each year, he would run an article detailing a personal list of his top Irish sporting figures.

Dan Langan was Mr Oil in Ireland as the Head of Caltex, later to become Texaco. He had played rugby with Clontarf and won one Ireland cap in 1934. He was one of those larger-than-life characters. When the suggestion was put to him, he put the resources of Caltex behind the idea. It became the major sports award in Ireland. Since then, the proliferation of awards from all sports organisations has diluted its profile, although it still lives on.

The Caltex Awards, now known as The Texaco Sportstars Awards, were established with the various Sports Editors of the national press as the judges and, today, follow almost the same formula.

Initially, the rugby and cricket overlords would not allow their players to receive awards because there was a perception that it would have been a breach of their amateur status. The award of the trophy would have been more than the value the players were permitted to accept as expenses. Anyway, I was co-opted onto the panel as the Head of Sport at RTE in 1972. I asked: Why should Texaco be concerned about the Rugby Union's rules and regulations?

As far as I was concerned, the panel's brief was to research and then select the ten sports and, from there, select the ten sports people of the year. Whether the players wanted to, or were allowed to, accept the awards was immaterial. The panel should make the decision irrespective. From there, it was down to the relevant sports bodies whether or not to enter into the spirit of the Texaco Awards.

This debate proceeded in the middle of the Mike Gibson and Willie John McBride era. It was crazy to carry on with the Awards without mention of some of our elite sportsmen. Whether they could accept the award was neither here nor there. It was our mission to select the winners, someone else's decision as to whether or not they should accept. This common sense attitude prevailed eventually, much to the delight of Dan Langan.

It is fascinating to recall the first winners in 1958. Caltex eventually became Texaco, before the 1970s when the IRFU eventually allowed rugby players to accept their awards.

1958 Caltex Award Winners.
Athletics: Bertie Messitt
Boxing: Freddie Gilroy.
Cycling: Gene Mangan.
Gaelic Football: Jim McKeever.
Golf: Harry Bradshaw.
Horse Racing: Vincent O'Brien.
Hurling: Tony Wall.
Tennis: Eleanor O'Neill.
Soccer: Noel Cantwell.

The philosophy was correct. It didn't really matter whether the players accepted the award or not, as long as they were nominated.

Chapter 20

HERE'S FRED!

Roger Fowler Wright is a name to conjure with. He was the sports editor of *The Sunday Telegraph* in London. He was also one of the nicest gentlemen I have ever encountered in the newspaper business. He was very sympathetic in his attitude towards Ireland. I was writing a column for the *Herald* for half of my working day, sub-editing there for the other half.

The Telegraph announced they would be bringing a new newspaper into the world – a birth of sorts – the Sunday edition of the paper. I wrote to them offering coverage of Irish events on a Saturday afternoon. They replied in acceptance of my offer. For the first two editions, I was asked to do a match report for them. There was a ridiculously early deadline of 5pm because it had to be in for the first run of the newspaper, which probably had an Irish circulation of two, including the one I bought.

A month into the publication, I was invited over to London where I met Roger Fowler Wright for the first time. He offered me the position of Irish sports correspondent for *The Sunday Telegraph*.

"What I want from you are opinion pieces," he said.

"What about news stories?"

"What about them?"

"I thought you would want me to break stories."

"No. I want you to concentrate on the opinion and feature side of the argument."

"Well, I could certainly manage that."

There was a lull in the conversation. In that time, it occurred to me I would require some guarantee of tenure or, at least, to know how much money I would be paid. After all, I had a solid, pensionable job in the *Herald* with Independent Newspapers. It was going to take a sound financial offer to take me away from that security. As we walked down Fleet Street – the facade of *The Telegraph* building was in my eye-line – he almost knocked me over, emotionally, with what he had to say.

"How much would you be willing to offer me?" I asked.

"Why should we talk about money when there are more important things in life, like fishing and golf? This is *The Telegraph*, old chap. Do you think it is going to close down?"

"Well, no."

"Well then?"

"It is just that I would like to have something solid to tell my wife, Madeleine, when I return home."

"How does £1,300 sound?"

"It sounds acceptable to me."

"Well, there we have it."

In fact, it was more than double what I was earning at home where I got IR£10 a week. It was an incredible offer. I was to continue happily for more than 30 years, although there were adjustments to the contract over time to accommodate my ambitions on radio and, later, television. Each of the sports editors who followed Roger was helpful and seemed satisfied with the service. None, however, had the same charisma as Roger.

• • • • •

The contract with *The Telegraph* allowed me the time to develop my interest in broadcasting in the 1960s. When Michael O'Hehir was appointed the Head of Sport to the newly created Radio Eireann in 1961 – which quickly became Telifis Eireann, then Radio Telifis Eireann – he had to give up The Vaseline Hair Tonic Programme. It was then introduced, for a short few months, by myself and George King, the sports editor of the Sunday Independent. We had the run of the programme until my hair, or lack of shine from it, got in the way.

Then, there was The Belvedere Bond Programme. It was a straightforward general standard music programme. DJ Fred was in the groove. Not for long, though. It lasted for one series.

Michael O'Hehir knew my work at the *Herald* from his time in the Independent and from the pieces he had commissioned for The Vaseline Hair Tonic Programme. The advent of RTE provided an exciting opportunity for Michael as Head of Sport, with Philip Greene as his assistant, to set up a real sports department.

Fronting sports for television on a nightly basis was the popular Irish High-Jump champion and record holder, Brendan O'Reilly. He had won a scholarship to Michigan State University and earned a degree in Dramatic Arts before returning to Ireland to work in advertising and film. Personable and unflappable, he was ideal as the anchor man in this new world of television.

Michael did not have editorial people and he felt there was a need for someone to do organisational work with regard to programming on radio. I was drafted in on contract to be the sports organiser and my main thrust was to develop the radio side, while Maurice Quinn came in as the first staff journalist to head up the editorial and scripting arm of RTE.

I requested permission from *The Telegraph* to pursue this avenue. Roger saw nothing wrong with this additional focus. He felt it would increase my profile and benefit them. The first time I did a match for *The Telegraph* was a hockey inter-provincial down on Londonbridge Road, near Sandymount. The newspaper was under the mistaken illusion that this was on the same scale as a similar fixture in the United Kingdom.

Came the day and came the hour.

I made my way down to the ground early to check the teams and 'suss out' where the nearest telephone might be so that I could deliver the copy on time. I had to take an assistant who could gallop off with the half-time copy while I oversaw the second half. It was probably one of my brothers-in-law, Cyril or Des White. They were my first 'runners'.

Anyway, we drove down Shelbourne Road and turned the corner onto Londonbridge Road to be met with a cluster of giant posters, each festooned with a photo of yours truly. If there was one, there were hundreds lining the route from Shelbourne Road to the hockey ground.

'FRED COGLEY IS HERE – READ THE SUNDAY TELEGRAPH.'

I later contacted Roger Fowler Wright to let him know that the campaign was just a tad over the top. 'The Fred Cogley Poster Show' eventually ran its course. It was a move 40 years before its time. The last thing the patrons needed to see was my beaming face as they made their way to the match. I was mortified.

Chapter 21

RADIO TELIFIS EIREANN

The establishment of RTE in 1962 was such a revelation for the country and for Michael O'Hehir, Phillip Greene, Brendan O'Reilly and Maurice Quinn. Initially, there were only six people in the sports department. The key member was Oonagh Gormley. She had been secretary to the great Billy Morton in his office on Berkeley Road. She was the cornerstone, lynchpin, everything in the department. Oonagh put order on the place because you were dealing with, mostly, journalists and actors – people with little real knowledge of administration and organisation. Phil Thomson, a BBC TV producer, was seconded to RTE sport. His personal assistant, Esther Byrne, completed the original team. I was offered a temporary contract to write scripts for Brendan's nightly Sports News.

The atmosphere and spirit was phenomenal. It was new. It was exciting. Everyone was pulling together. There was a get-up-and-go buzz about the place and you fed off that positive energy. There was a drive to show what could be done in all areas, whether it was technical, presentation, design or all the skills of the game of video/film journalism.

It was a microcosm of society in a way. For the first time in Ireland, a disparate group of people from all parts of the country assembled to put together a schedule of television programmes. I saw it as a community in action.

Behind the scenes, there was so much happening "on the hoof" as the late Bill McLaren might say. As video tape had only just been introduced films were transmitted from a tele-cine machine and news bulletins were illustrated with film clips. They had just come to terms with audio tape, which had been introduced during the 1950s. While there were only two big video tape machines for the whole of RTE, most programmes went out live. This was a particularly hazardous occupation. The drama programmes that went out live were often mild compared to the drama behind the scenes. The clashes of personalities between the various people in the production, from the director to the actors to those in lighting and design, made for drama of a different kind. Yet, it worked – somehow.

As far as the sports department was concerned, there was no recorded coverage. It was all stored on film. There were some remarkable cameramen who did incredible work. A friend of mine in Cork, Joe McCarthy, was helping me out with photos for my articles in *The Sunday Telegraph*. He would ring me every Wednesday to see what article I was working on and furnish *The Telegraph* with a photograph which complemented it.

We developed a smooth liaison. One time, in 1963, there was a schools' athletics event in Cork. Brendan O'Reilly wanted to transmit some of it for his Junior TV Programmes. I had become the sports organiser. I rang Joe. He had a camera, but not a movie camera. I explained the story.

"Could you borrow a Bolex 16mm camera? There might be one in the local pharmacy," I said.

"Leave it to me. I will see what I can do."

The film arrived by train the next day. Joe had never shot a moving picture in his life. It was the beginning of a new career. He became one of the most prominent cameramen to work for RTE. Later, he set up his own TV company in Cork. It all arose out of that one conversation.

Film cameramen Sean Burke and Eamon O'Connor were remarkable in what they achieved with the inefficient equipment they had to handle. They shot some incredible work on the Cycling Tour of Ireland, the Ras Tailteann and on the motor rallies. The director, Michael O'Carroll, drove a Renault 16 with Eamon O'Connor, from Limerick, on the bonnet of the car as he tried to get a close-up shot of multiple 'Ras' winner Shay O'Hanlon, a great competitor. Away from the camera, Eamon was an able amateur magician and a sword swallower. He truly was a man of many talents.

.....

Shortly after television had started, Madeleine and I, and our dear friends Tom Graham and Stephanie O'Reilly, as she was then, went to a formal dress dance at The Gresham Hotel. I happened to have a dance with Stephanie when, suddenly, a woman I had never seen before started to look at me in that way you recognise someone, but you are not sure where from.

She made her way over to us on the dance floor.

"You're on television, aren't you?"

I was slightly embarrassed. As if I had to get used to this sort of thing, I explained to Stephanie that, now and again, people made their introductions because they see me on television in their living rooms. This was a completely new experience to me. My head was swelling slightly. You see how easy it is to get ideas about yourself.

"Can I introduce you to some friends that have come up from Cork and Kerry?" the woman said.

"Certainly," I said graciously, my head expanding all the time.

Stephanie, obviously puzzled, accompanied me off the dance floor towards a small group of strangers. I was really starting to float on air. I was about to be introduced as some sort of celebrity. The chest was puffed out. The chin was raised.

"Look who I've found on the dance floor – Jerome O'Shea."

Jerome was a former Kerry footballer. Not only that, he had appeared as the presenter of an early Gaelic games magazine programme initiated by RTE. He was well-known, better known than I was at the time, in terms of his profile. What could I do ... but grin sheepishly.

Many years later, Jerome O'Shea was introduced to me again, this time as the father of Ireland rugby International, Conor O'Shea, now making such a name for himself as the Director of Rugby at Harlequins in the English Premiership, and I took the opportunity to tell Conor how his father had inadvertently spoiled my early moment in the limelight.

• • • • •

My general philosophy in life has run along the line of 'treat others as you would like them to treat you'. I don't believe in the stick, whacking people for the mistakes they make. We all make mistakes. That is the way of life.

From school days, I had been a member of the Pioneer Total Abstinence Association. Although my association with the organisation was a passive one, I was proud to wear the pin. It is one thing to tell someone what to do, quite another to show a person indirectly by the way you conduct yourself that there is another way to live life. You don't have to drink to have fun.

It was a pleasant novelty in those days to get a bit of recognition. But, there were times when you could be surprised. I came out of the Radio Telifis Eireann studios on Henry Street one evening and was standing at the corner of O'Connell Street waiting on a friend.

There was a man there. He looked at me for a while. I could only assume he was trying to figure out who I was, that I was vaguely familiar, but not quite a regular 'face'.

"Ah, it's yourself, isn't it?" he said.

"Well, that depends on who you think I am," I smiled.

"Are you the fella that reads the sports results? I'm sure I recognise you."

"Well, yes. I am one of the team. Fred Cogley."

"I thought so. I knew I recognised you from somewhere. I'm an alcoholic you know," he said, out of nowhere.

"Oh, I'm sorry to hear that."

"There's no need to be sorry. I have been on the dry for the last six months and I have you to thank for it."

"Oh, really! How's that?"

"I was looking at you one day on the television and I noticed you had a pioneer pin on your jacket."

"Yes. I am a member of the Association."

"Well, I said to myself 'if that feckin' eejit can do it, anyone can do it'."

Well, you have to take the rough with the smooth.

The only criticism I had of the Association at the time was that it was quite inactive, low-key about spreading the message. There should have been greater emphasis on young people meeting up and having fun without the need to imbibe.

I felt the Pioneers could have galvanised their energies better to create a fun environment away from the drinking culture, the excess. Overall, it was a good organisation that encouraged temperance, if not total denial. It was a very important part of my extra-curricular activity, to lend a hand where possible to promote abstinence, having seen the problems created by over-indulgence.

A personal attitude of mine, for whatever reason, has always been the absolute terror that I would wake up one morning and not know where I had been or what I had done the previous day. That has been something right through my life. I certainly wouldn't be able to cope with that comfortably, accept it and put it to one side. That is just the way I am made.

I guess I saw a lot of journalists who drank quite heavily. They had come through a tough time in the War. Some had served in combat. They were hard times, trying to keep a family together on wages that were a joke, and with little or no holidays. There was all of that and the attending stresses and strains.

Some of them overdid the bottle. I would see the men who hadn't made it and turned to drink for comfort, solace or a distraction, and the men I was working with on a daily basis who were able to survive without feeling the need to escape their daily lives.

When I started out in my working life in the newspapers, I was surrounded by a lot of non-drinkers in the business, like Michael O'Hehir, Mick Dunne and Micheal O Muircheartaigh. They never pontificated about it. They just preferred to stay alcohol free. If you are a drinker in Ireland, your companions are likely to keep asking until you say yes, whereas they won't even ask if you don't drink at all. The Pioneer pin became a physical manifestation of what I felt and I did not have to repeatedly turn down the offer of a drink every night I went out and about. It was a practical decision. Over time, I got out of the habit of wearing the pin. I regret that it seems the more affluent our society becomes the greater the dependency on alcohol. Now, more than ever, there is a real need for a renewal of the Pioneers.

• • • • •

In those early days of Telifis Eireann, greyhound racing enjoyed a greater profile than it does today. In the 1960s, Paddy O'Brien did the racing commentaries on television. He was a radio producer by trade, known by his real name Padraig O'Neill. His primary role as a features producer meant he wasn't allowed to be a broadcaster on television. Those were the restrictions of the day, reflecting the civil service pedigree which was part of the inheritance. No one could cross the Rubicon from producer to presenter. He could employ people to broadcast. But, he couldn't do it himself, supposedly because there was a fear people would abuse their positions.

So, for the purposes of his television broadcast work, Padraig assumed the name Paddy O'Brien when he did the sports results or greyhound racing. It apparently didn't bother anyone that he might be recognised in the new world of television. On one occasion, Paddy was attending a greyhound awards ceremony in the heart of Tipperary. He brought his wife with him. The girl at hotel reception was quite excited about coming into contact with this 'TV personality'.

"Ah, there you are Mr O'Brien. It is great to meet you. Can I shake your hand?"

"Of course, of course ... we would like to check in now."

"Sure. Just sign here,"

He took the pen and signed in "Mr & Mrs Pádraig O'Neill".

The girl turned the register around. She looked at it. She looked up at him with a knowing look.

"That will be fine Mr O'Neill!" she winked.

• • • • •

When it came to the 'dos' and 'don'ts' of the newly established Radio Telifis Eireann, there were always the costs and accounting to be taken into consideration. In those very early days, Michael O'Hehir was anxious for RTE to have a 'Highlights of the Year' programme at the end of the year. But, there were complications, like the cost of tapes. We couldn't cut the tape, which was two inches wide and run on an Ampex machine. The programme was recorded as if it were live. Once started, we couldn't stop. If you did, you had to go back to the top of the programme and do it all over again.

Video editing was unknown. If the two-inch tapes were cut and then soldered, the tape was considered unstable and, therefore, useless for future recordings. If there were glitches, they stayed in unless they were absolutely unusable. There was no auto-cue. You had your script to lead into a piece of video tape or film and you had to execute a proper roll-in so that the speed of the insert would be seamless.

For example, if I was introducing highlights of the match between Ireland and England at Twickenham, I would have to give a five- or six-second lead-in so that the film operator would have time to press the right button to roll the film in order that it would come in at the right time, at the right speed. Similarly, if it was video tape, it was a 15-second roll in. That meant 45 words had to be counted down for every Video Tape Recording (VTR) insert.

We had no action replay. But we decided to be creative by using the two big Ampex recording machines, working in unison. BBC and ITV had managed to import new video disc equipment, which was very sensitive and hugely expensive. It was way beyond our budget, of course.

This didn't stop us. Somehow we came up with this idea of recording the match on one Ampex machine and, as the tape came through, we would feed it off the machine and seven or eight guys would stand around the videotape room feeding the tape around the room through their hands and back onto the second video machine to play out the salient piece.

In rugby, for instance, when a try was scored, we would immediately feed the tape from machine 1-to-2. This took all of ten seconds – just enough time. Thus, we had our not-so-instant replay. Although it ran at normal speed, it was better than nothing. It lasted long enough to eventually embarrass the technical side of the house to find a way to buy a video disc machine from somewhere. In fact, it wasn't until the '80s that slow-motion replays became commonplace. The old two-inch tapes were replaced by small cassettes. At last, it was possible to keep full match recordings indefinitely. No more would we endure the frustration experienced when we wanted to go back on some highlights from Ireland and England at Twickenham in February of 1964, a

Five years old and enjoying my first Punch and Judy show with friends. That's me, second from the left, and my mother is standing behind me, also second from the left. It was a birthday party for a local girl, and when her mother politely asked me if I would like to use the toilet, I replied, 'No, thank you very much... I'll wait until I get home before I get sick!' I thought I was being a polite, little gentleman!

My grandmother, Madame Bannard-Cogley, and her pet dog 'Props'. Also (below) is her membership card issued after the founding of the Gate Theatre, which interestingly, is 'Membership Card No.1'.

1st Sept. 1928.

The Directors of the Dublin Gate Theatre Studio acknowledge with thanks the receipt of One Pound entitling Madame M. Bannard of 113 Stephen's Green to FOUNDER MEMBERSHIP of the Studio for the 1st Season at the Peacock Theatre, Dublin, commencing Oct. 1928.

Hilton Edwards
Director.

Founder Member No. 1
R. No. 4

The holder of this card (which is not transferable) is entitled to TWO Seats for each production during the 1st Season and to the purchase of addition-al seats at the special rate of (2/4 plus 6d. tax) 2/10 each. These seats can be reserved in advance upon request, but it is necessary that this card be pro-duced before tickets can be issued.

A new production every two weeks. Produced upon a Sunday each play will be performed for 12 nights including Sundays. There will be no performances on Thursdays and no matinees.

Box Office Telephone :—1577 Dublin.

(Tickets not purchased by members for themselves and their friends, 3/6 unreservable.)

Seat issued for :—
1st Production Peacock

1st Seat	OCT. 1928 24
2nd Seat	21 OCT. 1928
1st Seat	9 T OCT. 1928
2nd Seat	1 OCT. 1928
1st Seat	1 8 NOV. 1928 24
2nd Seat	1 8 NOV. 1928 25
1st Seat	
2nd Seat	

Peacock Theatre, Dublin.

THE DUBLIN GATE THEATRE STUDIO
(In Association with the Gate Theatre Studio, London).

Directors :—Hilton Edwards, Micheál MacLiammóir, Gearóid O'Lochlainn, D. Bannard Cogley.

Founder Membership Card.

No. 1

My father, Mitchel Cogley (on the right) leading a wolfhound into Croke Park for the opening parade of the Tailteann Games, in 1924. Alas, the second wolfhound did not make it into the stadium as, when the band struck up, the dog took off and its handler was last seen careering down Jones's Road... A tough experience for a 14 year old!

The Olympic Stadium, Tokyo, 1964... The start of a Special Sprint Challenge which attracted only a very select crowd. My father, Mitchel (on the left) and his dear colleague, Dave Guiney, himself an Olympian in 1948 (P.S. Both were disqualified for failing to finish).

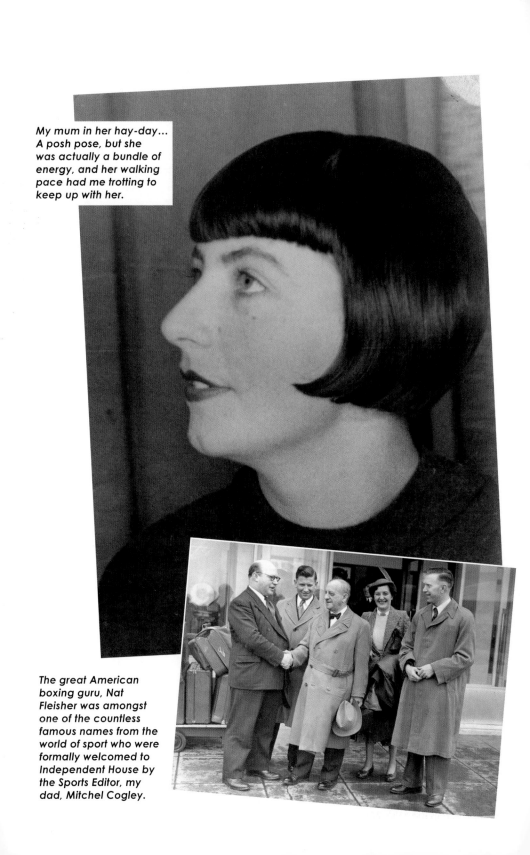

My mum in her hay-day...
A posh pose, but she
was actually a bundle of
energy, and her walking
pace had me trotting to
keep up with her.

The great American
boxing guru, Nat
Fleisher was amongst
one of the countless
famous names from the
world of sport who were
formally welcomed to
Independent House by
the Sports Editor, my
dad, Mitchel Cogley.

Mum and Dad in the mid-'70s ... always in good humour, well, nearly always!

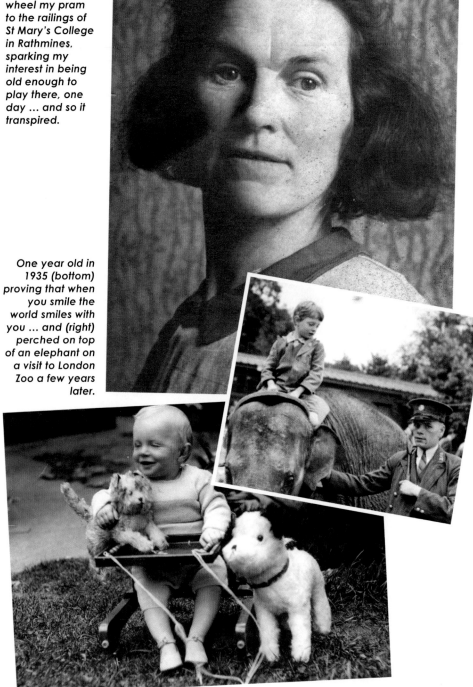

Annie Walsh in the mid-'30s... She'd wheel my pram to the railings of St Mary's College in Rathmines, sparking my interest in being old enough to play there, one day ... and so it transpired.

One year old in 1935 (bottom) proving that when you smile the world smiles with you ... and (right) perched on top of an elephant on a visit to London Zoo a few years later.

The successful St Mary's College Under-14s in 1948... What would we have looked like if we had lost?

A win in front of the field at St Mary's, in 1950, was easy ... until the cigarettes slowed me down.

SENIOR CUP TEAM 1950 - 1951

St Mary's College Senior Cup team 1951-52. You may notice the lack of trophies, but we had the best of fun.

My first year on the St Mary's College Senior Cup team... If only that drop-kick had gone over, we could have beaten 'Rock (so near and yet so far!)

'Our gang', or most of them, posing in Beverston about 1953! In the front (seated on the ground) is John Bowden (RIP). Ken Sparrow (RIP), is flanked by Kay Carroll (RIP), Pat Purcell, Stephanie O'Reilly and Kitty Purcell. At the back are the 'heavies', Don Purcell (RIP), Tony 'Rocky' Woodhouse, yours truly, and Pat Fitzpatrick.

A stroll around St Stephen's Green... Madeleine and I are caught by a 'street photographer' as we stepped out in the 1950s.

The RTE sports department (TV and radio) gathered to bid a fond farewell to Oonagh Gormley on her early retirement in the mid-'80s. There are some well-known faces here, and it was one of the very few occasions when people working on such a hectic out-put could come together in one room. An historic day!

Bill O'Herlihy and RTE friends at a party in the mid-'70s.

*In the pink...
The Pioneer
magazine
cover after my
appointment as
RTE's Head of
Sport.*

JANUARY, 1973 – PRICE 5p.

PIONEER

INSIDE THIS ISSUE   FRED COGLEY
THE IRISH LANGUAGE

My Mum did not enjoy the best of health in the latter stages of her life, but she was never happier than when surrounded by her grandchildren. In the front (from left) Madeleine, Muriel, Mitchel and me, and (back) David, Michelle, Denise and Niall.

When Pat Fitz, or Fitzer, became Fr Pat Fitzpatrick CSSp, we gathered to congratulate him.

Three generations in Irish media, with my father being honoured for his services to sports journalism, flanked by Niall and myself (both of us also 'honoured' to have been Head of Sport in RTE in our time).

Three of the greats honoured for their services to Irish journalism,
Paul MacWeeney, Mitchel Cogley, Michael O'Hehir.

An outing for a Taverner's cricket match, RTE v The Press in
the Phoenix Park... with international, Godfrey Graham and
renowned tenor, Frank Patterson in our side, how could we lose?

The historic Irish rugby team led by manager, Eugene Davey, bolstered by the 'Langers'... Freddie Fox's gang of supporting alickadoos and media en route to Australia in 1967.

The early days of the Links Golfing Society in the 1970s, with me asking a few questions of singer, Val Doonican. Also there are Paddy Finnegan and the brains behind the 'Links', Cecil Whelan - Cecil and the 'Links' raised millions for charities.

The remarkable Irish sporting all-rounder, Dr Kevin O'Flanagan with my dearest friend, Tom Graham. Kevin was amongst the last amateurs to play for Arsenal before he and his brother, Michael, won senior international caps for Ireland in soccer and rugby.

Interviewing three times major winner, Padraig Harrington.

South African golfer Mark McNulty is flanked by journalists, Frank Johnstone, John Redmond and yours truly.

The Irish Golf Writers' team prepare for their annual Four Nations Championship... Colm Smith, Philip Reid, Joe Kelly, Liam Kelly, yours truly, and Greg Allen. What's more... We won (I think!)

Ireland's Triple Crown winning captain, the legendary Ciaran Fitzgerald, takes time out to have a few words with me after Ireland's 'clean sweep' of five tour wins in Japan in 1985.

Augusta, Georgia, 2004... My most memorable golfing experience? Well, if you really insist on asking, let me tell you about the time I played Augusta National!

The precious invitation from Augusta National Golf Club.

AUGUSTA
NATIONAL
GOLF
CLUB

Monday, April 12, 2004

Fred Cogley
7:37
1st Tee

Please present this card at the Main Gate (Gate #2) for
entrance to the Club grounds and at the tee.

Those bunkers which the great Bobby Jones wanted at Augusta National can be troublesome.

match made memorable for a great try by right wing Pat Casey. It was Mike Gibson's first year on the team and he was in Cambridge University at the time. It was the start of his brilliant career. He initiated a great movement from inside the Irish 22, all the way up field, inter-passing with centre Jerry Walsh, and it was Casey who shot under the posts for a try that sent this commentator almost hysterical.

Sadly, the full match recording of the game had been quickly wiped afterwards because the tape had to be reused. However, some years later, a short excerpt was discovered on a news archive. Lo and behold, the original black and white coverage of that try was featured, along with the high-pitched commentary from yours truly. Whatever about the voice, the try has lost none of its magic – a worthy entry among rugby's greatest tries.

• • • • •

There were many great characters that roamed the corridors of RTE. One such man was the wonderfully named American, Burt Budin. He was a man who thrived on the electricity generated by live television and played a role in the ongoing success of The Late Late Show. A needle-sharp TV director, he thrived on calling the shots on live programmes.

Burt used to say: "Anyone can do the job when everything is going well. I earn my wages by knowing what to do when things don't go well."

He was also a real prince of the one-liners. Whenever there was a problem that needed sorting quickly, Burt would comically intervene with the immortal words:

"Leave it to me. I'm the guy of whom President Kennedy once said: 'Who?'"

• • • • •

On two nerve-jangling days, I have been close-to-later than acceptable in my career. Both of them came to pass at Twickenham. The Eurovision network of countries was developing its sports committee. It put forward the idea that the host nation's main broadcaster would look after those broadcasters visiting from other countries for major events.

In the early 1960s, we were very kindly invited by the BBC to their broadcasting centre, a building near White City. After a short briefing, I was treated to lunch and then rather grandly offered a chauffeur-driven car to Twickenham. Things were going beautifully as I was introduced to this huge Austin Princess limousine. I asked my English colleague, Mike Dolbear, did he want to join me. He said he couldn't because he had to take the French guys to the game. I pitied him for a moment as I sat into the back seat on my own – King Fred was on his throne for the day, being driven in state, straight into the ground. I was even tempted to try the royal wave as we swept out of television centre.

In the limousine, the driver was obsequious.

"What route would you like to take sir?"

"I am in your hands. I will leave it to you," said I.

"Very well, sir."

The match was starting at 2.15pm. We set off at 12.15 from the television centre. It was a relatively short run. There was a lot of traffic building up. The car slowed to a crawl. I had my match notes on my lap and my heavy winter coat over me for this International between Wales and England. The incomparable Gareth Edwards was scrum-half for Wales.

I looked at my watch. It was 1.30. I began to see that the limousine was struggling to make it to the ground on time.

"Which way is the quickest way to Twickenham from here?"

"You go through the village and you turn right. Then it is a straight run up to the ground."

"You know what, the traffic is jammed. I think I will walk the rest of the way."

"Very well, sir."

I jumped out of the car with the assurance from my driver that the stadium was only a skip and a hop away. There were thousands of people around going left and right.

It was 1.45. I saw a policeman: "Excuse me, do I go left or right for Twickenham stadium?"

"Neither. You go straight ahead."

"Fine."

"How far is it?"

"Oh, about two miles."

"WHAT! TWO MILES! You must be joking."

"I'm afraid not, sir."

I had half-an-hour to run two miles, make my way into my commentary position and ready myself for transmission. A panic ran through me. I set off with my notes tucked inside my winter coat, bumping into people willy-nilly with the sweat pumping out of me. Eventually, the stand rose above me at touching on 2.10pm. I knew where I was. I talked my way through the gate as I heard the national anthems being played out inside the stadium.

In those days, the commentary position was right at the back of the upper deck of the stand. I galloped up the steps, falling into my seat. I was met with the beaming face of Mike Dolbear.

"What happened to you? Where have you been?"

I was soaked through in perspiration. I sat down. I put on my headphones.

Immediately, I was met with the words of Michael O'Hehir from the RTE studio.

"We thank Bill McLaren for his kind words before the start of the match. We now go over to Twickenham for our own match commentary from Fred Cogley."

Whew, it was an experience not to be repeated. Sadly, it was.

· · · · ·

In November 1993, Mike Horgan, Tony Ward and myself were on the way to Twickenham for an autumn International between England and the All Blacks. We got into our taxi from The Kensington Close Hotel at 10.30am. Tony had been out to buy toys for his kids. There would be a royal presence at the match. Call it paranoia, but we were slightly anxious that three Irishmen with bags would be seen as suspicious at a tricky time for The Exiles living in London.

All of a sudden, we were trapped in traffic gridlock. The driver spun around and delivered us at Paddington Station for the train to Twickenham. I was starting to have flashbacks to the previous match there in 1968. The supporters spotted Tony and wanted an autograph when we hadn't time to write our own names.

We did not have tickets. It was déjà vu. We took off out of the train station at the other end. We raced up to the barriers at the home of English rugby. There were security forces and police everywhere. We pleaded to be allowed in. Luckily, someone in authority recognised Tony with all his baggage and waved the three of us through unchecked.

This time, the commentary position was located to the front of the upper deck. You had to climb up on the front of the stand and make your way out onto a platform and descend into what you could only call a boat. When we got to it, the New Zealand broadcasters were already on air. They were blocking our way. We just threw our bags on top of them and plunged down into the boat, whipped on our headphones to hear my son Niall, a producer in RTE at this point, laconically say.

"Welcome to Twickenham guys. You are on air in 30 seconds."

It was another near miss, another potential disaster avoided.

Chapter 22

IN BED WITH 'THE BRAD'

The Links Golf Society was originally founded by the remarkable Cecil Whelan in the winter of 1966. Three professionals, Christy O'Connor Senior, Watty Sullivan and Jimmy Kinsella, and 27 amateurs played golf and sat down for dinner, all for the purpose of raising money for charity. The princely sum for that first evening came to IR£13 and 10 shillings in old money.

Since then, the Society has raised, and continues to raise, enormous sums of money for different charities as an organisation that has been staging Pro-Am events for the better part of half a century. Cecil continues to lead a dedicated committee, bringing together some of the biggest names in the world of golf, business and sport. The Links has also been a factor in the development of golf in Ireland, channelled through the efforts of Cecil.

It was at one of their events where I managed to get talking to Christy Senior about his outstanding record in The British Open.

"You must regret what happened at Royal Birkdale in 1965. It must have been the greatest disappointment of your career to come within a hair's breadth of winning The Open?"

In fact, Christy came up two shots short of Australia's Peter Thomson in tying for second with Ryder Cup team-mate Brian Huggett. It was the closest he would get to a Major title.

"No. Funny. That was the one British Open I was delighted I didn't win."

"Ah, come on, Christy. You can't mean that. Don't be pulling my leg."

"No. At the time, I knew I had blown it. I was very disappointed at the end of the final round. I was totally dejected. Instead of going through with my plans for the next week, I told Mary (his wife) to pack the bags.

"She asked where we were going. I said we're going to London to catch a late night flight home. I had lost my appetite for the game. I felt I needed to be back where I felt most comfortable.

"The twins, Peter and Christopher, were at home with their grandmother. When we got back, in the middle of the night, Mary went in to check on them. One of them was missing. Mary looked to see if he was in with his grandmother. He wasn't.

"We started to search around the house. I found the kitchen door open. I went out into the garden. I walked over to the shed. I opened the door. Christy Junior was sitting there with what looked like a bottle of lemonade up to his mouth. It was actually weed killer. We rushed the child into hospital where he was pumped out. It was a terrifying time that immediately put my personal, professional disappointment into perspective.

"So, you see, if I had won that British Open, we could have lost our son."

•••••

In amateur golf, we have produced many remarkable players, including Jimmy Bruen, Cecil Ewing, Tom Craddock, Joe Carr and many others. What Joe achieved was quite remarkable in his day. It was at a time in the evolution of society and sport when amateur golf was seen as superior, the number one in comparison to the professional game.

Joe Carr's dominance of the world of amateur golf for a period through the 1940s, 1950s and 1960s was quite unique. He won the British Amateur Open three times in 1953, 1958 and 1960 and the Irish Amateur Open four times in 1946, 1950, 1954 and 1956. He was a Walker Cup player on ten occasions from 1947 to 1965.

Because of the huge demands golf places on technical resources we couldn't broadcast it on RTE all that extensively. We covered one tournament every year where all the outside resources – the trucks, the cable, the camera towers – were driven to a venue for live transmission. Ideally, we needed well-informed and objective commentators, who would have a feeling for the finer points of the game. On a once-a-year basis, it was hard to train anyone for the job, but I was asked if I was willing to lead the team.

Basically, I was the television man. I provided the background music, so to speak, to setting up a play, purely through the statistical translation of information – how tall he is, how heavy he is, how far from the green he is, where the bunkers are – to the viewer. I could never dream of analysing the swing or offering a guess at what club he would intend to use in terms of his shot selection.

We were looking for someone with a renowned reputation to comment on the intricacies of the game. We were lucky enough in the early days to get John Jacobs, who was one of the great teachers and analysts of the game in the world. John had worked with ITV and he stayed with RTE for several years. His expertise was sorely missed when he was no longer available to us.

John soldiered long and hard on the United States PGA Tour for twelve years, from 1968 to 1980. He came close to winning, finishing second three times, but could never quite break through. He had to settle for five career victories, away from the tour spotlight. He later went on to far greater success on the Champions' Tour where he won the Senior PGA Championship in 2003.

Anyway, I topped-and-tailed, set up the scene. I would identify the players, give the geography of where they were and relay the scoring to the audience at large. John would then come in and provide the technical knowledge.

After a while, we couldn't afford to foot the bill for his fee because John was becoming a valuable commodity for foreign broadcasters with far deeper pockets than RTE. So, we were on the lookout for a viable replacement.

The Irish Open was first played in 1927. It was closed down for financial reasons from 1950 to 1975, except for a solo event in 1953 when it was won by the Scotsman, Eric Brown. It was replaced by the Carrolls' Irish International in 1963 until the Carrolls' Irish Open was reconstructed in 1975 when Christy O'Connor Junior won at Woodbrook.

I was Head of Sport in RTE and I was ambling around Portmarnock at the Irish Open one year. Joe Carr was there as a spectator. He never turned professional. He was not interested in the pay-for-play aspect. At the time, he earned a crust as the front man for a clothing business. Anyway, we ended up shoulder to shoulder behind a green.

I discussed the possibility of Joe joining RTE as an expert analyst. I felt he would be ideal for commentary, not only because of his own record but also because he was such a pleasant personality. I asked him if he would be available to work for RTE.

"Do you mind if I say no?" responded Joe.

"Could we not persuade you? We would like to have you in the commentary position."

"Thank you for the offer. I must decline."

"Can I ask you why you are turning us down?"

"It is simple. I wouldn't feel qualified to talk about the professional game or even hint at a criticism."

"Really?"

"Yes."

I thought this was simply remarkable for a man with his success and record, albeit in the amateur game. He had finished eighth at the Open Championship in 1960. He was the first Irishman to be honoured with the captaincy of the Royal & Ancient Golf Club of St Andrew's in 1991 and was eventually inducted into the World Golf Hall of Fame in the Lifetime Achievement Category in 2007. It was a sign of his humility that he genuinely felt he would not be competent enough to talk about what was going through the mind of a professional player. His livelihood did not hang on the shots he played.

It was a lesson for myself in so many ways, and for journalists in general, who can be hyper-critical of players in different sports when they themselves might not have been able to understand why a player wasn't playing well, why a player was playing to particular instructions and so on.

Fortunately, when Peter Alliss retired from the tour, he joined our commentary team for a spell. But the BBC had a priority call on his services. They recorded their Celebrity Golf series in the same week as the Carrolls' event in Ireland. So, as the years went on, RTE had to move between analysts. It was able to call on the services of many of the top players in the game internationally and domestically, like Tony Jacklin, Christy O'Connor Junior, Des Smyth and Ernie Jones.

I find it difficult to admire criticism from people who have not been there, who have not played at the highest level, and how they can comment so harshly and unwisely, forgetting what they say or what they print can be very hurtful, not only to the players involved, but to their mothers, fathers, wives, husbands, children and families. The very humanity of the game can be lost in the scramble for media outlets to sell their wares through ill-tempered judgement or cheap-shot comments.

I look back to my father, Mitchel, and his generation. I don't remember nasty, critical comments in the writings of the better journalists. It was more constructive, not molly-coddling or weak. It was never bitter. It was just better.

• • • • •

Harry Bradshaw and Christy O'Connor Senior played together in the Canada Cup, later to become the World Cup. When they won the Canada Cup in Mexico in 1958, they returned to Ireland almost unnoticed. There wasn't quite the level of laser-eye treatment by the media of sportsmen back then that exists these days.

I was beavering away at the *Herald* one morning. When Harry and Christy arrived back in the country, I was given the task of finding Harry and doing an interview with him all about their success in Mexico. I found out from a few golf buddies that Harry had arrived back in Ireland on that very day. He was at home in Raheny, so I hopped on my bicycle and cycled out to his home.

I knocked on his door. His wife opened it.

"Hello, there. I am Fred Cogley from the *Evening Herald*. I wonder would I be able to talk to Harry about the Canada Cup for my newspaper?"

"I'm afraid he's in bed," she hesitated.

"Oh, of course! It was a long flight home. I'm sorry for troubling you.

Perhaps you could let him know I called?"

"Hold on a minute," she smiled.

"Okay, sure."

A few minutes later, she was back at the front door.

"He will talk to you now."

"Are you sure? He must be jaded."

"I am. He'd love to have a chat."

She walked upstairs. I followed on, right up into the bedroom. Harry was there. He was a gentleman to his fingertips. He showed such generosity of spirit to a scruffy reporter, who arrived into his bedroom to do a piece for the *Herald*. He did it all with the patience of a saint.

Can you imagine turning up to the door of some of the top sportsmen in today's greedy world to do an Interview in their bedroom? But, even then, it was a unique experience to interview the world champion in his bed. I suppose I realise how Al Capp, the American cartoonist, felt when he talked to John Lennon and Yoko Ono in theirs.

In subsequent years out in Portmarnock, Harry was always there to greet people. He was a real gentleman, known plainly and simply as 'The Brad'.

Chapter 23

A CALF NAMED MADGE

Late in the game, Ireland rugby legend, Willie John McBride, got a bang where it hurts most for a man. He was lying on the ground, moaning and groaning. Out ran a very attractive physiotherapist to examine the extent of his injury.

As soon as she arrived on the scene, Bill knew he would get a slagging from the rest of the players. Seeking to avoid any embarrassment, he refused immediate attention. The physiotherapist was insistent that she had to carry out an examination due to strict medical and insurance guidelines. Eventually, she agreed to wait for him in the medical room after the match to prevent any further embarrassment on Bill's part – or parts.

True to his word, he turned up to see her. She was waiting for him. He was told to lie down on the bench and this 'very attractive' physiotherapist began to examine the injury, such as it was.

He winced once or twice.

"I know this procedure can be embarrassing," she said.

"Ah, no. It's alright," he boomed, in his deep Ballymena accent.

"In case you feel uncomfortable, do you remember your '99' call for The British and Irish Lions?"

"Yes. I remember it."

The '99' call in South Africa was the trigger for all The British and Irish Lions to weigh into a punch-up in a one-in, all-in ploy in order to prevent the referee from sending off any one individual.

"Well, in the event you feel any pain or sensitivity, you can call 99 and I will stop the examination immediately."

"Very well then. That's fine ... 1, 2, 3 ..."

·····

Willie John was central to Ireland becoming the first northern hemisphere nation to win a Test match in the southern hemisphere when Australia was beaten 11-5 at the Sydney Cricket Ground on May 13, 1967. This is an achievement that can never be removed from legendary Irish figures like full-back Tom Kiernan, fly-half Mike Gibson – who went on to even greater feats in the centre – and the incomparable McBride. The memory of this feat came flooding back to me when Ireland managed to get the better of Australia at the 2011 Rugby World Cup.

None of these former greats ever got to share in a Triple Crown success, but the victory in Sydney was a significant piece of Irish rugby history. Tom Kiernan had taken over the captaincy from Noel Murphy, who couldn't travel. Eugene Davy, who played for Ireland in the 1920s and '30s, was the manager. Des McKibbin was the assistant manager. That was the entire support staff, although Dr Jamsie Maher, and several other 'alickadoos', were among a tiny travelling group of supporters.

There was a fortnight run-in to the test match. We were in Brisbane to prepare for the start of the tour. The Irish three-quarter, Pat McGrath, from UCC, was confined to bed because he had developed 'an allergic reaction to grass'. He was isolated. There was a doubt about his recovery for the first tour match. We were reassured he would make the test match. Otherwise, the management would have to go through the rigmarole of sending home for a replacement. There was a daily update on the condition of McGrath.

As my contract work for RTE then did not cover such an expensive lifestyle, I freelanced myself out to various agencies, newspapers and media interests to pay my way. Peter McMullan, then from the *Belfast Telegraph*, and myself were the first dedicated journalists to travel with an Irish rugby team. 'The McGrath Mystery' seemed to fade even before the opening game.

We were aware of the privilege and responsibility it was to be almost 'extra members' of the official party and, yet, we had to retain the element of independence. As rugby reporters, we were there to cover only rugby matters, i.e. team selections, match reports or commentaries and team or management interviews.

Ireland warmed up for the Wallabies with a trip to the seaside to play in the wonderfully named Wollongong Stadium in New South Wales. There were two lasting memories from that game. The first was the performance of Terry Moore. He was a big back-rower. The St Mary's No. 8, Denis Hickie, went out on tour as the heir apparent to Ken Goodall, who would shortly move into Rugby League. We all believed that Denis was a shoo-in for the test until Moore played his way into the Irish back row with a blinder of a game in Wollongong that was good enough to seal his selection for the test match.

The second memory was an amazing drop goal, not from the fly-half, not from the scrum-half or full-back, but from the tight-head prop, Sam Hutton. I can still see the ball sailing through the posts from near the left-hand touchline and the lads congregating to clap him on the back. I will never forget the smile that spread across Sam's face. It must have been the highlight of his rugby career. He certainly talked about it for long enough afterwards.

· · · · ·

The manager, Eugene Davy, announced Pat McGrath had recovered in time for the test match. It was later that I learned there had been nothing wrong with McGrath at all. As a recently qualified doctor, he had taken advantage of his trip down under to fly to New Zealand to attend a job interview. The players actually concocted the elaborate 'allergy' story, without the consent of Davy and his assistant, Des McKibbin. Needless to say, it would have been sorely frowned upon.

Subsequently, there was no mention of this mysterious allergy to grass. McGrath played in the test match and played very well in the centre beside

Jerry Walsh, scoring one of Ireland's tries on a blazing hot day. As far as I know, McGrath accepted the job and never again played for Ireland.

Australia 5: Ireland 11, Sydney Cricket Ground, May 13, 1967.

Ireland XV (v Australia): Tom Kiernan; Alan Duggan, Jerry Walsh, Paddy McGrath, Niall Brophy; Mike Gibson, Brendan Sherry; Phil O'Callaghan, Ken Kennedy, Sam Hutton, Willie John McBride, Mick Molloy, Mick Doyle, Terry Moore, Ken Goodall.

Although there were two matches left on the schedule against Sydney and an Australian Selection in Melbourne, the test victory was the obvious highlight. Even the lone defeat to a weak Sydney side could not tarnish the test win, though, in trying to explain it, I raised the hackles of some of the travelling Ireland party.

In fact, there was a suggestion made to black-ball me. After the test on Saturday, the celebrations understandably carried on into the start of the following week. Some of the Irish players had not been back to their quarters for those three days. They staggered out onto the pitch, some still, how shall we say, way short of match fitness. Some didn't know where they were, never mind what they should be doing, and others only woke up on the pitch. It simply wasn't acceptable.

My report in the *Evening Herald* and for RTE went something like this: "Ireland's rugby team, buoyed up by their great test victory last Saturday, had celebrated the win not wisely, but too well. Consequently, they failed to produce anything like their best form and lost to an ordinary Sydney side ..."

That was as far as it went. But I was told I had broken confidence. I was called aside by the manager, Eugene Davy, and informed the squad was withdrawing all co-operation for the remainder of the tour, which now only stretched to one match.

I was totally taken aback by this protest, having soft-pedalled my report, which explained the main reason for such an outlandish defeat.

"What are you talking about? I used no names," I said.

"The lads felt you were unfair to them given the win on Saturday," said Davy.

"You might explain to the players that I didn't go into detail and then they might realise how lucky they were."

That was where the episode ended. Fortunately, no damage had been done. I was totally unaware of any deterioration in my relationship with any of the players. Ireland went on to finish the tour with a resounding win in Melbourne. There were eight or nine supporters and two journalists on that tour, which had been a huge success in almost every respect. The supporters party, including senior IRFU members, like Dom Dineen, were few enough in numbers to be useful to the team in the official party and not too many to be a burden on the management.

The 'Hangers On' were brought together by Freddie Fox, who owned tobacconists in Dublin and London. Freddie was a great organiser. The players were invited to every bun fight and social gathering in Australia. These were a complete distraction from the team's match preparations. But, Freddie's little cabal or 'The Langers', of which I was one, stepped into the breach to fill out the appointment book as unofficial representatives of Ireland along with one or two injured players.

· · · · ·

On another occasion in 1970, when the Irish team was announced, I was very critical of Roger Young's selection and 'smited' him from on high on television. It was rather over the top. When I eventually came off air, there was a phonecall for me. I took it. I was met with a surprising chill.

"Hello."

"Hello. I am Mrs Young. Roger Young's mother!"

"Oh, hello Mrs Young."

Ooops, I thought, *how do I get out of this one?*

"Hello, yourself! I have to say I am very disappointed with what you had to say a few short minutes ago. You know, it isn't Roger's fault that he has been chosen by the Irish selectors. They picked him. It has nothing to do with Roger, other than he wants to play for Ireland. If you need to criticise anyone, I suggest you aim it at them."

I was back-pedalling quickly and without great composure, trying to placate her.

"Yes, I see your point Mrs Young. Perhaps, my criticism was aimed in the wrong direction."

"Well, yes, I think so."

"I'm terribly sorry if I have upset you."

Then, there was what I thought was the sound of her crying on the other end of the phone.

"I must say I apologise for any hurt ..."

Then, I could make out a giggle, not a sob. I was confused and didn't know what to do. Straight away, I was put out of my misery. It was Molly O'Hehir, Michael's wife, pulling a fast one on me.

She taught me a lesson I have kept stored with me to this day. It is that when you are in a public capacity, whether writing for newspapers or on radio or television, you just have to respect other people, their feelings, their families, their friends. You have to be very careful in what you say and how you say it. There is a way of getting your opinion across. My father, Mitchel, always took the approach – 'if you didn't play well, you weren't mentioned'. When in doubt, leave it out.

Of course, the demands of writers and broadcasters have changed and the aims have altered. It is all about the big scoop, the new view, something different, something new, more often than not, something raw, something controversial.

There is no need to play games with people's sensitivities. Amateur sportsmen and women, whether Gaelic footballers or hurlers, for instance, are doing their utmost at an activity they love. They don't want to make mistakes. They don't want their names etched negatively into the papers. They don't want to be criticised wildly on television. Reasonable criticism and fair comment is one thing; shooting off thoughtlessly at the mouth is another.

In 1985, I remember Mick Doyle, as Ireland coach, saying that he would like to discuss, before a match, the sort of tactics he was going to employ, so that the players could be judged by the media with the proper facts about what Ireland was trying to achieve and how they went about it rather than uninformed comment from journalists.

Some of the media experts took exception to this. They felt Doyle was trying to manipulate them. They didn't want to know. I, for one, felt it was a very good idea to have such a rapport with Doyle, even though it could have created more problems than it would have solved.

While a coach can detail his out-half to kick the leather off the ball in the first-half, the papers the next day will be full of vitriol on what the fly-half should have done, blaming the player rather than criticising the faulty game plan of the coach. The deliverer of the message is being nailed for carrying out his instructions. If the media had known the game plan, they would have been better informed to make a judgement call on how the player carried out the plan.

• • • • •

When you are involved in the media, it is very often a two-way street. You may have to make contact with people at all hours of the night. Or, indeed, they may have to make contact with you. Some people take it as part of the job and others take it as more than an inconvenience.

It was in the early days of RTE, the mid-'60s. The phone rang at three o'clock in the morning. I answered the call drowsily.

"Hello."

Back came a big barrel of a voice over the phone.

"Is that you Fred?"

"It is. Who is this?"

It was clear this man had had one or two too many, in celebration as it turned out.

"Listen, I'm running out of names. I've just had another baby. We're trying to find a name. Would you believe a cow has had a calf and I need a name for it, too."

"What? Who is this? What are you talking about?"

"It's Gordon Wood here, Fred."

It was Keith Wood's father. He was one of the great prop forwards, a British and Irish Lion. He was a character. The calving by the cow had cut short the celebrations of his new baby.

"What's your wife's name Fred?"

"What?"

"Your wife! What is her name? We're running out of options."

I put the phone down.

"Who was that?" my wife asked.

"Gordon Wood."

"Oh, the rugby player?"

"Yes."

"What did he want?"

"He wanted to name his newborn after you ..."

Madeleine wasn't very impressed by the timing of the late night call. I didn't mention the choices. He may have been looking for an option on the name of the calf.

Chapter 24

DR JAMES 'JAMMIE' CLINCH

Doctor James 'Jammie' Clinch was an uncontainable character, at times a terror of a personality. We invited him on television back in the late '60s into the early '70s as one of our first rugby experts. By then we had seen the back of most of his wilder days.

As a player, he won 30 caps for Ireland and further enhanced his rugby career by playing twelve times for The British and Irish Lions on their tour to South Africa in 1924, without making a test match breakthrough. This did not deter him. He did not object to filling in at full-back against Rhodesia and The Border Bulldogs when the Lions' thin resources were torn by injury. In fact, he also played at second-row seven times on that tour and once each in all three positions in the back row. I suppose you could say he was one of the original 'dirt-trackers'.

Jammie was one of those once-in-a-lifetime personas. He took a scenic thirteen-year journey to complete his medical degree. The Dubliner was mostly capped for Ireland as a back-row forward. He had a ferocious reputation as an unbreakable blindside. His career was punctuated by his legendary disregard for others' reputations. This was best illustrated in the Five Nations at Twickenham in 1929.

Ireland won there for the first time at the seventh attempt. Jammie was one of the heroes of that hour. The story goes that he had a few words with the out-half, Eugene Davy, just before the kick-off.

"When you get the ball, sky-rocket it to the full-back and we'll look after him."

Early into the game, Davy lined one up, sending up a towering Garryowen. The English full-back, Thomas Brown, had a reputation for being, how shall we say, slightly unsure under the high ball. As he waited for it inside his 22, Jammie led the stampede of the Irish cavalry.

Five yards away from the full-back Jammie let out this cowboy-like roar: "YYYYYAA-HHHOOOOOOO!!!"

The full-back was smashed into smithereens and Ireland went on to make history, winning by the slimmest of margins (6-5) to make a breakthrough that has been a common occurrence at Twickenham ever since the turn of the millennium. After that, there was an addition made to the laws of the game that banned shouting at an opponent. It lives on today.

Jammie was a wild man. He qualified as a doctor, but he couldn't hold down a job because of his reaction to alcohol. He would devour a few drinks and become a danger to those around him. Rosslare held a special place in his heart. It was his hideaway. Despite the fact that he was banned out of every pub in the village, there were enough people there who understood how to handle him. He used to stay at The Iona Hotel on the beach.

Jammie used to clear places by merely walking into them. I was a witness to one incident. There was a dentist named Johnny Atkinson in Donnybrook. He was a great man. He would venture down to Rosslare on his holidays. He and his wife, Mary, knew Jammie. It seems they were often given the unwanted responsibility as the designated chaperones.

By this time, Jammie had carved out a career as a gynaecologist in Wales. Indeed, he was credited with giving birth to the entire infamous Pontypool front row of Graham Price, Bobby Windsor and Charlie Faulkner.

He was often heard to say: "If I had known how they would turn out, I would have thrown them back."

Anyway, Jammie never touched a drink in Wales. It was a different matter when he came home on his holidays. He was the old tearaway again. One night, he was in the golf club. He was just beginning to get rowdy. Johnny took care of him by taking him out of the place. Johnny spotted the impending danger and brought him back to his room at The Iona Hotel. It was located right beside the back door. Johnny saw him to bed. Jammie's most loyal friend at the time was his dog. He was stationed outside the back door. On guard. Unfortunately, the dog was trained to prevent intruders from breaking in, not a guest from breaking out.

The next morning. We were having breakfast. The dining room was fairly full. Suddenly, the door was flung open. There was Jammie. He had a big voice.

"AT-KIN-SON, AT-KIN-SON," he bellowed.

We all froze. He bolted over to us.

"You didn't look after me last night."

"What are you talking about? I put you to bed," said Johnny.

It was only then we noticed Jammie was drenched from head-to-toe.

It quickly transpired that Jammie had woken in the night. He sleep-walked out to the beach and lay down there to fall back into a deep sleep. The tide came in to wake him up in a state of near drowning. He thought he had been abandoned at the beach. We were all terrified, afraid he would smash up the place. He was eventually persuaded to calm down. He had sobered up by then.

There was another incident when England came to Dublin and he took their captain out for a spin in his car on the Friday. It turned into a hair-raising experience. There were two tramlines in Rathmines, one coming into the city centre, one going away from it. Jammie was not the most patient man in the world. He decided to overtake the tram in front of him. He made an impulsive manoeuvre, only to see the incoming tram approaching. It was too late to react. The impact came. Jammie 'jammed' his car between the two trams.

The English captain's nerves were destroyed. He didn't have the best of games the next day.

Chapter 25

CHICKEN COOP COMMENTARY

When travelling abroad, visiting radio and television commentators were always at the mercy of people in charge of domestic organisation, who didn't really give a damn about them. Oftentimes, in looking after their own, you are viewed as an irrelevance, independent of them, an afterthought. This did not apply at the BBC, where they always went out of their way to provide all visiting broadcasters with the best possible assistance. In truth, modern media facilities are a world away from those times.

In the mid-20th century, the media facilities at venues in any town or city were crude at best. No matter what country you went to you could find yourself hoisted into a commentary position that wasn't quite what you would have wanted or expected. One such place was Wollongong, a seaside city located deep in the Illawarra area of New South Wales in Australia.

Before the first test match in Ireland's history-making test win over the Wallabies in 1967, Ireland played New South Wales Country there. I was invited to share the radio commentary with the ABC (Australian Broadcasting Corporation) commentator, Bill O'Reilly. It doesn't matter where you go, you will find something weird that provides, in hindsight, an everlasting memory.

I was brought up into a tower that was basically the Judge's Box for greyhound racing at this stadium. There was a slit, no more than six inches wide for the photo-finish camera. It was the only way we could see the pitch – through this narrow gap in the wall. There wasn't enough room for us to sit side-by-side.

We devised a workable plan. He was smaller than me. He sat on the main seat leaning forward and I perched myself on the top of the back of his armchair with my feet delicately situated either side of him. Believe it or not it worked quite well for a while. It all unravelled when he got excited at one stage, jumping up off the chair. My weight was too much. The balancing act was over. I went flying backwards. I ended up sprawled all over the floor of the Judge's Box. Yer man, O'Reilly, convulsed into laughter. Fortunately, there were no expletives. At least, I heard none.

· · · · ·

My first experience of the French way of doing things came at the historical Stade de Colombes. Getting there was always quite an experience because it was in the suburbs. The commentary position was not unlike one of those window cleaning platforms you see attached to the side of a skyscraper. It hung from the top of the stand. You climbed up a rope ladder into the position.

When that became too dangerous, or someone had fallen from it, or a microphone had been dropped down onto the crown of an unsuspecting VIP's head below, we were moved to the running track, or cycling track, or whatever the heck it was between the pitch and the crowd. It may have been a less treacherous position to find, but a worse view from which to carry out commentary.

Further, the French were always difficult at providing the suitable commentary technical support, like a microphone that worked. Invariably, you had to check and double-check all the details. There was usually a problem somewhere along the line. It could have been the French or Irish Post Offices. They were in charge of the lines that transmitted the commentary back to Ireland.

For whatever reason, whether it was the Prix de l'Arc de Triomphe at Longchamp or a rugby International at Stade de Colombes, as it was in those days, and even later at the Parc des Princes, there was always some technical difficulty in getting a satisfactory connection back to the RTE office.

On one particular occasion, I went over to Paris for a France-New Zealand International in 1967, the last to be staged between the countries at Stade de Colombes before the French and All Blacks re-engaged at Parc des Princes six years later. My commentary position was arranged ahead of time. They were expecting me. I arrived to check things out at the ground the day before the game. I could see they had placed me on the running track that surrounded the pitch, along with the other TV broadcasters.

So, on match day, I arrived early, had a quick sandwich and took up my position only to find there was no communication with RTE. As this was no great surprise, given the French Post Office was involved in the matter, we had a standby arrangement. If we had no solid communication, we assumed there had been a telephonic breakdown, but that the actual commentary circuit was working. Our plan was that, as soon as the anthems were finished, the commentator would begin his commentary. This was a safety net that worked most of the time. I didn't panic too much. I knew the French way.

There was no point in complaining about the fact that we were expected to work sitting on the running track, separated from the baying crowd by a thin fence. It's a lonely place to be, although the great Welsh out-half Cliff Morgan was nearby, working for BBC.

We could just about see the knees of the players, never mind their faces. The French camerawork for rugby wasn't all that great. It leaned more towards the artistic than the practical. There could be a slow-motion shot of a handsome French player tying his shoelaces at the same time that they were carving up the Irish midfield. It did little to assist our commentary. The touch judge and a host of French photographers were haring up and down the line, blocking our view of the pitch. Much of the commentary that day was done by consensus. Cliff would look at me as I'd point at a name in the match programme and nod at him. He would return the compliment. And so it went until I hightailed it out of there straight after the final whistle.

"Get me out of here, I'm a commentator."

When I got to the airport, I tried but failed to make contact with RTE. The phone system in those days was not quite what it is today. Eventually, I established contact with home by phone when I got to London on my way to the connecting flight to Dublin.

"Oh, there you are," piped Madeleine.

"Yeah. It's me. Did the commentary work okay?"

"We didn't hear a thing,"

"Oh, for God's sake. That's crazy. All that effort for nothing."

"Well, at least, the Garda Siochana and Interpol will be delighted to hear you are safe and well."

"How do you mean?"

"When there was no word of your commentary coming through, the office got onto Paris, to the Rugby Union. They were told that the Irish commentator hadn't arrived for the match."

The commentary circuit had been put in place, but no one came to use it, the French had said. It transpired that, previously, the only contact with RTE was when the Irish rugby team was playing. Long before television, there was radio and, on this occasion, when they got the booking from RTE for a television commentary, they didn't twig that this was a different thing. The French Post Office assigned the commentary connection to a radio line in the press box in the middle of the stand, which was a long way from where I was for the game. Meanwhile, French Television had set up the TV position on the track and they assumed the TV commentary would be fed into the TV centre and then onto a direct circuit in Dublin.

Thus, when the RTE office was put through to the French technician at the ground, he relayed the message that the commentator was nowhere to be seen. The knock-on effect prompted RTE to contact the hotel. I had checked out. As far as Dublin was concerned, I was lost somewhere between the hotel and Stade de Colombes.

The Head of Sport, Michael O'Hehir, was working at Leopardstown. Word reached him that 'Cogley was missing in Paris'. His secretary, Oonagh Gormley, intervened. She contacted her brother, Eamon O'Doherty, who was a senior officer in the Garda Siochana. He dialled up Interpol. The French had received no report of a missing Irish commentator. There had been no accidents reported to them. In the meantime, Cliff Morgan and I were working away at the game.

Months later, in the office, I got a card from a man in Hong Kong. He was in the American navy. He had picked up my commentary and wrote a card in appreciation. Somehow the signal went somewhere. Strange world.

•••••

In 1991, George Hamilton paid a scalding price for his excitement at the old Lansdowne Road as his namesake Gordon Hamilton raided down the left wing for what looked like Ireland's winning try in the World Cup quarter-final against that wonderful Australian team led by scrum-half Nick Farr-Jones and the Davids – Lynagh at out-half and Campese on the wing.

Hamilton the commentator sprang to his feet to celebrate what briefly looked like a golden moment until his head hammered off the lowest of low ceilings. Full marks to him, he continued in his work with a splitting headache, made worse by Lynagh's plunging try for their 'get out of jail card' ahead of cracking the All Blacks in the semi-final, back at Lansdowne Road and a one-dimensional England in the final at Twickenham.

Despite Hamilton's argument with the ceiling, there wasn't another ground in the world that I visited that had such a good vantage point for commentators. You were right in the middle of the crowd. You were close enough to the pitch. You were high enough to get a wonderfully panoramic view of the game without meeting with the clouds. It was absolutely perfect.

The tearing down of the old and the construction of the new is done in the name of modernisation. The Aviva Stadium, opened in the autumn of 2010, is certainly a magnificent structure. There was a great deal of nostalgia over Lansdowne Road. It had its charm. It also had its drawbacks. The faded pictures of the old pavilions are a distant memory with the players emerging out of the old Havelock Square. The terraces were so cramped, so close to the action. I don't think the magic has been lost at the new venue. We saw that when Leinster played Munster there in the Magner's League match in October, 2010 and when Ireland tore up England's Grand Slam grand plan in 2011.

Chapter 26

TWO-CAR FUNERAL

Malcolm Brodie was the Sports Editor of the *Belfast Telegraph* for several years. He was a remarkable character. He had a touch of a Scottish accent running through his brogue, even though there was no mistaking he was from Northern Ireland and a committed supporter of the Northern Ireland soccer team. In his capacity as a journalist, he had so many contacts in the sports world. He was an 'expert' on the development of sports and the sports-related stories that broke around them.

He knew everyone and everything, from the greatest to the smallest. He was travelling to furthest South America with Northern Ireland in the 1960s in the days when communications systems were not as sophisticated as they are now. Basically, it was one step up from the carrier-pigeon. Anyway, Malcolm was at the airport in Belfast. The journalists congregated together, waiting to be called for their flight.

"I have some unfinished business," he announced.

Malcolm scurried off to make a phonecall to one of the newspapers he did extra work for at the time. He had copy they needed for the following day. Eventually, he was connected to a copy taker. He was a little tetchy as boarding time was fast approaching. Anyway, in the heel of the hunt, the other journalists nearby could hear Malcolm start to dictate the Dunmore – the Shelbourne Park of Belfast – Dog Card for the next day's paper.

"The Dunmore Dog Card. The first race. The 525 Yards ..."

It was such a nothing piece of work. But, Malcolm gave it more than the respect it deserved. That was him. He treated every piece of work as if it was a major scoop.

The next thing: *"Calling all passengers to London en route to Buenos Aires. Calling all passengers ..."*

"Oh God, I will have to finish this later. I will call back in a few hours," he told the copy taker.

That was fine. The group loaded into the plane. Some time later, they disembarked the plane, slightly weary for the experience. Malcolm hurried to the nearest phone at Heathrow.

"Now, where were we?"

"The third race."

"That's right. That's right. The third race is the ..."

On another day, in a faraway land, Northern Ireland was playing in Russia, or somewhere equally remote in the 1960s. His greatest concern was the timing of the match. He wanted to make his evening deadline at all costs. He checked out the schedule.

All going well, the match would end at 4pm Irish time. He had to be talking to the copy taker by 4.30pm to make the first edition. Of course, telephones were few and far between back then. There was no phone at the ground. He decided to make an arrangement with the hotel for a taxi to collect him directly after the final whistle.

"I need a taxi to pick me up at precisely 4.05pm outside the ground and bring me back to the hotel."

"That is no problem, sir."

"How long will it take?"

"Ten minutes, sir."

"Are you sure?"

"Yes sir."

"I can't afford to be late."

"You won't be, sir."

"Very well."

Malcolm called the Belfast office to let them know he would be back at the hotel, in his room, ready to give copy at 4.30pm. They agreed to call him. He even made a dry run the day before the game to choose the point of pick-up.

All went well. He was picked up at the hotel. He was taken to the agreed meeting point. He went to the match. Northern Ireland were leading 1-0 with two minutes left to play. He left the Press area and slipped down to the exit from where he watched the game come to a natural conclusion. The final whistle was sounded. Malcolm scarpered for the meeting point. The taxi was there. Happy days!

He was back at the hotel at 4.15pm. Up the stairs he ran at top speed.

"Is there any sign of that call coming through for me?"

"Not yet, sir"

"Let me know immediately when it does."

"Of course, sir."

The 'ts' had been crossed, the 'is' dotted. He sat on his bed to construct the beginning of his report. The phone rang.

"Hello."

"Your call to Belfast, sir."

"Hello. Hello. Hello."

There is a voice at the other end. It is one of the girls on the switchboard.

"Ah, it is yourself Malcolm! How are you doing?"

"Never mind that. Put me through to the sports desk."

"Who won the match?"

"Forget that. Just put me through!"

There is a short silence. A young girl at the desk picked up the line at the other end. She was new.

"Hello," she said.

"Hello, Malcolm Brodie here."

"Who?"

"Malcolm Brodie!"

"Who is that you say? The line is bad."

"M-A-L-C-O-L-M B-R-O-D-IE!"

"Oh, I'm sorry. He is not here. He is at the Northern Ireland match in Russia."

And the line went dead.

Happily, Malcolm recovered his sanity in time to file his match report, and all was well...

• • • • •

In 1969, The Ryder Cup was held at Royal Birkdale in Southport, near Liverpool, where Jack Nicklaus conceded a 'missable' putt to Tony Jacklin in what turned out to be the first draw in the history of the great competition. It was followed by The Alcan Tournament in Portland, Oregon, which was due to be played in Ireland the following year 1970. This was a tournament of champions and a core group of Irish media hounds had been asked to travel to Portland, Oregon, to see how it was put together and what we could learn before it came to Ireland.

There was one guy who seemed to be in control of the whole operation. I wanted to know what sort of guy he was. I made an inquiry about him to one of the American journalists at Birkdale.

"Who is this guy? What is he like?"

"I'll tell you what he's like. He is the only guy I know who could f**k up a two-car funeral!"

It was an expression I had never heard. But, as far as the broadcasters were concerned, it was well wide of the truth in this instance. The Alcan was a big success at Portmarnock in 1970 and in the supporting 'International' event – this was for those who didn't qualify for the champions' competition – there was a memorable win for one of Ireland's gentlemen of golf, Paddy Skerritt.

• • • • •

That same year, I received a phonecall from a man called Jack Murphy. He was the source behind bringing fully automated ten-pin bowling to Ireland. He built the Stillorgan Bowl. He wanted to expand it, but ran into planning difficulties when he wasn't prepared to kowtow to the 'demands' of those in authority. If it wasn't going to be played by the rules, Jack wasn't interested. Consequently, all his efforts remained restricted to Stillorgan and his ambitions to expand had to be shelved.

He formed a close relationship with The American Machine and Foundry (AMF) Company. This was a large recreational equipment business in the United States which looked after the installation of all the machinery required to kick start The Stillorgan Bowl. The Bowl was then well established. Jack and his family ran the operation to the highest professional standards.

Anyway, I got a phonecall in the office at RTE from Jack, who had an American friend staying over in Ireland. He wanted me to meet him to discuss a golfing project. I went to the old Jury's Hotel in Ballsbridge. Paddy Flynn, the sports editor from the *Evening Press*, was there too, although he wasn't all that interested in golf.

The American turned out to be Victor Kalman. He was very outgoing, a force of nature really. He had been employed as a media link man between AMF and their various clients. Anyway, Victor started talking what I considered at the time to be complete and utter nonsense.

"I am going to open a golf course on a virgin island in The Bahamas in six months' time."

"Really?"

"You see, I represent the Grand Bahamian Development Authority. It has bought a parcel of land on the Grand Bahama Island with exclusive rights to develop a world-class golf course, hotels etc, etc."

He spoofed and spoofed with that loud American twang, blasting away with apparent certainty about how he was going to transform a bare, coral island into a world-class golf resort in half a year.

And it got better.

"Gee, Fred, you have to come over and see it. It is going to be something to behold."

I was sitting there, twisting in my seat, looking at Paddy Flynn and my watch, wondering where they got this 'looney tune' from. He was talking the talk. I just wanted to walk – out the door. But one doesn't want to be rude.

"The Bahamian Open will be played in November. You have to come out for that. You can stay at the Lucayan Country Club. The new course is called The Shannon, a sister course to the Lucayan. Well, The Shannon isn't actually a course at the moment. It is a coral island. But we will have it up and running in six months' time."

"You really must come down to Grand Bahama Island. We have a beautiful place right on the beach, green waters and white sands as far as the eye can see."

"Sounds wonderful!"

"And you can bring your wife as well. Why not come over for the official opening of the new Shannon course? It will be led by Christy O'Connor."

"Oh, that would be lovely Victor. I can't wait."

At the end of the meeting, we said farewell to Jack Murphy and drove Victor out to the airport.

"I am developing the Grand Bahaman Golf Society. When you come back from The Bahamas, will you lend your support to developing the Society?"

"Of course! You can rely on RTE."

What could I say? Eventually, we waved our goodbyes. I drove Paddy Flynn back into town. We sat in silence for a while.

"Paddy, that was something else! That guy blew in like a hurricane and left like a whirlwind. You don't take him seriously do you?"

"This guy is for real, Fred."

"Paddy! Come on! For openers, a golf course in six months' time is just plain crazy."

"I don't know about that. All I know is anything he has said to me before has been straight and above board and I've known Victor a long time."

"Well, so be it. If it works out, I'll see you in The Bahamas in six months so," I said, as a true non-believer.

A month later, out of the blue, came an envelope to the RTE office. I opened it. Inside, there was a full itinerary for a trip to The Bahamas, two air tickets, a booking into a suite at the seaside hotel, The Lucayan Country Club, and an invitation to the official opening of the new Shannon golf course. I couldn't believe it.

I arrived home to Madeleine.

"You are not going to believe this! You know that madcap American I was telling you about?"

"Yes."

"He has invited us out to the Grand Bahama Island. I have the tickets and the details of our stay."

We went there. Victor met us at the opening ceremony of the new Shannon golf course. I got a few nice interviews for RTE with Arnold Palmer and Christy O'Connor and wrote a few articles about the possibilities of the golf course and the plan for a link with Irish tourism and Shannon Duty Free.

It was sensational to see this golf course built out of nothing. There were something like 140 construction companies working this area of land. Sadly, not long after that, there was a change of government in The Bahamas. It became less European-focused in its outlook.

One year later, when we returned, there was something like five or six companies left in operation. Victor had wanted to generate more golfing traffic to The Bahamas using cheap flights and reduced membership fees, but it all fizzled out. The dream was never fully realised.

The lesson I learned was never to make judgements on first impressions. Victor Kalman may have given the impression of being something of a 'spoofer'. But, he was true to every one of his words. The Shannon golf course was officially opened on time as he predicted ... dug out, dusted and divot-free in six short months. The large contingent of Vic's media connections and friends – this included English Heavyweight hero Henry Cooper – were there in 1970 to see Christy O'Connor rifle the first ceremonial drive down the middle of the fairway.

The Professional Players staff at The Lucayan complex was headed up by Harry Obitz, a burly, seasoned golfer who looked after the requirements of two clubs – the established Lucayan and the newly opened Shannon. As part of their promotional activities, they arranged a short tour of Ireland and the United Kingdom.

The idea was to generate interest in visiting The Bahamas. To this end, Harry and his team of professionals would put on a one-hour show, entitled The Swing's the Thing. Several venues in Ireland agreed to provide facilities for the show, starting at what was then the John Jacobs Golf Centre at Leopardstown and including Tramore, Lahinch and Galway golf clubs.

It turned out to be a most entertaining and informative show. While many of the spectators expressed the wish to travel to The Bahamas to join the Grand Bahama golf society, it all came to an end when the development company behind the project geared down their efforts. We heard no more thereafter.

Chapter 27

ENGLAND OUR FRIEND

Rugby is, at its core, a battle of minds and bodies. Retribution and revenge can be useful tools in arming players with the kind of ferocious intent that is necessary to overpower a foe equally large in size and deep in strength.

IRELAND 14 WALES 0, Lansdowne Road, March 14, 1970.

This was the day Irish rugby saw Ken Goodall for the last time. What an impact he made in the space of three seasons. From his debut as a 19-year-old against Australia in 1967, he developed into a fine athlete with a gift for the game. He was a beautiful footballer, lanky and slightly ungainly in his running. Just as he was about to reign indefinitely at No. 8 for Ireland, he decided on the road less travelled. He moved to Rugby League, like Paddy Reid from the Grand Slam side of 1948, never to return.

In his last appearance, the Derry man produced one of the finest individual moments in Irish rugby, showing his superb athleticism to rip through the Welsh defence, denying them a second successive Triple Crown in the process. It was a cameo that will live long in the memory. He took a wayward kick out of defence, chipped over the head of Barry John, collected the ball on the other side and left Gareth Edwards and J.P.R. Williams gasping for air on a charge that took in half the length of the pitch.

There was more than just a game at stake, however, and Goodall was seen as the hero of the hour in a game carried out as the bitter after taste from a brutal encounter the year before.

WALES 24 IRELAND 11, Cardiff Arms Park, March 28, 1969.

The significance of this was as revenge for the previous year's defeat in Cardiff when Ireland were going for the Triple Crown at a stadium that could only accommodate 29,000. The Arms Park was being rebuilt. It was also the year Charles was crowned as The Prince of Wales at Caernarfon Castle later that summer. He was present to be introduced to the players in a welter of pageantry and brouhaha.

It was a strange game. There was no one on the far side of the stadium. The stand was under construction at the time. There had been a great deal of angst generated in the Welsh media about the Irish team and how their forwards had lived on the edge of the laws of the game. Noel Murphy was seen as an 'agent provocateur'. He was eventually singled out and levelled by second-rower, Brian Price, in his last International season, in the early stages of the game.

In the middle of an early maul, Noel Murphy was seen to receive a punch. He reeled back and collapsed in a heap in full view of the crowd. The referee didn't do anything about the incident other than bring play to a halt so that Noel could be attended to quickly. There was some suggestion that if the punch had landed plum, Noel would never have got back to his feet. Afterwards, Noel insisted he took one fair-and-square in the 'mush' – the face, to you and me.

That one incident unsettled everyone and everything. We were waiting for a dust-up at every ruck and maul. It didn't actually erupt until later on, when London-Irish hooker, Ken Kennedy, was taken out. I still recall Ken lying on the ground while Old Belvedere's Paddy Madigan patrolled the touchline, ready to realise a dream by being called in as a replacement hooker for his first, and what would have been his only, cap. Ken was groggy and should have come off. But he refused. He carried on and Paddy was destined never to play for his country. How crestfallen he must have been to come within one miraculous recovery of an International cap. The Irish were beaten. The Triple Crown was lost. The game went down as one of the uglier ones between the two great Celtic rivals.

•••••

Sometimes it is impossible to keep sport and politics apart. I was convinced Ireland could have won the Triple Crown, Grand Slam, the whole shooting gallery in 1972. It was the year of 'Bloody Sunday'. The troubles in the North had escalated. The atmosphere was fraught. There was a great fear there would be a reprisal south of the border. Scotland and Wales withdrew from their fixtures in Dublin. There was a great deal of ill-feeling generated because it was felt various aspects of the British media had contrived to scare the visitors away from Ireland. First, it was Scotland's decision not to come. Although Judge J.C. Conroy led a delegation from Ireland to convince the Scots there was no danger to players or supporters, it was all to no avail. Scotland said 'no' and Wales followed suit.

That Irish team was one of the best we had ever fielded. They were all on top of their game. It was littered with Lions. We had the front row of Sean Lynch, Ken Kennedy and Ray McLoughlin; Willie John McBride in the second row, Fergus Slattery at the back. Behind the scrum, you had the half-backs, Johnny Moloney and Barry McGann, Mike Gibson at the peak of his powers, the unflappable Tommy Kiernan at full-back.

Having beaten England and France away, we were already on a roll. We had our best chance of capturing our second Grand Slam since 1948. Sadly, it was not to be. The French were gracious enough to come to Dublin in April to be soundly beaten again in an arrangement to generate much-needed revenue for the Irish Rugby Football Union.

I remember at Twickenham, there was a protest during the course of the game where several people quietly walked onto the pitch to signal their disgust at what had happened on 'Bloody Sunday'. It was one of those occasions, when, as broadcasters, we had tried to anticipate how we would react if something serious had developed. The BBC cameras were covering it. One had to be very careful about the commentary that would accompany such pictures. As it was, the protest was dignified and quiet and low in numbers. The players were able to complete the game to give Ireland another deserved win at the home of English rugby.

The following year, there was huge pressure on the English Rugby Union and their players, brought about by aspects of the media in the United Kingdom, who seemed to spend a great deal of time trying to persuade the players not to travel to Dublin.

The English Union and the players insisted they were available to travel to Dublin to fulfil the fixture. This they did. It provided one of the most memorable moments in my career. When the English ran out onto Lansdowne Road from the pavilion corner, they were given a tremendous standing ovation. It was one of those moments, something similar to that at Croke Park when England came out at GAA headquarters in 2007.

· · · · ·

Prop Brian 'Stack' Stephens was a farmer from Cornwall. He played for England 25 times between 1970 and 1975. He was in something of a hole. He needed a favour.

"Is there anyone going to the airport? Stack needs a lift," an English official requested.

"I have a car outside. I would be happy to leave him out there," I said.

On the way, we got to talking. The conversation went something like this:

"What was the atmosphere like in the English dressing room?"

"We were in the pavilion. We didn't pay a lot of attention to what was going on outside. We had a game to play. We were intent on focusing in on winning the game."

"You didn't feel the atmosphere in the ground?"

"No. We were psyched up, ready to go. We went out onto the pitch so determined to smash the Irish team."

"So, what happened to you?"

"As we ran on, there was this wave of goodwill that seemed to envelop us. I have no recollection of the first 15 to 20 minutes of the game. I was totally drained emotionally by the way the crowd responded to us when we came out. We were ten points down before I woke up."

Legend has it that the ovation lasted for a full five minutes. That's as maybe, but I don't think it was quite that long. What is on the record is that Ireland registered another good win over the 'auld enemy', who, for this occasion, had become our greatest friend. The embargo had been ended. Normal service had been restored.

Chapter 28

LIVE COVERAGE

The Sunday Press, November 3, 1974

Headline: TV HEAD OF SPORT FRED COGLEY REPLIES TO G.A.A. CRITICISM.

MORE LIVE COVERAGE – THE ANSWER.

I believe, and history proves me right also, that the best promotion any game can get is 'live coverage'. The best example of this in Ireland was in the case of rugby, where practically all of that sport shown on television during the past ten years has been live transmission of matches.

This has led to a tremendous growth of rugby throughout Ireland, in areas where it had no tradition, which has been quite staggering.

Recorded games shown later on have not got the same impact at all. Soccer is a good example of this. So, if I had my choice of all the G.A.A. games in a year, to do as I wished with them, I would take the five live days we now have, St Patrick's Day, All-Ireland semi-finals and finals and, in addition, the semi-finals and the finals of the National Leagues, some provincial championship games and the provincial finals. I would show all these games live.

This I would regard as the best possible service that RTE could do for the G.A.A.

It is bad that RTE should be broadcasting MORE live soccer and rugby at present than our own national games and this is caused mainly because of lack of permission by the G.A.A.

If I could get the permission from the G.A.A. for more live televising, then I would be prepared to sacrifice some of the other events now being shown.

I would be against the G.A.A. having their own programme each week devoted to their games alone. I believe that would be 'ghettoising' the G.A.A. and cutting it off from other sports.

My idea is that by showing Gaelic games in general sports programmes we can show those who may not have much interest in the games that football and hurling are as good, if not better, than any other sport.

By putting G.A.A. games into a programme on their own, all you are going to do is preach to the converted.

I'm not all that sure that the Sunday Sports Show is something that should concern the G.A.A. all that much as the period of the show (October to the end of January) is a season which is virtually closed for Gaelic games.

If there were no Sunday Sports Show the number of times on which the G.A.A. games would feature on Sunday nights during that period are relatively few.

During that time of year, the amount of sport of the right quality available for television in Ireland is very limited. Hence, we decided to provide a more leisurely-type programme.

I think some of the things said by G.A.A. people about the Show have been overstated and they are inclined to pre-judge what way an event will be handled. Also, the fact that it is during the G.A.A. close season means that they are not going to be all that involved in it anyway.

As regards the possibility of a G.A.A.-style Match of the Day on RTE, apart from the technical difficulties involved for us, it is worth remembering that very few Gaelic games have the sort of crowds or atmosphere that the English soccer games have on a Saturday.

How many G.A.A. games have forty or fifty thousand at them?

A more accurate comparison for the G.A.A. to consider is the BBC 2 "Rugby Special" on Saturday nights – games which have relatively small crowds in fairly large grounds. That would apply to 80% of G.A.A. matches.

•••••

Sean O'Siochain took over from Padraig O'Caoimh as the General Secretary of the GAA in 1964. He helped to build the Association into an impressive force. He was the ideal man to carry the GAA through to a more enlightened perspective in terms of its relationship with the media.

He came at it from a different angle, having moved in the entertainment world as a ballad singer. He toured the United States four times. He had an ease, a familiarity around publicity. He was more approachable than Padraig O'Caoimh, a private man. It must be noted that the GAA was the first of the big Irish sports organisations to agree to permit a limited number of days for matches to be televised live – the two All-Ireland finals, the two football semi-finals, the Railway Cup Inter-provincial finals on St Patrick's Day.

In contrast, the IRFU and the FAI were very suspicious of the emergence of RTE and how this would affect their attendances at matches. They wanted to know what compensation they would receive financially if they allowed the cameras in. Their expectations were far above RTE's capacity to meet them. Michael O'Hehir's difficulties with the IRFU and FAI were defined, more or less, by the financial aspects of what might accrue to the organisations. For the first few years, in the mid-1960s, there were no domestic live shows. In many cases, in fact, RTE's only coverage was shot on a single film camera.

Some of the legends of sport have been diminished by television because viewers can see that the bodies are merely human whereas the mythical performances of Mick Mackey and Christy Ring in hurling were probably not as brilliant, not as super-human, as read about in the papers or heard on the radio. The imagination of the writers of Gaelic games, and sport in general, and the vivid words of Michael O'Hehir on radio transported readers and listeners to a land of heroes, lifting them out of the ordinary into a world apart. They added mystic to the matches.

I had the great honour of meeting Mick Mackey and Christy Ring at various functions. They were great characters. Their genuine interest in all things sport transcended everything. They would have seen me as someone from the rugby world. They were always full of chat about the oval ball at a time when the GAA's 'foreign games' ban was in operation. It seemed to me to be kept alive by the officials and a portion of the supporters, who had either long since given up the game or had never been a part of the playing of the game at a high level. It was felt the 'foreign games' issue was a bandwagon they could be noticed on. Consequently, it lived on until 1971.

I remember Pat Fanning, the President of the GAA at the time, in my early days as Head of Sport, and how excited he was to feel that, at last, the ban was going to be left behind. I had great admiration for Pat as he helped the official movement away from the dark days. The ban was lifted, gone in a very peaceful, orderly, civilised way. That was the end of it.

It was a little like the more modern attitude towards the visit of the English rugby team to Croke Park in 2007, which was no more than we should have expected. And yet, on the day, it was such an occasion. You felt so proud that everything was so emphatically pro-Irish and pro-rugby, while not anti-English, by a crowd which wasn't asked to sing Amhran na bhFiann, but did, which wasn't asked to stand quiet for God Save the Queen, but did. It was just something that showed the better part of us – the real us – rather than the nonsense that has caused so much pain and anguish over the years.

I also remember talking to the GAA in the 1960s and early 1970s when every single County Board Annual General Meeting was reported extensively in the newspapers. At almost each and every one of them, someone would raise the roof with a criticism of RTE about the coverage, or the way Gaelic games were discussed. Radio wasn't giving enough air time. Television wasn't giving enough air time. Some of the criticisms were justified. It was more the manner in which they were put. The grass roots were not happy and, to some extent, Croke Park had to reflect these views back to us.

In turn, RTE had to send back a response to explain our shortcomings, bemoaning that fact that the facilities were simply not there. We didn't have the money to do what they wanted us to do. The lowly punt only stretched so far. It was all to placate people who stood for a rant at RTE and were using the platform to win personal publicity.

Of course, some of the criticisms were justified. When I was in 'The Chair', we managed to strike an agreement where RTE, as a national organisation, and the GAA, as a national sporting organisation, should work on the area of co-operation rather confrontation. We had a mutually beneficial arrangement. I remember Con Murphy in Cork was very helpful in the organisation of the details. A positive attitude pervaded all our discussions from then on. It was so much more helpful. We were in it together, to some extent.

Later, when Liam Mulvihill succeeded Sean O'Siochain as Director General, we were able to extend and improve our coverage, although it took two decades to convince all sections of the GAA that live coverage of more games would help to promote the GAA better than any other marketing tool.

• • • • •

RTE's technical people devised ways that allowed us to use outside broadcast cameras for recordings. This led to multi-camera coverage and, ultimately, to The Sunday Game.

When I succeeded Michael O'Hehir, he was perceived, wrongly, as a GAA man. He was a sports journalist, first and foremost. He specialised in Gaelic games and Racing. He wasn't a dyed-in-the-wool devotee of one sport. He had a very wide appreciation of sport and its value to the wider community.

As Head of Sport, Michael had a very catholic outlook, a general, widespread interest in sport. He knew what was what. The GAA was the only big organisation to embrace live coverage of their own sports events with a sense of expectation, a sense of adventure, not a negative feeling that it would be harmful to them.

That was a great advantage for RTE, in the initial stages, because the GAA, encouraged by Michael's suggestions that live coverage would promote the game, embraced the new approach, particularly in view of the coverage of soccer on BBC and ITV which was streaming into the country at the time.

• • • • •

Initially, the Irish Rugby Football Union was loath to allow live television coverage of Internationals at Lansdowne Road. However, RTE was showing live matches in the first years of existence through its connection with Eurovision, the European-wide broadcasting partnership. There was live airing from Twickenham, Cardiff, Murrayfield and Paris. But we were restricted to showing delayed coverage from Lansdowne Road. It was just plain crazy. But it took time to agree the terms.

RTE's first live match from Twickenham in 1962 was unique in a number of ways as Willie John McBride started for the first time, along with scrum-half Johnny Quirke, out-half Gerry Gilpin and prop Ray McLoughlin. Unfortunately, it was an unhappy occasion for the fledgling Irish squad as England won clearly, 16-0, on an afternoon when no less than nine players made their International debuts.

It was only in the latter part of the 1960s that RTE expanded its expert analysis when Ronnie Kavanagh and Karl Mullen came on board as assistant commentators and the IRFU became a party to the Five Nations television committee. Once on board, they accepted the value of live coverage and, in co-operation with the BBC, RTE gained access to Lansdowne Road for live television transmissions.

We moved into a bright, new era in 1972. By that time, the IRFU had warmed slightly towards live coverage of their International matches. RTE worked in co-operation with the BBC. They were the senior partners in the sense that they covered Scotland, Wales and England. They also had BBC Northern Ireland. The BBC had a four-way interest and their contract covered Northern Ireland and the Republic of Ireland. France had a separate television rights arrangement. They always had their own way of doing things.

The established practice was for the BBC to organise and to sub-let the Irish rights to RTE. This led to difficulties with copyright issues and needed clarification, although the arrangement was, in practice, beneficial to RTE.

In the end, the BBC sold the Irish rights to RTE. In exchange, RTE provided the machinery and the necessary staffing. It would save the BBC the expense of moving their 'tools of the profession' over and back across the Irish Sea. This would be RTE's contribution to the contract. It saved the BBC considerable money and gained control of Ireland's home Internationals for RTE. It worked out favourably for all parties. It was a happy arrangement until 1973 when I took over from Michael O'Hehir as Head of Sport.

You see, one problem remained as far as rugby coverage was concerned. RTE was effectively a sub-contractor to the BBC. This meant that there was no formal acknowledgement of RTE by the five Rugby Unions. In order to regularise it, I met the International Rugby Board (IRB) in London. We didn't want to upset the apple cart or reinvent the wheel. We just wanted to make sure all was in order contractually, with RTE responsible for all aspects of coverage at Lansdowne Road.

There were some very nice gentlemen on the IRB Committee, some were very toffee-nosed wondering what this upstart from 'Eire' was on about. The conversation went something like this ...

"To simplify the matter, I will put it like this. There is a television bus which goes into Twickenham, Murrayfield, Cardiff Arms Park and Lansdowne Road. It is pretty well the same bus, driven by the BBC. RTE sit on the bus as a passenger at the British venues.

"Well, all we want to do is drive that bus at Lansdowne Road and let the BBC become the passengers. It will be the same bus. We just want to drive the bus in our country. It is proper that an Irish event should be covered and controlled by the Irish broadcaster."

"That sounds very reasonable."

I admired the fair-minded man who carried out the negotiations for the BBC. Michael Dolbear was his name. There was another man, Peter Dimmock, who was Head of Sport at BBC. He was a great admirer of Michael O'Hehir. He was also very helpful in the early days of RTE Sport. We wouldn't have matured as a sports department as quickly as we did without his assistance.

Subsequently, on retiring from the BBC, Peter was working as a consultant for sports bodies in general in the television game. He got involved in arranging for RTE to relay the Match of the Day programme. It was the first time we had been able to show English football on RTE. It was such a complicated business with so many interests involved.

On behalf of the Football Association and the League in England, Peter was in the business of selling to as many customers as possible. The rights for overseas sales, as distinct from British domestic programmes, were held by ITV. Ironically, ITV took BBC pictures and sold them onwards. ITV had a constituent partner, UTV in Northern Ireland, whose signal was receivable in the Republic of Ireland. They had an interest in it. The FA and the English League were happy to allow RTE to take the coverage. The BBC was happy to allow their programme to be sold to RTE. ITV was quite happy as well with the arrangement. So far so good.

But UTV had to be asked and convinced. We eventually negotiated with UTV not to invoke their veto as part of the ITV family. We had cleared the stations and the football partners, the whole kit and caboodle. But, another hurdle emerged.

The Football Association of Ireland (FAI) entered the equation. They got in touch with the English League, objecting to RTE's securing of Match of the Day. They feared the damage it would cause to the domestic football scene in Ireland. That was another argument we had to get around. The negotiations were repeated and repeated until we eventually got it through.

In subsequent years, it didn't seem to get any easier every time we tried to get access to live coverage. We managed it for a season – one live match on a Saturday afternoon. Everyone had their corner to fight. As the costs escalated it became unworkable. In later years, RTE settled for a Match of the Day-type compilation of Premiership highlights, which continues to attract huge audiences as Premier Soccer Saturday.

· · · · ·

In 1972, RTE was able to send a full team of 20 personnel, headed by the Athletics commentator, Brendan O'Reilly, to the Munich Olympics. I was the team leader. Phil Greene was our specialist reporter and radio commentator.

It was while we were in Munich that it emerged Michael O'Hehir had resigned as Head of Sport. We were all shattered. I was seen as his right-hand man for the latter part of his career in RTE. He had often discussed his unease or unhappiness with aspects of his role at RTE. He explained he thought he would be more content as the General Manager of Leopardstown Racecourse.

We had argued 'the devil you know is better than the devil you don't know' in an effort to convince him to stay with us. Michael felt he was not being listened to at RTE and that the powers-that-were did not appreciate the value of sport. When Michael's departure was confirmed, the speculation began as to a likely successor. I was relatively young. I hadn't seen myself in that position. Yet, when it happened, I was perceived as the natural successor as

Head of Sport by some, but not by others.

Michael wasn't a meetings man. I was often asked to attend when he was 'unavailable'. I had represented RTE at the foundation of the Eurovision Sports Broadcasters' seminars twice a year, established in 1969, purely as a stand-in for Michael. It turned out to be another string to my bow when the interviews were held for the new Head of Sport.

In 1973, I was appointed Head of Sport for radio and television at RTE in succession to Michael O'Hehir. He had a worldwide reputation as a commentator and sports broadcaster. His presence had been a great advantage to the fledgling RTE at the time. He knew the people who made all the decisions at the BBC. He was able to approach them on a personal basis in a way no one else could. He had opened the doors and had left a vibrant sports department prepared for further growth.

·····

In the mid-1970s, we had an Australian producer/director, Jim George, helping with our production. Tim O'Connor, Maurice Reidy and Mike Horgan were the key members of the sports editorial team. We were struggling to justify our regular Sunday night sports programme, as only limited camera facilities were assigned to us. Tim suggested we forget trying to cover hurling and other sports with a single film camera. Instead, he pointed out that we could inject some humour into a studio-based programme. Ergo, The Sunday Sports Show was launched. Tim was the inspiration, while Jim George managed to get it all to air. Irene Fenton was the first female presenter of this controversial experiment when she joined Bill O'Herlihy for the second season. I had been involved for the first season. I wanted to give it an imprimatur as Head of Sport. It was just a matter of 'flying a kite'. This was a show examining the funny side of sport in a sardonic way. It could have been developed further.

Tim and Jim had ambitious plans for its future. But the facilities just weren't there. They found it hard to keep it fresh. They were restricted to 'make do and mend'. They eventually had no options to expand the horizon of the programme. Sadly, it ended after two seasons.

Nonetheless, it had left its mark and a bundle of memories. One day in my office, Tim and Jim were there shooting the breeze, chatting about forthcoming events.

"By the way, I heard that the Irish athlete, John Joe Barry, died in America," said Tim.

John Joe was a great middle-distance runner, also known as 'The Ballincurry Hare', who dominated the Irish scene in the 1940s. He was distinguished for his fair hair and his preference to run barefoot. He doubled up in the 1,500 and 5,000 metres at the London Olympics in 1948.

"Really?"

"So I heard."

"Would that make a feature for The Sunday Sports Show?"

"It would ... a good one, too."

"Are you sure he has passed away?"

"Ah, I don't know what you are talking about. I never heard of him. I never knew he was alive until now," said Jim, the Australian in the room.

"John Joe was a great Irish athlete, a double Olympian. Apparently, he died in America," I said.

"Hold on a minute. I will make a few calls," said Tim.

Lo and behold, The Ballincurry Hare was nowhere to be found in the obituaries. But, a priest had announced from the altar in Tipperary that John Joe had passed away in America. The gospel according to this priest spread like wildfire. The absence of a death notice was nagging at us. He was last known to be living in Philadelphia. We contacted a police department there. Happily, it transpired that John Joe was still very much alive.

Tim and I spoke to him on the phone.

"For God's sake, don't tell anyone you are alive John Joe!" was our request, as we now worried about keeping the story under wraps until the following Sunday night.

He took it all very light-heartedly and agreed to 'play dead' for the time being. I was detailed to fly out to Philadelphia one Saturday. There was a film crew there to meet me at the airport. We went to John Joe's house and carried out a lovely interview for The Sunday Sports Show.

John Joe had such fun reading the reaction to his 'demise' I had brought with me from Ireland. Rumours of his death had, indeed, been greatly exaggerated. It was perhaps too much to hope that we could 'hide the story' for long enough. John Comyn, in the *Irish Independent*, had had his suspicions. He guessed we were up to something when he learned RTE had booked one-day return tickets to the United States. He was first out with the story. But, we had the man himself.

• • • • •

Around this time, I had the worst experience in my entire working life. It happened while I was attending a programme meeting in the radio studios in Henry Street. Although I had been at that sort of meeting many times before in the absence of Michael O'Hehir, who was not a lover of these gatherings, it was the first time I attended with full responsibility for what would be agreed.

Everything was moving along fine. Suddenly, there was a knock on the door.

"Fred. There is an urgent call for you."

I left the meeting to be told there had been a helicopter crash with members of the sports department involved. I just froze. I returned to the meeting and shattered everyone with the news. I sped back to the office in Montrose.

The plan had been to shoot a film about the famous horse trainer Vincent O'Brien's stables at Ballydoyle. Jim George brought with him another young sports director, Michael O'Carroll, who had done some remarkable work with cameraman Eamonn O'Connor at motor rallies and on cycling tours. Consequently, Eamonn was chosen for the Ballydoyle assignment. As Jim was not happy to fly, Michael and Eamonn teamed up on board the helicopter.

It seems Michael and Eamonn were intent on flying low over a gallop to give the impression of a jockey's eye view. There was some sort of interference, a wire of some kind, and it tipped over the helicopter. I never experienced anything like the worry and concern we had for those involved. Their injuries were severe, to say the least. Fortunately, there were no fatalities, but one shuddered at the thought of the possibility. It was a miracle they all survived. Thankfully, there were many more years of safely generated excitement ahead of them.

• • • • •

As ever, money was tight in the 1970s and 1980s, forcing us into making difficult decisions. On one such occasion, the choice came down to whether we would spend the available budget on covering the Barbarians against the All Blacks at Cardiff Arms Park in 1973, or hold off to spend it on one of the Five Nations Championship matches not involving Ireland.

In those years, Ireland had a very strong team with the likes of Fergus Slattery and Ray McLoughlin and Willie John McBride and Mike Gibson. Later in the season, if Ireland was in the running for the Championship, the England-Wales game could have been pivotal. The choice rested between covering one or the other. My argument was that the Barbarians-All Blacks was essentially an exhibition match. Therefore, I decided to skip the Cardiff match so that we would have enough in the budget to cover England v Wales in the Championship.

As we all know, the match between the Barbarians and the All Blacks turned out to be one of the greatest exhibitions of rugby ever seen, but not on RTE television, or so some of my learned friends remind me from time to time. I still say it was nothing more than an exhibition. These are the things that happen when you have to make a decision between what were, at the time, two valued choices. Unfortunately, I cannot blame it on anyone else. It was my decision. In the context of the job, I felt I was right. History and hindsight have combined to prove me wrong, considering the strong Irish influence through Ray McLoughlin, Willie John McBride, Fergus Slattery and Mike Gibson.

Remember the teams in that memorable match? Well, here they are!

The Barbarians: 15. J.P.R. Williams (Wales); 14. John Bevan (Wales), 13. John Dawes (Wales, capt), 12. Mike Gibson (Ireland), 11. David Duckham (England); 10. Phil Bennett (Wales), 9. Gareth Edwards (Wales); 1. Ray McLoughlin (Ireland), 2. John Pullin (England), 3. Sandy Carmichael (Scotland), 4. Willie John McBride (Ireland), 5. R.M. Wilkinson (uncapped-England), 6. Tom David (uncapped-Wales, capped against France later that season), 7. Fergus Slattery (Ireland), 8. Derek Quinnell (Wales).

All Blacks: 15. Joe Karam; 14. Bryan Williams, 13. Bruce Robertson, 12. J.A. Hurst, 11. Grant Batty; 10. Bob Burgess, 9. Sid Going; 1. Graham Whiting, 2. Ron Urlich, 3. Ken Lambert, 4. H.H. Macdonald, 5. Peter Whiting, 6. Alistair Scown, 7. Ian Kirkpatrick (capt), 8. Alex Wyllie.

• • • • •

The other big decision that I most regret was when Munster played the All Blacks at Thomond Park on Tuesday afternoon, October 31, 1978. We had planned to cover the match which, in itself, was something of a novelty at the time. Rugby coverage was largely confined to the Internationals because there were very few other games that would attract an audience to justify the expense of mounting an outside broadcast.

Looking forward to the game, it had promise. But it wasn't the be-all and end-all that legend has since made it out to be. It was still a spectacle that would make a very good advertisement for Munster and Irish rugby. We were sure Munster would give the All Blacks a good run for it. The outside broadcast unit was booked and pencilled in until RTE, in their wisdom, decided to celebrate the establishment of the second channel, RTE 2, with a live broadcast from the Cork Opera House.

Because we only had one outside broadcast unit, those-on-high were afraid that the unit would not be able to make it from Limerick to Cork the following day if there was some sort of unforeseen delay.

In order to cover the rehearsals, and the subsequent live show, it was decided to scrap the planned live transmission of the Munster-All Blacks match. We just had to swallow that one. Instead, a small film camera was sent to record the greatest one-off non-International match in Irish rugby. All that remains of the match is that single camera, twelve-minute reel of action. That was a great regret for us in the sports department. Once the date to open the second channel was set in stone, the Munster-All Blacks match became a secondary interest.

There had been a major corporate effort invested into acquiring the second channel, which was very important for the structure of broadcasting to enable RTE to develop a wider array of programming. At that time, we were so constrained by the single channel. It had to be everything to everyone. It had to have sport in it. It had to have news in it. It had to have entertainment in it. It had to have drama in it. It was sardines-in-a-can television.

As a national service, you simply couldn't accommodate everything adequately on a single channel. There was a great effort put into persuading people that the second channel should be awarded to RTE rather than to have it as a separate commercial entity in its own right. For the greater good, it was the best thing that could have happened. As a sports man – oh, how I wish we could have given Munster's shock of the All Blacks a better television platform.

Chapter 29

BRENDAN O'REILLY

Brendan O'Reilly was one of the really colourful characters in Irish sport for years. He should have been on the 1956 Olympic team. He was originally chosen as the Irish High Jump record-holder, but he was kept off the plane because they hadn't got the money to send him to Melbourne. He was at college in Michigan State University. It was a huge blow to him because, if he had been made aware of the lack of funds in time, he would have been able to secure sponsorship support in America.

In almost 30 years in RTE, Brendan built up a library of 'out-takes' from getting locked out of the live news studio to having to kneel behind the news desk when his chair broke. Sometimes the errors were self-induced. Sometimes they were the result of other people making mistakes. But he never acted the prima donna. His gentle sense of humour made him one of RTE's most popular personalities.

• • • • •

Tragically, dozens of people were killed in riots in Mexico City just days before the 1968 Olympics. The National Strike Council organised a mass meeting at La Plaza de las Tres Culturas in protest against a military occupation of the National Polytechnic Institute. The Mexican government became aware of what it viewed as rebellious behaviour and sent out armoured tanks to ring-fence the square, whereupon the army fired into the protestors, women and children among them.

It quickly became worldwide news. The Olympics were even mooted as being in doubt. Luckily, or unluckily, Brendan O'Reilly had been dispatched to Mexico to prepare for the games. He was actually there. On the spot. The news department wanted an eye-witness account from their RTE reporter.

The phone in Brendan's hotel room rang out in the middle of the night.

"Hello."

"Hello, Brendan! Is that you?"

"It is. Who's this?"

"It's the RTE newsroom in Dublin."

"W-H-A-T? Do you know what time it is? What do you want?"

"Can you give us a minute-and-a-half report on the riots in the city?"

"Riots? City? What riots? In which city?"

"The student riots have exploded and there are reports of a number of people being shot in the streets."

"Hold on a minute."

Brendan rolled back the blankets, spun onto the floor and walked over to the window in his room. He opened the curtains and looked out onto the street. There was no noise, no sign of any disturbance. He leisurely made his way back to the phone.

"I'm sorry. But, I haven't seen anything. There are no riots on the street outside my hotel."

"Well, there are people being killed somewhere in the city as we speak."

"Really? That's dreadful. What are the international news agencies saying?"

The gentleman in the newsroom read out one agency report.

"Tragedy has struck Mexico ..."

Quick as a flash, Brendan reached for his pen and paper.

"Hold on a minute! What was that again?"

"Tragedy has struck Mexico ..."

Five minutes into the report and a subsequent conversation, Brendan told the news man he was ready to make his report.

And so it went...

"Tragedy has struck Mexico ...."

The coup de grace was his sign-off.

"This is Brendan O'Reilly with an eye-witness account from the heart of Mexico city."

And Brendan went back to bed.

· · · · ·

At The Olympics, Brendan was sent to cover the games with one cameraman, the total RTE crew. He was asked to do a piece for promotional purposes for 'The Games', including the details of the opening ceremony. No problem. The film was sent back. It arrived into the editing room. There was a fair bit of excitement around the place. We all sat down to see what he had produced.

Brendan appeared on the screen. The camera was focusing in and out. The setting was somewhere in the vicinity of the Aztec Stadium. Then, we heard the cameraman.

"Okay, Brendan, we will start with a shot of the Aztec Stadium and we will widen it out. I will drop my hand and you can start."

"Fine. Ready to roll."

"Five. Four. Three. Two. One."

"Hello. Welcome to Mexico City. I am standing outside the Aztec Stadium, the focal point of the opening ceremony for the Olympic Games, which will be held here on Thursday evening, eight o'clock Irish time."

Then, you could see his head slowly turning in the middle of his introduction, eyes fixed firmly beyond the camera and the cameraman.

"You will be able to ... You will be able to ... You will be able to ... Jaysus, Eamon (the cameraman) would ya look at your one's arse?"

Alas, we never got to share the sight, but, after a slight pause and another take we got our promotion piece.

There was another time at an athletics meet in Belfield. Brendan was chatting to someone. The camera platform was at the end of the straight. They were lining up for what was the 220 yards, or 200 metres, race. He was to do the commentary. He had his start list prepared.

"Brendan! Brendan! The 220 is about to start."

He quickly climbed up the ladder to the commentary vantage point. He sat down. The gun went.

"The men's 220 yards on the inside lane is ... (he reads the list of runners)."

As they come around the bend, he is still commentating.

"Joe Bloggs in lane four is still going well in front. Peter Smith challenging ..."

Brendan takes a look up from his script to see the runners approaching him.

"Ah, Jaysus, they're women."

Brendan was so talented in so many ways. He had a kind of Rock Hudson-esque stature and build. He was an actor. He had an Equity card. He starred as Detective Inspector Michael Roarke in the classic children's film, 'Flight of the Doves', one of his many appearances on film and in the theatre. Across the Spectrum – his one-man show of poems and song – was presented on stage and also on RTE radio. He was a multi-talented man.

Brendan was very artistic. He wrote a book on Michael Collins. He was too good at too many things to be recognised as a specialist, or an expert, in one area. He was probably more theatrical at heart than a hard-core sports lover. At the end of it all, he didn't get anything like the recognition for a man of his talents. I have to say, one of the criticisms of RTE in general is that they really didn't look after their prized possessions back then. He was kind of overlooked by some of the senior staff, who should have known better, because of his easy-going manner. As a front person for RTE, meeting people out and about, he was fabulous. I don't know whether there was an innate jealousy. It is one of the aspects of Irish life that can get to you from time to time.

Brendan and his friend, hurdler Eamon Kinsella, made great efforts to bring about unity in Irish athletics in spite of various threats to himself and his family at a time of dissention within the sport. The fact that they were with the AAU (Amateur Athletics Union) disenfranchised them from an element of the opposition at the time, which was the NACA (National Athletics & Cycling Association). The division of our island politically generated all sorts of difficulties for sports bodies. While we had to abide by the rules of international sports authorities, it was a pity our small population had to get embroiled in arguments over flags, anthems and birth places.

Over the years, there was also bitter rivalry between The Cycling Bodies, CRE (Cumann Rothaiocht na hEireann) and NCA (National Cycling Association). They had their various interests. One would compete internationally. The other would only compete against Communist countries – who were not affiliated to the world governing body. It goes on and on. Politics and sport are simply incompatible bedfellows.

Very often, Brendan suffered for being seen as a proponent of one side at the expense of the other. In order to compete internationally, athletes had to be affiliated to the AAU. Therefore, you were 'persona non grata' as far as the NACA was concerned. This made it difficult for him. He persevered. Eventually, the athletics and cycling bodies repaired the damage. The animosity that had blighted progress was left behind.

Chapter 30

"I'LL GIVE YOU A LIFT WHEN I FINISH THIS PINT"

Long after his playing days ended, the legendary Wales out-half Cliff Morgan was invited by the British army to speak to the troops stationed in Germany as a well-known commentator and personality of the BBC. He often recounted, in his inimitable way, the bizarre accidental experience he had over there.

He arrived in Germany safely. He gave his usual entertaining presentation. Then, he collapsed unaccountably. He was unconscious. The army personnel were very concerned for him. They summoned an ambulance. They carried him to the infirmary. There was an orderly sent with him to wait for the ambulance.

Meanwhile, Cliff came-to on the stretcher. He was unable to move. He was paralysed of body and speech, but he could see and hear everything. As he lay there, the orderly rushed around making sure all was prepared for the medics. He was in such a panic that he slipped and fell hard, smashing his head off the floor. Blood came gushing out of a wound. He lay there motionless.

The ambulance arrived on the scene. Immediately, they saw the orderly on the floor, blood pouring out of him. They picked him up. Cliff was lying on the nearby stretcher. He couldn't move. He couldn't speak. He couldn't tell them they were there for him, not the orderly.

The medics never checked the stretcher and it was only when they got to the hospital that someone spotted the problem.

"Who is this?"

"Cliff Morgan, the guy we were sent to bring back."

"That's not Cliff Morgan."

They had to return for Cliff – in an 'orderly' fashion of course.

Happily, the orderly and Cliff recovered from their ordeals. Cliff has since spent many years recounting the stories that accrued from his time as a player, a renowned broadcaster and administrator. None have been quite as extraordinary as that incident in Germany.

• • • • •

I bought a new car at the back end of 1975. Well, it was new to me, but it was second-hand. It was lovely, a big three-litre Rover. Or, so I thought. The reality did not quite work out the way I first envisaged when I took ownership of it

Munster were marked down for one of their many ferocious encounters with a touring southern hemisphere country. This time it was Australia. I made my way down to Musgrave Park in January of 1976 for the match.

I drove two colleagues and one or two from BBC Northern Ireland, including Joy Williams, their Head of Sport. I noticed there was something amiss with the new car on the way down to Cork. I quickly put that out of my mind, as you do. After the match, I had to drive my colleagues from BBC Northern Ireland straight back to pick up their cars in Dublin on the way back to the north.

The Australian scrum-half of the time, Rod Hauser, had lost his contact lenses. He needed to get to Dublin quickly for the following day to acquire a new pair of spectacles. I was asked if I could take him as a passenger. We really hadn't any room for Hauser. The only place he could park his backside was on the hand-brake in the front. Rod accepted the short straw.

When we got to Cahir, in Tipperary, I saw my engine over-heating. There was smoke and foam rising from within. It came to a stop. No one on board knew enough about cars to examine the patient. We abandoned it somewhere on the road into the town. Later, I found out to my financial cost the extent of the damage. I had blown the engine, the head gasket, all of it. There was a crack in the engine block. It was like a washing machine gone mad. We were in a jam. Eventually, we walked into a pub. There had been a wedding. There were a few stragglers still there hanging around.

"Excuse me lads! Do you know the best way to get to Dublin? Our car has broken down. Does a Cork-to-Dublin bus pass through here?"

One of them, somewhat the worse for wear, needless to report, piped up:

"No, you won't get a bus. I'll be happy to give you a lift … when I finish this pint."

Those were different times. We got into his car. We managed to make it back to Dublin in what was undoubtedly the most frightening drive of my life. However, our Aussie passenger, Hauser, the scrum-half, got his hands on his new lenses and, of course, Australia beat Ireland a few days later. If anyone noticed Rod walking a little crooked during the game you now know why.

•••••

When Joy and myself were the respective Heads of Sport at BBCNI and RTE, we tried to develop a cross-border exchange. It was fraught with difficulty. The biggest crowds attending sports events in Northern Ireland were flocking to the GAA matches, but there were very few of the matches being shown on television in the North. There was common agreement between the two of us. We were trying to develop more coverage on RTE and Joy wanted the BBC to benefit from the popularity of Gaelic games in Ulster.

Anyway, one of the big stumbling blocks was the attitude of official Northern Ireland. It was not sympathetic towards sport being played on a Sunday, as well as it being seen as 'too Irish'. This would have upset the delicate balance of the time. Poor Joy couldn't get any 'joy' out of that endeavour! Fortunately, she lived to see both BBC Northern Ireland and UTV give GAA extended live coverage. A great sports enthusiast, Joy was respected as a thorough professional, not just by her peers, but by sports people North and South.

• • • • •

I was on my way back from Geneva to Cardiff for a Five Nations match in the mid-to-late 1970s. I was to meet my editorial assistant in London on an overnight stay at The Tara Towers Hotel and travel down to Cardiff the next morning. I arrived at the Hotel in London, went to the room, sat down to my work.

The next thing, there was a knock on my door. It was this chap, my assistant, who we will call Mick, to save any embarrassment. He came in. It was his first trip as the production assistant, handling the technical side of work. He had recently joined the sports department. We exchanged pleasantries.

Then he suggested something I didn't expect.

"Will you come into my room, I want to show you a few presents I got?"

"What do you mean?"

"You'll see. It is just a few things for the kids."

"Fine."

We walked across the corridor. He opened his door. I followed him in. I stood there in the middle of the room, waiting to see these presents.

"They're in here, in the bathroom."

I thought this a little strange. Still, I walked into the bathroom.

"Well, what do you think?"

I didn't know what to say. There, in the three-quarter full bath, were these baby 'alligator' reptiles swimming.

"What in the name of God are those?"

"They are for the kids. They are into ...".

"Wait a minute! We're going to Cardiff in the morning. This is a bit much. What are you going to do with these?"

"Don't worry. They won't interfere with anyone or anything."

Ten minutes later, we communed for an evening meal. It was a slightly edgy atmosphere because I wasn't altogether happy with this predicament and how it was going to work out.

Anyway, we wished each other goodnight and retired to our rooms at around 9.30pm. Ten minutes later, there was a knock at the door.

"Ah, there you are, Mick. Something up?"

"I have a slight problem. One of my reptiles has gone missing."

"Close the bloody door!"

"What will I do?"

"I don't know what you can do! I don't care about the bloody thing. Just go away! I will see you at seven o'clock sharp for the first train to Cardiff."

I barely slept a wink with visions of this miniature alligator crawling into the bed.

The next morning, I arrived down to reception at 7am. Mick was there with his bags. He was holding two or three plastic bags, containing the reptiles. He took this opportunity to inform me he also had a toad, a giant frog, in a box. This was the sum total of his baggage.

Anyway, we made the train and arrived into position in Cardiff without too much excitement or anxiety. In those days, the commentary area was on a platform hanging out of the roof of the stadium. You had to walk out on the roof and climb down a ladder into the seating. The match went smoothly. The arrangement was to leave the stadium as soon as possible to make the train back to Reading for the connection to the airport for a late flight to Dublin. We climbed out of the stadium, literally, and made it to the nearby railway station. The train was filling quickly.

Who did we see but the BBC rugby commentator Peter West. He waved us on to take seats beside him. We sat down. Peter was smoking his pipe as he always seemed to do. He turned to Mick.

"What have you got in the bag young man?"

"Don't ask!" I said.

It was too late. Mick was rooting around in one of his bags. The next minute, there was anguish.

"My toad! My toad!"

He could not find the toad. We mentally traced our steps all the way back to the climb into our commentary seats. It turned out the toad must have fallen out of his bag as we climbed down into his position at the match.

Can you imagine? Some unsuspecting Welsh supporter, or supporters, were probably tucking into a 'toad in the hole' when a real live toad plonked down on his head as if it had fallen from the sky. If you ever hear of a supporter recounting how he was struck by a flying toad in Cardiff, you'll know where it came from.

"A toad? What else have you got there?" asked Peter.

"Baby alligators. Would you like to see one?" said Mick

"No, he wouldn't. Forget it. Put the bloody things away," I intervened.

It didn't seem to have an effect. Mick pulled out one of the baby alligators and put it on the table. Peter looked at it in astonished silence.

"My apologies, Peter. But, I did warn you," I said.

"Would you mind putting it back in the bag?" said Peter.

That wasn't the end of it. We still had to pass through security at the airport at a time in London when the Irish were looked upon with some suspicion.

"You're on your own on this one, Mick," I said.

I was still close enough to overhear the conversation between Mick and the airport customs official.

"Show me the bag!"

"I wouldn't open that if I was you."

"Why?"

"I just wouldn't."

The customs official stood straight and looked Mick in the eye.

"What exactly are you saying?"

"I have reptiles in there."

"You have what?"

"Reptiles. You know, baby alligators."

"Open it yourself," said the customs official.

He opened the bag wide enough for the official to peer down inside it.

"Get on that plane as quick as you can," he said.

It was clear. He just wanted Mick and his reptile friends out of the country as fast as possible. I must say I didn't blame him.

Later, I brought my full authority to bear by insisting that Mick never, ever accompanied me to another match. I simply didn't need to have livestock or wild animals along for the ride. Whenever I see any mention of Peter West, I think of Mick and that day on the train.

Chapter 31

1978 WORLD CUP

I was asked to represent the European broadcasters at the 1978 World Cup, in Argentina. I was stationed in Cordoba, the Athlone of Argentina, right in the middle of the country. It is a beautiful place. My job was to ensure that everything at the venue was up to the standards required under the Eurovision umbrella, to organise the supply of tickets to all the rights holders and to check that all the commentary positions were satisfactory.

I was the head of the delegation. I arrived two weeks before the opening of the World Cup to set up the office. I went to Buenos Aires and met the other European Broadcasting Union (EBU) representatives for the various venues. I was dispatched to Cordoba. I was totally on my own with nothing more than the address of the appointed office and a hotel booking.

I found the building, a central sports club. Our office was on the top floor. It was an empty room. I was scratching my head, contemplating how I was going to organise the operation. There were only five or six matches to be broadcast, it wasn't a heavy workload, but everything had to be right for the hundreds of radio and television personnel on their arrival.

There was a knock on the door. In walked a very attractive girl. She was from the Argentinean television booking office. We would be working closely as all our commentary circuits would be ordered through her office.

"Are you local? Where are you from?"

"No. I was born and educated in Spain."

"That is a long way from here."

"I got married to a man from Argentina and we came here. Where are you from?"

"I am from Ireland."

"When I was in Spain, I visited your country."

"Oh, really? Whereabouts?"

"Well, I was at school in your capital city."

"That is a coincidence. I am from Dublin. What school were you at?"

"It was one on the outskirts, in a little village called Rathfarnham."

"Was it one of the Loretos?"

"Yes. It was Loreto Beaufort."

"I have two daughters studying in Beaufort at the moment."

"Really? That is amazing. I stayed in a house on the main road into Rathfarnham."

"What number?"

She mentioned the number of the house.

"I live right across the road from there."

It was an incredible coincidence. We just laughed out loud about it. The Eurovision broadcasters got the best possible service from Cordoba for the tournament.

• • • • •

For the World Cup, a driver was assigned to me by Eurovision. His name was Solomon. I am sure he was a member of the secret police. He was a great guy, as far as I was concerned, because he seemed to have a free hand whenever I needed anything. If I asked him if he could arrange for the sun to shine at midnight, Solomon would somehow try to fix it.

On a motorway in Cordoba, there was a huge crowd going to a game. We were held up. He decided to cross over into the middle of oncoming traffic. He drove like a bat out of hell, with lights flashing, in their fast lane – not with the wisdom of Solomon I hasten to add.

I reckoned, quite reasonably, only a man of authority could break the law with such little thought for it. If I had any problems with advertising in the stadium Solomon would simply say.

"You tell me. I fix."

He was as good as his word.

I was having trouble at one match. I wanted three levels of advertising reduced to two, as per the Eurovision guidelines for the World Cup. I asked the stadium controller, an army general as far as I could make out, could he do anything about it. This was in the time following the death of Juan Peron in 1974 when successive military juntas held control over the South American country. There was always a feeling that 'Big Brother' was watching.

Solomon went to move the offending advertising on my behalf. The general told me the agent in charge of the advertising would be along.

"There is serious concern here. The contract with European television has certain stipulations about the amount of advertising to be shown and its positioning," I said.

The agent looked at the general and shrugged.

The general said: "How much are you paying for the rights?"

I said: "It is huge – 30 million dollars (or some such amount). If you break the agreement, you'll lose a lot of revenue."

Then the general asked the agent: "How much are the others paying for the advertising?"

He said: "75 million dollars."

"Very well! The advertising stays."

End of discussion.

Later, I couldn't help but smile as I watched the coverage of the World Cup final in Buenos Aires between Argentina and Holland as it was transmitted back to Ireland. At one point, the camera moved to a shot of the scoreboard. Instead of the score, it read: 'Brazil Coffee'.

I often wondered how they managed to orchestrate that one. And there was me worried about my triple-decker advertising in Cordoba. Someone, somewhere got a few free coffees for that stroke.

I wonder? Could it have been my friend Solomon?

•••••

A European-wide broadcast, and the complications that ensued because of the different – and sometimes competing – interests of the different bodies from the different countries posed many teething problems that required all of my patience. The individual broadcast problems of a small country tended to be overlooked or hindered by the pan-European policy. The 'Big Boys' really ruled the roost. The requirements of the smaller countries had to be watered down. I found this out in the early days of the Sports Working Party in Geneva, where all the European broadcasters were represented.

The whole question of advertising came up regularly and how it was important for the state or national broadcasters to protect the signal they were issuing around Europe because each country had its own laws and regulations. Each had to make sure, as far as possible, that the picture was kept 'clean'. There were great discussions on how to decide how much advertising could appear, where it could appear around a stadium or, indeed, on the jerseys of players, which was a total 'no-no' in the beginning. The height of the lettering on jerseys and tracksuits was another problem, which took hours of lively discussion before being put off to the next meeting.

Eventually, there were guidelines drawn up as to what was permissible and what wasn't. In order to be good Europeans, the Irish broadcasters had to apply these guidelines to sports covered in Ireland. Of course, the sports organisations here were very anxious to give their support sponsors as much help or visibility as possible. Even though RTE couldn't pay serious money to, say, the GAA, for the rights, they could still insist on limiting the advertising to fall within the confines of the European guidelines. The sports organisations were immediately placed between the rock of resistance that was RTE's stance and a hard place in terms of disappointing their sponsors.

Apart from the rugby and soccer Internationals, there were various events staged here, like the World Cross-Country Championships in Limerick in 1979, which was won by our own John Treacy, the man from Villierstown in County Waterford, currently employed as the Chief Executive of the Irish Sports Council. There was also the World Show Jumping Championships at The RDS in 1982, which were threatened by the guidelines.

However, when American programmes, such as a world heavyweight title fight, came onto our screens, the incoming coverage was plastered with advertising. The European broadcasters were then faced with a dilemma. Do we show the event or not, regardless of the advertising?

You were left with a situation where the broadcaster, RTE, would try to impose the guidelines, and the ultimate sanction was to withdraw coverage, which would have been disastrous. In the case of, say, an All-Ireland final, RTE wouldn't have had the courage to deprive the viewers of such a must-see event. A balance had to be struck between the GAA and RTE over advertising rights. Happily, their cooperation and understanding ensured that no big game was ever stopped over the issue.

When it came to the smaller sports, hockey, badminton, for instance, they had little or no bargaining power at all. Consequently, the EBU rules were enforced wherever necessary. Alas, it always works against the small guy. That is the nature of the business.

· · · · ·

The whole question of advertising and the primacy of a 'clean' picture for the TV audience brought about quite a few bizarre situations. I remember the World Show Jumping Championships at The RDS in 1982, which was eventually won by the German, Norbert Koof. Bank of Ireland were very big supporters of staging the competition. For that, they wanted as big a return for their investment as they could get. Quite right, too. They wanted their logo on one of the jumps. But, of course, it was unacceptable to have advertising in the arena.

Anyhow, they agreed to the terms of our conditions. They could only have three individual spaces for their logo around the perimeter of the arena. On the final day of the competition, I got a call from our RTE producer, Justin Nelson.

"You better get down here Fred!"

"What's wrong?"

"You have to see this."

"See what?"

"Just come on down."

Over the pocket gate of the entrance to the jumping arena, Bank of Ireland had erected an archway-shaped sign of their logo. This wasn't in the agreed plan. It meant RTE couldn't show the horses entering or exiting the arena. There was no other option but to take it down. There was a stand-off. The bank didn't want to take it down. We weren't willing to broadcast because of the transgression of the guidelines and our undertaking to the European Broadcasting Union. The event was being televised to Great Britain and Europe. We saw it as trying to pull a fast one. They argued it did conform as it was outside, or on the edge of, the arena. Eventually, they removed the sign. It was either that or the plug would have been pulled. It was all very unsatisfactory.

It often reminded me of the clever way people manipulated the advertising game. For instance, Christy O'Connor Junior always wore the flat cap. In any one-to-one television interview, he would receive a question and immediately lower his chin into his chest so that the logo on his cap would be visible to the TV viewers. The same sort of thing occurred more recently when Brian O'Driscoll would take a gulp from his Powerade energy drink every time he was seen on television in a post-match interview.

· · · · ·

Still, in 1978, the prominence of advertising was a hot topic in Europe. We had to be careful as we prepared to relay the Monaco Grand Prix. A lot of the racing cars carried advertising to increase their investment. We had to be sure it didn't run counter to the law in Ireland.

On this particular day, I was at a function. I was assuming the Presidency of the St Mary's College past pupils' union at an annual general meeting in Rathmines. I got a call from Tim O'Connor, my eventual successor as Head of Sport at RTE, as the race began. He had spotted a problem.

"There is a car in the race carrying the Durex logo. What are we going to do?" asked Tim.

In addition to religious and political slogans, it was illegal to advertise condoms in Ireland at the time. Imagine. We were due to go live a half-an-hour into the race. We were joining it nearly halfway through. We decided to put off a decision until closer to the time. If the car was in the lead, we were banjaxed. If it was down the field, it would barely be noticed. As it transpired, five minutes before our transmission, the self same car's engine blew up. There must have been a leak somewhere. Tim relaxed. Our programme went out on time and our little drama petered out.

· · · · ·

That same summer my youngest daughter, Denise, and her friend, Jill Regan, a neighbour, appeared one evening. I was minding the house. We decided to go to Stillorgan for a bite to eat at The Swiss Chalet. I parked the car there. We went in and ate our meal. Afterwards, I suggested I would pay the bill while they were in the toilet and we would meet in the car park. It was an August evening. The darkness was starting to take over.

I decided to play a little trick on the girls. I saw them just leaving the restaurant. I found a hiding place near my car and stooped down between two cars, out of sight, wondering how the girls would react if they thought I wasn't there. I waited and imagined where they were on their short walk to the car. I waited to hear them discuss where I had got to. I heard nothing. I rose slightly to check where they were, spying through the windscreen of the car I was kneeling beside. I was met with this startled face looking out at me.

It was a fella with his arms around his girlfriend. Her head was tilted back against the window. I could see his eyes grow wider and wider looking out at me, looking in at him. I could read his lips.

"You're not going to believe this! There is a guy looking in at me!"

I was transfixed. I couldn't very well stand up and tell the gentleman I was just hiding there waiting to frighten two little girls. It was one of the most embarrassing moments of my life. I quickly made my way to the girls, who by the way, were calmly waiting for me by our car.

"Dad, where were you?"

"You wouldn't understand! Get in the car quick girls! We gotta get out of here."

Chapter 32

WARD AND CAMPBELL

The Tony Ward-Ollie Campbell question wasn't unique.

There was the kind of precedence any self-respecting judge would not have dismissed. Mike Gibson emerged as the greatest Irish prospect since Jack Kyle, the icon of the 1940s and 1950s. Although others, like Mick English, came along to threaten to don the mantle, no one could reproduce Kyle's charismatic style of play. As a private person, Kyle didn't do anything away from the game to attract the attention that was sent his way. It was purely down to what he did on the field of play. He didn't court the crowd. He wasn't a showman and, yet, he was the supreme entertainer. He is still revered 60 years later. He has all the attributes that should be the hallmark of a solid gold, super-star. He is quiet, self-effacing, self-deprecating.

Ireland waited in hope more than certainty that a man would come along to compare with Kyle. Ulster's Mike Gibson grabbed attention by making his mark for Cambridge University against Oxford in the annual Varsity match. He was immediately tipped as Ireland's next out-half. He exploded onto the international scene. On his debut against England at Twickenham in 1964, he was instrumental in creating one of the greatest-ever tries for Ireland. He pierced the English defence from the border of his own 22, bursting clear before reversing to Jerry Walsh, who scythed right, before switching the ball, once again, to Pat Casey, who rounded it off under the posts, the move having swept in Z-shaped fashion up the field. This was at a time when neither Ireland, nor anyone else for that matter, except maybe the French, ever played this sort of effervescent rugby.

Gibson was hailed as the next Jack Kyle. He wasn't very big. He was wiry, without being bulky. It was his electric acceleration, his strength in the tackle, his ability to split a defence, which was part-speed, part-footwork, that made him special. Ultimately, it is difficult to pinpoint what separates the exceptional from the excellent. It is like saying: what makes a great singer? It is a combination of things.

Gibson was set to command the out-half position for the next decade. The emergence of Cork Constitution's Barry McGann encouraged the Irish management to think twice about Gibson's pre-eminence at No. 10. Ireland lacked depth in other areas. McGann made his International debut against France in 1969 and would represent his country 25 times. He was more solidly built than Gibson and quick over a short distance. The feeling was that there should be room made for both of them.

While McGann was an out-and-out fly-half, Gibson had the superior skills set to operate in a number of jerseys. He played in three positions for Ireland over his 15 years, a then-record Ireland total of 69 caps, further embellished by 12 tests for The British and Irish Lions over the time travelled of five Test tours.

There was a feeling that he was somewhat strait-jacketed at No. 10, that if he were to move out one, he would have more room to express his talents. Relatively out of the blue, McGann came into the side to improve the overall picture. It made sense to accommodate both men. They made it work between them, Gibson going on to become a sensation in the centre for The British and Irish Lions in New Zealand in 1971, making room for Wales' Barry John at No. 10.

If it hadn't been for Barry McGann, Mike Gibson mightn't have become the best centre in the world, nor Barry John the best fly-half in the world, because Gibson's move allowed room for 'King' John, the brother-in-law to Wales forward Derek Quinnell, who was also on that tour, and uncle to Gavin, Craig and future two-time, British and Irish Lions No. 8, Scott Quinnell.

• • • • •

Fast forward ten years from Barry McGann's debut, when Ireland travelled to Australia with Tony Ward as European Player of the Year. Ollie Campbell was brought out as the understudy. I went out to provide television commentary on the two Test matches. I missed out on the first part of the tour. Little did I know of the controversy that was about to reverberate through Irish rugby.

My journey out, just before the first Test in Brisbane, was enhanced by the company of the late Bobby Ganly. It was just the two of us. We landed in Hong Kong where we couldn't believe our eyes when we read of Tony Ward's 'demotion' in the English-speaking newspaper there. It was just unbelievable. It was the biggest shock in the selection of an Irish team – before or since.

"What? What? It can't be right!" cried Bobby.

"What? What is it?"

"Tony Ward has been dropped by Ireland."

It was stunning news. At the time, it was a sensation everywhere, not just in little old Ireland. Ward had been playing well on the tour. So, indeed, had Campbell. But Ward was the man in situ. He was considered the best player on the team, the most vital cog in the machine.

The idea that he would be demoted on a hunch of the Irish management was bordering on ludicrous. Jack Coffey was the manager. Fergus Slattery was the captain. Mike Gibson was towards the end of his illustrious career. There had been the suggestion Gibson preferred to play outside Campbell. I don't know how true that was. There were all sorts of stories bandied around, about how the tendency of Ward to play off-the-cuff wasn't in keeping with the management's playing policy.

I spoke to a number of the junior players, the less experienced Ireland Internationals, off the record when I arrived in Brisbane. I knew what the senior players – the old hands – would say. They would toe the management line. But the younger players also felt, quite honestly, that going for Campbell was the right decision on a playing basis. This was a surprise to me. One of them actually told me he didn't think the management on tour would have the courage to make the decision they did.

The main problem was that it was badly handled. Tony was totally unaware this was going to happen. Mike Gibson was in the twilight of his career. He was fingered as one of the people who expressed the view that Ollie Campbell was the better option. Gibson was stationed at No. 12, leaving Ward nowhere to go. It was most unfortunate. I still think it would have been so much better to accommodate all three of them.

Even so, the pressure on Campbell to deliver must have been immense. He started off in a blaze of glory in the first Test by kicking everything in sight; four penalties, two conversions of a pair of tries from that wonderful scrum-half, Colin Patterson, and a drop goal to boot. He did it all. Ireland won 27-12 at Ballymore and Ollie had justified his selection. It still wasn't enough to quell the controversy. The outside observers felt Tony had no reason to suspect his position at fly-half was under threat. It was great to have Ollie there as a viable alternative. That was all. Or so we thought. For Ireland, it was the making of Campbell and the beginning of the breaking of Ward's international career.

The management had taken a monster gamble. It paid off more handsomely than they could have foreseen. The second Test at the Sydney Cricket Ground was a low-scoring, chances-at-a-premium affair. It came down to the battle of the No. 10s. Australia's Paul McLean cleared the crossbar once; Campbell three times, from two drop goals and a penalty for a second historic victory and a 2-0 whitewash.

From then on, Ollie was firmly established in the team. It turned out to be the key decision in bringing Ireland the Triple Crown in 1982. The greatest disservice to both men was that Ireland could not, or would not, try to make room for both of them. Sure, it was tried once or twice, but quickly dismissed as a non-runner when it didn't click immediately. It was worth persevering with for longer.

Over time, Campbell became indispensable. He maximised his talent as a superb goal-kicker, tactician and one of the best pound-for-pound textbook tacklers Ireland has ever had for such a light-framed man. Of course, Tony didn't exactly drift out of view. He had his days in the sun, too. No one will ever forget his impact for Munster against the All Blacks on that incomparable day in 1978. He was brilliant in the game as a supreme kicker and as the 'field marshal' behind his front-foot pack of forwards.

Now, suddenly, you had two world-class players, very different in their styles. It was said of Tony that his own team-mates didn't know what he would do next. He played it off-the-cuff. It was argued Ollie was more able to fit into the team structure and carry out a game plan.

There were also the stories about Tony getting too big for his boots, by appearing in the tabloids. This was madness. You only had to know Tony to see this was utter balderdash. He remains the least self-promoting guy. He had that something special. When he ran onto the pitch, the eyes of the public would move to him. He had charisma. I guess they call it the x-factor these days. It is something you can't bottle, or else everyone would take a good swig of it.

They are the two nicest men you could meet, fair-handed in how they deal with people. They loved the game and sport in general. The question lingers however: Why weren't they both accommodated? If you take them solely as players, how many genuine world-class operators does Ireland have at any given time? It wasn't that long ago that Ireland could not get by without Brian O'Driscoll and Paul O'Connell.

On return from Australia, Ollie and Tony were the two best players. No doubt. They should have been put in the team. My opinion is that Ollie would have made a brilliant inside centre as a tremendous tackler and clever playmaker beside the more mercurial talents of Tony. Those were the days when Ireland came together on Thursday and Friday. It wasn't comparable to the professional set-up where a squad could be bent into shape by the coach. You couldn't tinker too much with what you had. That was probably a factor to it.

There was also a lot of chat about how the senior players, especially the forwards, preferred to play with Ollie because they knew where the ball would be when they looked up after a scrum. They loved to move forward and that was what Campbell gave them. There was less certainty with Ward over where they would have to go for the next ruck. It could be forty metres forward. It could be fifteen metres backwards. That is what came with the high risk factor – big gains and big losses of yardage. In the years before, Mike Gibson and Barry McGann were accommodated. The same room was not given to Ward and Campbell with any degree of conviction.

When Ireland did opt to experiment with both of them, Tony was moved to No 12. I would have moved Ollie there. Look what Munster did to the All Blacks with Tony Ward at out-half. He was capable of playing the game conservatively, if required. He wasn't a renegade. To treat the European Player of the Year as a cast-off was just bad management. It was also the beginning of tabloid sports journalism in Ireland.

There was an element in the IRFU that did not want any one player to appear to be bigger than the game. It was seen as a problem rather than an opportunity, back then. If you attracted attention, you were suspect. It is in stark contrast to the way Brian O'Driscoll, for instance, has been marketed to spread the Gospel of Rugby in the country. The game is now partly built on personality and publicity. That is the way of professionalism.

For example, look at what Ronan O'Gara has done for the profile and success of the Munster brand. Where is Jonathan Sexton going to take Leinster and Ireland in the years ahead? When once the question of which man fills the No. 10 jersey was a bone of controversy, it is now a source of debate that only brings more attention and interest to Irish rugby.

Chapter 33

APARTHEID

In the late 1970s, our new colour outside broadcast unit arrived. It must have been a £IR1million investment. It came with all the bells and whistles imaginable for the time. It was sent to Pairc Ui Chaoimh for a Munster Championship match. As it was not going out live, we didn't have the vision links to transmit the pictures back to the network. A plan was devised. The match would be recorded in Pairc Ui Chaoimh and we would physically transport the tape back to Dublin for transmission.

We had a transport issue. If we waited to the end of the match, there was a risk of a car being delayed in traffic. The travel time to Dublin would have been three and a half hours, or more, in those days. The transport routes were not as direct as they are now. We decided to hire a boatman to take this valuable tape from the Pairc Ui Chaoimh side of the river to the far side where a motorcycle courier would speed it to Dublin. The match went well. The colour recording was apparently spectacular. At the final whistle, the valuable tape was whipped off the machine and dispatched.

Everything went to plan until the engine of the boat conked out halfway across the river. The boatman had to row the boat against the tide. He was getting wild and panicky encouragement from both sides of the river. It was an example of how the best laid plans can come undone by a faulty engine. The video eventually arrived at its destination. An edited version was delivered to air. So much for spending a small fortune on the latest gear when the weakest link in the chain breaks down!

·····

There was a great furore over the proposed Irish tour to South Africa in 1981. There were those who abhorred the Apartheid system, but maintained that ongoing contact was the best chance of influencing change. The door should always be kept open. There were those who felt the opposite. The players were just footballers and didn't want to get dragged into it. This controversy grew. It wasn't new. But the prospect of the Irish national rugby squad travelling to South Africa brought a spotlight to the issue.

Indeed, it was only revealed in January 2012, on foot of the 30-Year rule that allows for theretofore secret State papers to be released into the public domain, that the Irish government of the time applied pressure on the IRFU to cancel the tour to South Africa. There were threats made to reduce state grants to the IRFU. The vice-president of the IRFU, J.J. Moore, countered with the argument: "Would the Government not discourage the ESB from importing coal from South Africa, or discourage fruit imports from South Africa?"

At the time, we decided to host an open studio debate at RTE. We invited various factions to air their standpoints. It was very serious, very heated. It affected all the players and all those who objected to it. There were also many among the players who were either uninterested or unsure whether the tour should go on.

The programme went on air. Jim Sherwin took the role as presenter and agent provocateur. He was very competent. He extracted comments from both sides of the divide. It was a discussion that wasn't going to have a definitive ending. It could have lasted through to the break of the next day.

I would have had an open mind. I am not a political animal. My feeling was that sport had always suffered at the hands of politicians. They get involved, other issues become a part of something pure. You play the game for fun and relaxation and improving your band of friends. I wouldn't have had terribly trenchant views.

One would have to say, in the course of the debate, I felt the stronger, more correct views were to cancel the tour. In the light of hindsight, it was very difficult to justify the tour. There was only one legitimate point of view. That was the right one – to stay at home. Anyway, in conclusion, Jim Sherwin turned to the President of the IRFU, Bobby Ganly, in the front row of the audience. He wanted a simple 'yes' or 'no' answer to the question: should Ireland go to South Africa?

To put Bobby into a position where he had to give a definitive 'yes' or 'no' answer, Jim constructed the question in a roundabout, drawn-out manner he thought had placed Bobby into a corner from which there was no escape, ending in the final teaser.

"So, what is your view as President of the Rugby Union, Bobby Ganly?"

Bobby looked at him blankly.

"Would you mind repeating the question, Jim?"

You could see the blood drain from Jim's face. It was the last answer he expected. I burst out laughing. It was so incongruous and took the heat right out of the row.

Jim found his way back to the question by a shorter route to which there was a typical hurler-on-the-ditch response from the President of the IRFU.

As it happened, the Irish embarked on the seven-match tour and two Tests against the Springboks, which Ireland lost, by the way, at Cape Town and Durban. The first Test was made remarkable for that fact that Errol Tobias became the first black man to wear the Springbok jersey. The second was South Africa's 100th Test match in their long and storied history.

· · · · ·

In 1984, Munster played Australia in Thomond Park. There was an incredible fog there. No one could see anything or anyone. The game really shouldn't have been played. RTE went ahead with the television coverage. All you could see for certain was a white mist from the start to the end of the match, interrupted by intermittent clusters of shadowy figures.

The only camera that got any sort of perspective was the one on the ground. The unfortunate cameraman had to carry this weighty thing up and down the touchline and relay the information to us as he saw it. We only knew a try had been scored when we saw the players emerge into visibility near the halfway line. The only way we knew the conversion had been tagged on was from the restart. If it was good and true, the restart was from the turf. If it wasn't, a drop kick would set the game in motion again. That is how we worked out the scoring system. It was a hairy experience. It was on this day that one of the most memorable tries in Irish rugby was claimed simply because no one saw it.

"Who scored that one, Fred?"

"Munster, I think," was as good as it got.

In fact, there was no point in transmitting live except for the fact that our pictures, such as they were, were being taken by BBC in London and BBC Northern Ireland, who continued to go live. This put us at a disadvantage because if we opted out, our viewers would have turned over to the other stations. So we stuck with it.

The fog didn't lift. It could be said that the commentary was "even foggier than usual". But no one could dispute our opinions on the who, the what, the why, the where and the when of the match.

Chapter 34

FRIED ICE CREAM

I have had many opportunities to travel over the years, but not so many that it became a chore. George Hamilton, for instance, must enjoy travel. There must come a time, though, when the constant movement around Europe, and to further reaches, becomes more like work than wonder.

Mick Dunne, our Gaelic games correspondent in RTE, after many distinguished years of service to *The Irish Press*, had to travel the highways and byways around the country. He did a ferocious amount of travelling. Micheal O Muircheartaigh is another who must have clocked up enough miles to travel to Mars and back over the decades.

For me, the 1987 Rugby World Cup in New Zealand, and the 1978 soccer World Cup in Argentina, were very exciting. Like the tours with the Irish rugby team, each one was a unique experience. It wasn't as if I was on the move every week.

When the Ireland rugby team flew out to Japan in 1985 on the back of winning the Triple Crown, there was a small core of press workers – Karl Johnston from the later to be defunct *The Irish Press*, Barry Coughlan from *The Cork Examiner*, as it was then, Ned van Esbeck from *The Irish Times*, myself and my producer John D. O'Brien.

The Ireland captain, Ciaran Fitzgerald, caused quite a stir among the Japanese by introducing a few hurleys at one of the team's training sessions.

I suppose it would have been likened to a samurai sword in their eyes. The Japanese media was captivated.

There was an Irish Export Board, or An Bord Trachtala, representative there generating an interest in all things Irish through the platform provided by the visit of the rugby team. Later in 1985, the All-Ireland finals were shown on Japanese television, all arising out of this marketing opportunity and the appearance of Fitzy's hurleys.

The Japanese were very proud of the 'Bullet' train. It was new to us. They had a very un-Irish system. If you were travelling, as we were from Tokyo to Osaka, you would send your bags separately from the Bullet train, which apparently didn't lower itself to taking baggage. When you arrived at your hotel, the bags would be there waiting for you. At least, that was the theory as explained to our media group by our own 'organiser' John D.

Of course, this did not fit with the Irish psyche of 'keeping an eye on what you have'. We were never going to trust our bags to anyone given they contained our tools for work. They were far too important to let out of our sight in the middle of a city new to us.

We were informed that the trains ran to time. We didn't quite appreciate how strict the Japanese were about their time-keeping. It was all explained.

"You go to Entrance Number 27. You walk up the stairs, across the bridge and descend to Platform 23. Follow the signs as per your ticket. Then you go to Gate Number 4. You walk to Door B and stand there. The appropriate carriage door will arrive opposite where you are standing."

It was a degree of accuracy we didn't fully comprehend. We decided we wouldn't be late for our Bullet train. We trooped to the station with our baggage. We found the entrance, climbed the stairs and followed the numbers and letters as given. Miraculously, we came to a standstill at Door B.

The train was due at two minutes to the hour. To be sure, we arrived there ten minutes to the hour. The first train whizzed in and out at six minutes to the hour. Obviously, our train was the next one. When a huge metal train slid to a stop right where we stood, it advertised the exact number and exact letter on our tickets. We were in business.

The passengers attempted to make their way off the train in an obedient, orderly fashion. We were worried about the train leaving without its most precious cargo – us. Without further delay, we rushed onto the train, heaving our bulky bags on board, brushing aside some of the alighting passengers in our haste. We found our seats. There were people sitting there. We tried to explain how they were at the wrong 'Opera'. They would have to move.

Voices were raised. A big argument was threatening to erupt. Suddenly, an English voice broke into the heated debate.

"What seems to be the problem, gentlemen?"

"These people are sitting in our seats," I said.

"Are you sure?"

"Positive. Look at our tickets!"

"Yes ... well I'm terribly sorry ... you are on the wrong train."

"What do you mean? We can't be! Can we?"

"I am afraid so. Your tickets are for Osaka. This train is on its way to Nagasaki."

"What are you talking about? This is the right platform, the right door, the right train."

"No, no, no. Your train is two minutes to the hour. This train is four minutes to the hour."

We made an immediate apology. We bowed and scraped to the passengers and shovelled our bags out the door or else we'd have been on our way to Nagasaki. We extricated ourselves with all the speed of Shane Williams raiding down the left wing. When the Japanese said two minutes to the hour, they meant it. Precisely. They didn't have the Irish tendency for getting there around the right time.

I subsequently learned – my youngest daughter Denise lived in Japan for two years – they were so strict on time that if the underground train is even one minute late, the driver is fined. They don't hang around at rush hour. They even have what they call 'pushers' to make sure people are on the train properly so that the doors can close.

·····

One night in Tokyo, as we prepared to come home, we decided to go out for a meal. We found a restaurant. The cooking was carried out by a chef on a hot plate in the centre of the table.

"How you like your meat rare, medium or well done?" asked the chef.

"Well done, thank you," I said.

Then he sliced the meat and put on quite a display of skill, creating the various dishes we ordered. After that, the hot plate was cleared and cleaned. The next course was prepared in front of our eyes again.

Eventually, we looked at the list of desserts. We noticed one interesting option.

"Could we order the fried ice cream, please?"

The hot plate was fired up with cointreau. Brown sugars were added. Fresh mixed berries also. A slab of ice cream appeared in front of each of us. It looked like a pound of butter.

"How you like ice cream rare, medium or well done?"

"What?"

"How you like rare, medium or well done?"

"Ah, what the hell! Make it well done."

He dipped it onto the hot plate, into the berries and sugars. He flambéed to his heart's content. It turned out to be the nicest dessert I had ever tasted. I can still remember wallowing in it, all these years later.

Chapter 35

BILL MCLAREN

I walked into Mario's restaurant in Sandymount on the Green with my family five years ago, in 2007. In no time at all, this strange man approached our table.

"Fred, isn't it?"

"It is," I said.

"Excuse me. I wonder could I have a word with you?"

"Well, yes, of course. What is it?"

"My name is Peter Dwan."

"Do I know you?"

"Well, no. But I have something I think you would be interested in. Would you be able to meet with me some day?"

He appeared to be sane. I was intrigued. We exchanged telephone numbers. He apologised for interrupting and promised to call within a few days.

In time, the phone duly rang. We talked. We met in the Radisson Hotel at St Helen's, just off the dual carriageway near Stillorgan, for a chat over coffee.

"Now, will you come out to the car with me? I have that thing I was telling you about," he said.

"What is it?"

"You will have to wait and see."

We walked out to his car.

"I know you have been a great admirer of this man. It is something I have and I would be more than happy if you would take it as a gift."

I was totally bemused and confused. He opened the boot of the car and removed a very large framed article. It was, in fact, the authentic notes of Bill McLaren's final commentary from the 2002 Six Nations match between Wales and Scotland at The Millennium Stadium.

I couldn't believe it. It was such a lovely gesture from a man then unknown to me – Peter Dwan.

• • • • •

Bill McLaren came to broadcasting in a roundabout way. He was a school teacher and ambitious rugby player as a flanker for his beloved Hawick, earning a Scotland trial in 1947. He looked like climbing all the way to the top of the game before contracting tuberculosis which was nearly the death of him. The price he had to pay was that of his rugby career.

He was confined to a sanatorium for 19 months as part of his recovery. He survived the disease at a time when so many didn't. It was there he began the journey of a lifetime by commentating on in-house table tennis competitions for the hospital radio.

Six years later, he made his Five Nations debut, covering Scotland against Wales for BBC Radio, the very same two countries he would cover in his last commentary, 49 years later.

Another half-dozen years on, Bill was able to move into the space vacated by Cliff Morgan at BBC television. At the time, Cliff was so valuable to the BBC, as a name, that they wanted him on the management side of the department. He made the adjustment. Bill made the move from radio to television.

In a world where there was a lot of competition for recognition, Bill wasn't interested in a high profile. He was loyal, very loyal. When people asked why he didn't travel on the Lions tours, he had a reasonable explanation. When he was ill just after World War II, he was in the early days of his marriage to Bette, a charming lady, and in his early days as a teacher. The Scotland

Education Authority (SEA) continued to pay him in his absence. This made a deep and lasting impression on Bill. The BBC wanted him to develop his career as television started to take over. This would require Bill to end his teaching career. He would not do it, out of loyalty to the SEA for what they had done for him. That was the way he viewed life.

$$\bullet\bullet\bullet\bullet\bullet$$

First of all, Bill had this integrity that, no matter what he wangled out of players, whether appropriate or not, it would never be used against the sources. He respected the fact that they gave him their time. He always avoided controversy. The last thing he wanted to do was cause players trouble.

He also had a charming way of disarming players so that he could extract information. He would always have, in his coat pocket, a little tin containing round mints which he called his 'Hawick Balls'.

"Would you like a Hawick Ball?"

"Oh, okay."

"I just wanted to ask you a few questions, if you don't mind."

"Sure. No problem," said the player, through his mint-smelling breath.

You could say that Bill retrieved information from players as if taking candy from babies by giving them exactly that – candy.

He was always very generous in passing on information. His son-in-law, Alan Lawson, played at scrum-half for Scotland, perhaps finishing out the playing journey denied to Bill by his life-threatening illness. The rugby lineage lives on today through two of his grandchildren, Gloucester and Scotland scrum-half, Rory Lawson, and Edinburgh wing, Jim Thompson, coincidentally the son of Channel 4 Racing commentator, Derek Thompson. What a remarkable legacy.

Bill always brought his Hawick Balls with him wherever he went. I remember meeting him in South Africa at the Rugby World Cup in 1995. His wife, Bette, was at his side.

"I suppose you still have those Hawick Balls," I said, as a conversation opener.

"Just hold on!"

The hand disappeared inside his pocket.

"Will you have one?"

As he became established as 'The Voice of Rugby', people – players, coaches and supporters – were only too delighted to share time and information with him.

In those days, the Irish team had an end-of-week run-out at Greystones rugby club in Wicklow. Bill would have been booked into Jury's Hotel, beside Lansdowne Road, with the sizable BBC party. I would pick him up from the hotel and drive him out in my Renault 16.

"Now, none of this Ferrari, Le Mans, Grand Prix stuff, Cogley. Just get me there safely."

Sometimes, on my way to Cork or Limerick for a match, I would collect him and a few others, like Jim Sherwin or Tom Rooney, and regale them with the latest anecdotes about people. Some familiar, some not. Some true, some false. He would take out his notebook and scribble down the punch lines in what he called his 'Book of Irish Jokes'.

Apparently, when he was giving classes in school the following Monday, he would take out this notebook and start laughing in the middle of the lesson. When he went to retell the stories, alas, he would forget the beginning of the yarn, only remembering the punch line. It used to kill him. A punch line is little use without the proper preamble.

For all the laughs, come the stroke of two o'clock in the afternoon, Bill would be gone. He would be updating his notes. His charts for a commentary were akin to a work of art in their own way for the amount of research and detail that went into them.

There is an old adage – 'the best ad-libs are the ones you rehearse'. It would be true to say Bill put an inordinate amount of hours into his preparations. He would have had a library of statistics or facts in his head to do with players, rivalries between countries or the history of venerable old stadiums that he could pluck out at any given time during the course of a match.

He wouldn't bring them out at every opportunity. He was very aware of not over-crowding his commentary with too much detail. I have never heard a quote of his that was in any way inappropriate. It was always lyrical, poetic, incisive and entertaining. We had some great times over the years and all over the world.

• • • • •

Bill took over from Cliff Morgan and Peter West on BBC TV as the voice of rugby in the way that Peter O'Sullevan was the voice of racing. David Coleman was at the forefront in athletics. In terms of rugby, there was no one to match Bill for his style and the staggering preparation he put in. He used all these little humorous anecdotes. Still, what he would use in the course of a match was only a fraction of what he had prepared for each and every game. Of course, the surplus information could be stored away for use the next time, or in a different context.

The players respected him greatly because of his impartiality and his interest in the game. He never got involved in the cheapness that is part and parcel of so much of the reportage of matches these days. Fortunately, it hasn't crept into broadcasting in the same way it has into the print media.

Criticisms of television commentators tend to be 'he's talking too much'. Bill McLaren talked endlessly. But what he was saying was interesting. Viewers stayed connected. It is those who keep repeating themselves or who state the obvious, who are accused of speaking too much.

Chapter 36

'LA VILLE DE PARIS'

Bord Gais was the sponsor of the League of Ireland for a spell in the 1970s. The semi-state company ran a golf competition for the soccer writers, spread over the course of each season. It was a way of improving communication between the sponsor and the journalists. I wrote about soccer for *The Sunday Telegraph* and maintained my membership of the Irish Soccer Writers' Association for several years.

There were about six outings. There was an aggregate, overall prize. I happened to win it at Rathsallagh Golf Club, just outside Castledermot. It was a most unusual trophy. It was a very big replica of a 'tall ship'. My wife wasn't too impressed when I arrived home with what she described as a 'dust catcher'. It was one of my better golfing achievements, if not the only one. And the prize did look well on the sideboard at home.

When I retired from RTE in 1999, Madeleine and I, and two of our best friends, Tom and Stephanie Graham, decided to go on a world tour to celebrate my retirement and their good health – Tom had recovered from being ill for a while.

Off we went. In Australia, Stephanie, who had been part of the Irish Ladies' Hockey team that played in the International Conference there, had to renew long-standing acquaintances. While there, we went to the Melbourne Cricket Ground to find the seat Stephanie occupied when Ronnie Delany won the 1,500 metres at the Olympics. What a nostalgic moment that was. It took me right back to that morning in 1956 when I screamed out in delight, skipped out the door, hopped on my bicycle and raced to the *Evening Herald* for the adrenaline rush that breaking news can bring.

When we arrived in Perth, Stephanie met an old friend, Betty Foster, who was very hospitable to us in our time there, showing us the sights. Some years later, Betty embarked on a tour of Ireland and Great Britain. We endeavoured to return the favour she had granted to us by making her visit to Dublin a memorable one.

Betty's big target was to find some representation of The Battle of Trafalgar because her husband's family had been part of the British navy at the time. Her husband's grandfather had been master of one of the ships. She was searching for memorabilia or paintings of the ship. She was planning to search the British Museum for anything connected with his career.

One evening, we were chatting about this over dinner at our house. In the background was the ship I had proudly presented to Madeleine as my great golf prize years previously.

"Betty, is the ship you are looking for anything like that one up on the sideboard?" I asked.

"Yes, it would look very like that. What is the name of that ship?"

"I haven't a clue. Would you believe it? I have never looked."

"Do you mind if I have a look at it?"

"Not at all."

Betty got up and walked over to the replica ship. There was a long pause.

"You are not going to believe this? The name on this tag is 'Le Ville de Paris'. It was the French flagship at The Battle of Trafalgar. When it was captured, the captaincy was transferred to one of the captains of the British fleet. The captain who took over the ship was my husband's grandfather."

Betty had travelled all over the world looking for something that was residing in our dining room. We all looked at each other in astonished silence.

Of course, my buddy Tom Graham broke the stillness.

"It must be fate. Why don't you give it to her?"

Madeleine was quick in support.

"That is a great idea."

"Are you serious?" said Betty.

"Sure. Oh, sure. Fred doesn't mind, do you," said Madeleine.

"No. Not at all," I responded, less than enthusiastically.

My greatest golf prize was taken away and it is now resting appropriately in Betty's home in Perth, Western Australia.

Chapter 37

AUGUSTA

On the occasion of my 70th birthday, Niall, my son, and Tim O'Connor got together and used their contacts at the US Masters in Augusta, Georgia, to arrange for media accreditation for yours truly in 2004. It was always one of those sporting ambitions of mine. Not only that, they entered me for the media day draw, the winners of which would be invited to play the course on the Monday after The Masters.

There are a limited number of journalists allowed to play the course. My name was drawn out of the hat and I was invited to play. I couldn't believe my luck. The only spanner in the works was the weather. In previous years, Johnny Redmond, formerly of *The Irish Press*, won the same privilege. He bought a new set of clubs, new gear, arrived at Augusta only for the dastardly weather to ruin his dream. It was called off. He never got to play the course.

There was rain forecast for the Sunday night of The Masters. It duly arrived a few hours after Phil Mickelson's first Major win. A deluge, you would call it. I drove into the club car park on Monday morning feeling downcast about the forecast. I need not have worried. A drying wind took care of my fears. The rain stopped and the course was deemed to be playable.

To honour the occasion, I asked for a separate scorecard to keep as a souvenir.

"Sorry. No can do. One card per player! One pencil per player!"

Each day had its own individual scorecard. The club was precious about its image. There was a fear that the cards could be hocked as memorabilia.

From a personal point of view, it was my day at Wembley. I played with two men from Norwegian television and one from South Africa, a man named Naas. It turned out to be Naas Botha, the great out-half, who would have been world-renowned when he was in his pomp were it not for the Springboks' exclusion from international rugby due to Apartheid.

Based on the Stableford system, I scored 32 points, which started with a fluky par at the first hole. Augusta has a special quality built up over the years from the umbilical link to designer Bobby Jones and the players that have worn the green jacket, like six-time winner Jack Nicklaus and four-time champions Arnold Palmer and Tiger Woods, and for the fact that it is the only course on which a Major is played every year. Each hole has its own historical significance. It defines that beautifully alluring word – mystique.

• • • • •

While Augusta was an opportunity to realise a dream, the one constant in my golfing life has been the presence of the picturesque Grange golf club, just past Rathfarnham, in the foothills of the Dublin mountains, a lovely spot for an afternoon's play, so close to the city. It really is a place where you can get away from it all. It has been both a playground and a sanctuary for me since I became a member in 1968. The course places a strong emphasis on accuracy and delicacy for those who want to tame it. Of the many marvellous parklands courses, the Grange would rank as one of the most enjoyable to play, if not one of the most difficult.

In fact, I had the honour of playing with Tony Jacklin at one of Cecil Whelan's charity Pro-Ams out at Grange. It was another joyous occasion. Tony proved to be a gracious playing partner. At one point, he rifled his drive way, way down the fairway. There were a few spectators watching.

One voice boomed out.

"Gee, I've never seen anyone hit a golf ball as far as that."

"Ah, yeah, the older I get the further I used to hit them," chuckled Jacklin.

• • • • •

Years earlier, I played with Max Faulkner, the 1951 British Open champion, at Woodbrook in another Pro-Am. Few achieved the status of Max as a world-class player. He was father-in-law to Brian Barnes. He was an old-style professional, one of the top players on the European circuit in those days. We came to a particular hole. It was a relatively short par 4 with a right-angle approach to the green.

I hit my second shot. It came off the edge of the blade and flew across the green and straight into a field of nettles and briars and muck and dirt. It was a team event. As far as I was concerned, the ball was lost. I was slightly embarrassed in front of Max. We walked to the green.

"Okay lads, it is a lost ball. I'm out of this hole."

But Max ignored me. He climbed over a fence and went into the undergrowth in search of the ball.

"Max, don't worry about it. It's lost," I said.

"No, no! A ball is a ball."

The courtesy of the man! He came from a generation who grew up in hard times, where to waste anything was a sin. But that is not why he did it. He did it because that is what professionals did back then. It was another lesson. The bigger you are the nicer you should be.

• • • • •

I was down at a Pro-Am event that preceded the Kerrygold professional tournament at Waterville, in Kerry, in the late 1970s. Bob Hope was playing. He was into his 70s at the time.

Waterville could be beautiful one day, brutal the next. The day of the Pro-Am came. The wind was blowing and the rain had swept in. It was anything but hospitable. We were standing on a hill overlooking a valley. The club had given Bob Hope a buggy for the day. He was out there, hacking away in the wind and rain.

This lad beside me, Bobby Browne, was a young Irish professional at the time. He could be very serious. Bob Hope stepped out of the buggy and, after a few practise swings, let fly at the ball.

"Isn't he fantastic at his age to fulfil his obligation to play despite this weather?" I said.

"Ah, yeah, but did you notice the way he allows the left side to collapse on the back swing?"

Bobby went on to become a keen golf teacher to young and aspiring players out in Laytown and Bettystown Golf Club, dedicating a lifetime to encouraging generations of youngsters to learn the values and joys of the sport. You could see why.

• • • • •

Every time an athlete wins a medal, or a team celebrates a championship, the politicians seem to appear at their shoulders to claim credit, even though most of the athletes or sportsmen had to go abroad to achieve their goals. The sight of Charlie Haughey suddenly sharing the podium with 1987 Tour de France winner, Stephen Roche, springs to mind.

The Irish Sports Council has made an effort to provide support to sportspersons. But it is peanuts compared to what is actually required to sustain a lifestyle and make our best sportsmen and women competitive on the international stages. We have been poor supporters of the very activities that could help cut down costs in other areas. We wouldn't need the same level of medical care if the young kids in Ireland were given the right opportunity to play their way into fitness.

Obesity and diabetes have developed exponentially in this country at the same time that the very activities that would have limited these diseases have not received the requisite financial support. I know these are unprecedented times. The country is suffering. We should do everything we can to ease the pain. Sport hasn't been given the attention it deserves. The provision of facilities does help to give children, who have a talent in that direction, a basis for realising potential. It develops the expression of that talent. In America, for instance, basketball, baseball and American football, have offered a way out of the ghetto.

There are also grave faults in sport. Sometimes the machinations of the people behind the scenes in sports, like professional boxing, give a very bad impression of what it should be about. Enormous sums of money were generated by boxers who were used up and/or abused by promoters, managers and agents only to wither away in poverty once their gift had deteriorated. How much of Muhammad Ali's current illness was aggravated by his experiences in the ring I don't know. I am not a medical person. I suspect much of it.

Chapter 38

PAT RUDDY

Pat Ruddy had a dream.

In 1957, he came to hear how two Americans, Jack Burke and Jimmy Demaret, had sculpted The Champions Golf Club out of their sheer bloody-mindedness and the beautiful terrain in Houston, Texas. It was a world away. It may as well have been another planet for a ten-year-old boy sitting on a seat in the primary school of the tiny village of Ballymote, in County Sligo.

As a ten-year-old, Pat was already stealing time with his father, Sid, the local postmaster, as they motored away to Rosses Point golf club in the clapped-out old family Ford Anglia. The pessimism and restrictions of winter gave way to the optimism of golf days in the spring afternoons. A love of the game was stored up to last a lifetime.

Pat knew he wanted to make Burke and Demaret's dream his. It was way back then he first imagined creating a golf course. It took him 35 years to make it happen. I guess the longest journeys can be the most rewarding.

He spent half a lifetime visualising the possibilities of undulating fairways, natural bunker bowls and the shaping of perfectly prepared greens. For most, the dream remains just that, alive only in imagination. Here was a man who dreamed the dream into an obsession so strong it became his first thought when his eyes opened in the morning, his last when they closed at night.

I was not to know, when we first crossed paths at the *Evening Herald* in the 1960s, that this was a most remarkable man. He had a crazy notion that he would create his own golf club on a piece of land somewhere in Ireland. He drove the highways and byways in search of this dream. Golf was his passion; a golf course his pursuit.

• • • • •

Apart from his dreams, he became a respected writer, particularly on Irish amateur golf, publishing his own golf magazine and contributing to The Independent Group as a columnist. Gradually, he got immersed into the sport and business ends of golf. He was considered by many, including myself, to be slightly eccentric as a young man with the responsibility for a wife, Bernardine, and four young children, who scorned the security of a steady living to follow his own path. It is credit to Bernardine that she shared in his ambition or, at least, allowed him the luxury to follow it.

Pat decided he was going to build a golf course in the West of Ireland, many miles from anywhere. There is always a 'knocker' for any project and they were lining up all the way to the corner of Henry Street and O'Connell Street for this one. It was seen as a touch of madness. Anyway, he scarpered off to Sligo in the mid-1970s to embark on a dream that would not materialise – not then anyway.

The Sligo project was a learning process that threw many curve balls in Pat's direction. The endgame arrived when a river burst its bank to flood the plains then intended to be developed into a golf course. He would later recount this trying experience in his book, *Fifty Years In A Bunker: The Creation of a World Top-100 Golf Links at The European Club*.

Even then, he failed to forsake his sense of humour, recounting how a farmer down the road 'stole' or borrowed his brand new tractor one day.

"There were many challenging moments, like the day when one of our brand new tractors went missing. It took three days of driving around in ever-decreasing circles to find it parked outside a farmhouse, 10 miles away," he wrote in his book.

A conversation ensued.

"I think that is my tractor out in your yard?"

"It could be. I borrowed it."

"I would like you to leave it back now."

"I'm not finished with it yet."

With a little persuasion, he left it back real fast!

• • • • •

Pat held tight to the dream. Thereafter, I lost contact with him. He was going one way, I the other, only occasionally crossing his path at a function or golf-related event where he would share the latest update. The West of Ireland project hadn't worked out. But he was involved in two new projects for new courses, one called Druid's Glen, with the late, great amateur golfer, Tom Craddock, the other, St Margaret's, out near Dublin Airport. His reputation was growing in the industry. This was no fly-by-night.

His enthusiasm and his work ethic were infectious. He educated himself about the various strands of golf design and made an impact through sheer personal drive and ambition. He was a perfectionist and innovator. Through all of this, he craved his own golf course and, eventually, he built the remarkable European Golf Club from nothing into what is generally considered around the globe as a world-class course.

• • • • •

In 1984, Pat took off on a helicopter survey to unearth any prime locations on which to create a major new golf links. He came across the ideal stretch of sand dunes at Brittas Bay, pitched on the Irish Sea, 35 miles south of Dublin.

He waited with the patience of a saint for two years until this piece of paradise, disguised as low-value scrub land, came up for sale at The Abbey Hotel in Wicklow town. To finance the purchase of 300 acres of links land, between Wicklow and Arklow, he sold his car, remortgaged his house, cashed-in an insurance policy and waited with bated breath on confirmation of a bank loan.

"Listen, I have to know now," Ruddy pleaded to his loan officer over the phone on the day of the auction.

The banker could not confirm.

"We'll call you tomorrow," came the reply.

The land was not that valuable in a strictly agricultural sense. But there were a few local farmers who wanted to bid on it in sub-divided, individual plots as a grazing area for sheep. It turned out Pat was the only bidder who wanted to buy the entire parcel of land.

Ruddy was a golfer, not a gambler. But this was the moment he had been waiting for and he made his bid in lieu of the banker's decision. The bid was accepted and the banker was back with good news the next day.

In the meantime, there was more in it than Pat really wanted, so he approached the local farmers and offered to sell them plots. They ended up with a good deal for what they wanted and Pat ended up paying less than he expected for what he needed. Everyone was happy – even the bank manager.

We heard in the RTE office:

"Did you hear Pat Ruddy bought half the Irish Sea?"

We all knew so much that we knew nothing.

Between the hoppin' and the trottin', Pat and Gerry, his son, started out with one 20-tonne Volvo dump truck and a JCB excavator and built 90 per cent of the course themselves, adding two additional holes (both par 3s) just for fun, making a total of 20 instead of the usual 18.

He pushed the sand dunes from one side to the other. He sculpted the land into the shape he had imagined in his head for 30 years. You could say he was at the coalface. He built a little shed, like a Portakabin, where he would often eat and sleep.

On one occasion, Madeleine and I were on our way down to Wexford in the late 1980s. I explained the lengths to which Pat went to get this project up and running and how intrigued I was to see how it was progressing. So we stopped by.

All I really knew at the time was that Pat Ruddy was driving a digger around Brittas Bay.

Pat, as ever, had a pot of tea going in the shed.

"I would love to show you around some of the land. Would you like to see it?" he said.

"We would. We would."

We walked outside and piled into his beaten-up, old Nissan Bluebird which didn't appear to have any springs left. That didn't bother him even if it did bother my backside. He took off on what was one of the scariest drives of my life, speeding up and down the sand-based rolling hills like a roller coaster ride, all the time showing a schoolboy's enthusiasm for what he was making. We were swept along with him.

"This is where the third green will be," he said, as we accelerated over a blind hill. "And the fourth tee will be over there."

We were too busy trying to see where we were going and how we could survive the drive to fully comprehend his vision. By the end, we made our escape in case we were handed a shovel. Even then, my impression was one of awe at how much he had achieved.

Pat had to overcome numerous physical, financial and psychological obstacles, breaking his left foot three different times dismounting from machinery and withstanding the petitioning of local environmentalists to the European Union to stop the project.

The European Club opened on St Stephen's Day in 1992. It has since been placed in Ireland's Top-5, Great Britain and Ireland's Top-25 and the World's Top-100 golf clubs in various ratings. It has often been included, on international rankings, in the Top-6 golf courses in Ireland beside Portmarnock, Lahinch, Royal Portrush, Ballybunion and Royal County Down.

I would certainly include it as one of my two favourite courses from those I have played. The experience of playing at Augusta is something that lives in the memory. It is a sensational, parkland course. It has that 'wow' aspect formed out of sheer beauty and the historical significance of The Masters. My friends tend to cover their ears when it is mentioned for fear that I will remind them 'again' of that great experience.

The European Club is a more personal favourite. I still shake my head in disbelief when I stand on the 12th hole there and look out at the Irish Sea with one thought in my mind: "I know the guy that built this out of wasteland. He was one of us – a journalist – an ordinary Joe Soap, who would not be denied his dream."

In 2000, an amalgamation of twelve publications, spearheaded by America's Golf Magazine, listed the 500 Greatest Holes in the World. The European supplied three, the Par-5 thirteenth, the Par-3 fourteenth and the Par-4 seventh, which alone made the Top 100 list.

Pat Ruddy has received more than a dozen offers for the club, including a King's ransom of €40 million. They have all been turned down. What was once a dream is now 'A Family Treasure'.

Chapter 39

MY FAVOURITE TRIES

A lifetime in broadcasting and journalism has been signposted by the good and great moments in sport. It is the attritional nature of rugby that has made the greatest impact on a commentator in thrall to our heroes in green. From my days at St Mary's College, onto the train to Belfast for the 1948 Grand Slam and from the armchair of my home in Rathfarnham in 2009, there have been many abiding memories. I have set out my ten favourite Ireland tries, not necessarily the best, but those which have been embedded forever.

1. BARNEY MULLAN – Ireland 6 Wales 3, Ravenhill, March 13, 1948.

The most memorable, earliest try was when Ireland won the Triple Crown and Grand Slam in Belfast, in 1948. I was a schoolboy at the time. I distinctly remember the first try Ireland scored by Barney Mullan.

It was one of the great explosions of excitement. It was a miserable day. It had been raining. It was bitingly cold. Nonetheless, we paid little attention to this minor distraction as the ball was flashed across the three-quarter line to Barney Mullan on the left wing. He was a burly sort of lad, not a big man. He wasn't your typical lean, flying machine.

As you went into Ravenhill at the pavilion end, we were at the far end, diagonally across. We could see the overlap. We could see how it was developing. It came out to Mullan. He was suddenly hurtling towards us. It was a moment to live in the imagination. He made it over in the corner to give Ireland the lead. The excitement was total. It is indelibly marked in my memory. I will never, ever forget it.

2. TONY O'REILLY – Ireland 5 France 24, Lansdowne Road, January 26, 1963.

O'Reilly's direct opponent, Christian Darrouy, scored three tries in the game by a totally dominant France. It was left to O'Reilly to make Ireland's only impression with a fantastic try, right out of the top drawer. He got the ball under the old East Stand, facing the entire French team.

The angle of his run, the speed of it and the momentum generated by such a big player split the French defence in two until he was hit about ten metres out by two or three covering defenders. His bulk, power and the pace at which he was travelling carried the three Frenchmen over the line to score at the posts. It was one of the few times a standing ovation was given to a player for a piece of unaided, individual brilliance. Alas, it was our only joy that day.

3. PAT CASEY – England 5 Ireland 18, Twickenham, February 8, 1964.

It was the first season of a young Mike Gibson. He was at Cambridge University at the time. He had played very well in the annual Varsity match against Oxford. His remarkable career would span fifteen seasons and a then-record 69 caps for Ireland, the last coming in the second Test against Australia in Sydney, in 1979.

This try was sparked by a sensational move from deep inside Ireland's 22. On his debut, Gibson, at out-half, started it all off. Jerry Walsh was also involved as the two men combined to sweep the play deep into the England 22 where it was given to Casey, who raced away on an arcing run to the posts.

It was the early days of RTE. Listening back to my commentary of the time, you could almost describe my reaction as hysterical. It was certainly not the sort of objective observation we had been used to from the rather more aloof or restrained – some would say professional – British commentaries. In other words, I lost the run of myself. It was a great occasion, rounded off by a great victory and an unforgettable try from Casey.

4. KEVIN FLYNN – England 12 Ireland 16, Twickenham, February 12, 1972.

The Wanderers' centre made his Ireland debut in 1959. He was exiled from international rugby from 1966 to 1972. He was brought back into the fold to make a stunning impact at 32 years of age.

Ireland were trailing towards the end of the game. They were pressing hard against a stubborn England defence. There didn't seem to be an opportunity presenting itself until, suddenly, Barry McGann, Mike Gibson and Kevin Flynn combined. A sweet shimmy by Gibson created a slight hesitation in the defence.

England's David Duckham was marking Flynn, who faded a foot or two to his left and outside the reach of Duckham as Gibson drew the defence onto him. There was a half-gap. Flynn shot through it like a bullet to score between the posts to ensure an Irish win. It created such a fuss and a hoo-ha. It was one of those moments when apparent and looming defeat was turned into glorious victory with a sensational try. I am sure Kevin Flynn has it stored inside a scrapbook somewhere in a place of high honour.

5. TOM GRACE – Ireland 10 New Zealand 10, Lansdowne Road, January 20, 1973.

This involved two kicks, the first from Barry McGann, the second from Tom Grace. The All Black No. 8, Alex Wyllie, tidied up McGann's initial grubber only for Fergus Slattery to arrive like a train and rip the ball back on the Irish side.

There was space down the blindside. Scrum-half Johnny Moloney spotted it. He went right to find Grace raiding the flank. His lofted ball over the top turned it into a foot race with half the New Zealand backline, including Grant Batty, Bruce Robertson, Bob Burgess and Bryan Williams, which Grace won just before the ball reached the dead-ball line.

To this day, I am not too sure how close it came to the dead-ball line at the Havelock Square end. It was a perfect kick and 'Gracer' raced like his predecessor on the right wing, Alan Duggan. In today's game, there would have been a Television Match Official who would have been called in to give a definitive answer as to whether the ball was in or out of play. The referee, Meirion Joseph, was happy with it. Tom was certainly happy with it.

6. GINGER McLOUGHLIN – England 15 Ireland 16, Twickenham, February 6, 1982.

The ball was moved around almost basketball-like with Ciaran Fitzgerald breaking away from a maul on the blindside. Ollie Campbell carried into the 22. He magically moved the ball inside to Fergus Slattery, getting it back immediately and palming it off to his supporting No. 8 Willie Duggan.

It was still difficult to see where the try would come from. There were so many bodies closing in on Duggan. He slipped it on to tight-head 'Ginger' McLoughlin who, as he would say himself, dragged the Irish pack with him until I could announce they were "in and over".

Out-half Campbell made an almost impossible conversion. The wind blew straight into his face. He had to curl it in from the right-hand touchline. How he managed to get it over I will never know. It was vital. There was just one point in it at the end.

I had seen Ginger with the ball just fractionally before Ireland got to the line. Otherwise, everyone was totally obscured from view. As soon as they went over, I was luckily able to call out Ginger's name. Eventually, he emerged with the ball. I certainly hope he has that squirrelled away at home. He deserved that match ball. That try always comes to mind every time I see Twickenham.

7. TREVOR RINGLAND – Scotland 15 Ireland 18, Murrayfield, February 2, 1985.

This was a perfect tribute to coach Mick Doyle's creative style of rugby, which was new to Ireland. 'Doyler' had to take some flak for parachuting Paul Dean into out-half when he had established himself as a centre. Doyle had also handed the kicking responsibility to centre Michael Kiernan, a man not well-known for his expertise from placed balls. It was a gamble that could have gone horribly wrong.

The try most symbolic of this change of approach from the forward-oriented Triple Crown-winning side of 1982 was symbolised by Dean's soft hands and, in a way, his sub-standard kicking. He was picked to run the ball.

It seemed the entire Irish three-quarter line was involved in this wonder try. It came out from Michael Bradley to Dean. The loop with Michael Kiernan sparked the move. On return of the ball, Dean straightened the line, which was one of his greatest strengths. From there, the perfectly timed passes through Hugo McNeill and Kiernan gave Ringland enough room for manoeuvre on the outside to make it into the right corner.

Usually, the out-half has a tendency to run slightly across the field and, if he is in the move twice, as Dean was, there is rarely space to exploit by the time the ball reaches the wing. What is now taken for granted as Leinster's trademark wraparound move latterly imported from Australia was, in fact, born in that moment.

8. KEITH CROSSAN – Wales 9 Ireland 21, Cardiff Arms Park, March 16, 1985.

This was another one of those lovely movements that became typical of Mick Doyle's reign. Again, it was all about the injection of pace. Michael Bradley, Paul Dean and Brendan Mullin all played their part in moving the ball simply, quickly from right to left. It all hinged on a subtle, superbly timed short ball from Michael Kiernan to the full-back Hugo McNeill, who came into the line bursting through a gap in the midfield. It was good positive straight running and quick passing that ended with McNeill sucking in Wales full-back Mark Wyatt for the left wing flyer Keith Crossan to be propelled by his speed and low centre of gravity to the posts.

9. BRENDAN MULLIN – Ireland 13 England 10, Lansdowne Road, March 30, 1985.

While all of those were spectacular in their own way, there was another, not so wonderful one, which has stayed resolutely fixed in my mind. It was vital for its effect on the history of the game here.

It was Lansdowne Road again. It was England again. It effectively won the Triple Crown for the second time in four seasons and the Five Nations

Championship.

The English were frustrating us. We didn't seem to be on our game. They were able to use their big forwards to clamp down on us. We looked like getting a draw, at best, which would have been a terrible anti-climax.

The try came from the Irish pack scattering the English at a lineout. The disruption enabled Michael Bradley to provide Paul Dean with the time to hoof the ball straight down the field. The English full-back Chris Martin bent down and gathered the ball. He seemed to have plenty of time.

It looked like a basic tidy-up job. Martin misjudged the searing pace of Mullin, who, virtually alone of the Irish players, refused to give up a lost cause. He chased with everything he had. Martin dwelt a tad too long on his clearance. He didn't lift his head to see what was in front of him. He kept his eye on the ball, but not his surroundings. Mullin was closing in on him. As Martin put boot to ball, Mullin smothered the kick. It could have gone anywhere. Fortunately, it bounced kindly for Brendan and his momentum took him onto the loose ball for the try that kept Ireland in touch before Michael Kiernan's drop goal won the Triple Crown.

In setting up that vital score, I remember thinking this could be our last chance as Donal Lenihan took the ball into the England 22. The ball came back. I looked out across the pitch to see a clear overlap on the right. They could have scored in the far corner. Instead, I saw Michael slipping back for a drop at goal. If he skewed the kick, it would have been a disaster. Don't forget, this wasn't the easy execution it is today. The Gilbert balls were more round than the pointed balls of today. He had it all worked out. He hit it absolutely plum. It sailed over. Sensational. His name is written large in history for that one swing of his boot.

10. GORDON HAMILTON – Ireland 18 Australia 19, Lansdowne Road, October 20, 1991.

The thing I remember most about this one is that I was sitting up in the commentary box. I wasn't working. We had mixed and matched our broadcasting teams. George Hamilton, no relation to Gordon, was doing the game.

The commentary position in the old Lansdowne Road was probably the best in the world of rugby. It was close to the pitch. It wasn't too high. You got a great overall perspective of the game. The only problem was the low ceiling in the room. You had to crouch to get into the position. Once there, you were fine. But, if you stood up sharply, you were in danger of meeting the concrete ceiling. People often say I started my career with a full head of hair and it was all scraped off by the low ceiling at Lansdowne Road.

There were three points in it with five minutes left to play. The ball was moved from inside Ireland's half. It was kicked through under severe pressure for Jack Clarke to get the better of David Campese, who had scored two tries that day. Jack plucked the ball up and found Gordon Hamilton coming through at top speed. The flanker just about made the line, rolled over, sat up and jabbed his right hand into the air. There was bedlam at the old ground and George Hamilton, in his excitement, lost all control of himself, like any good professional would, jumped up and smashed his head off the ceiling. The scream of ecstasy was replaced by one of piercing pain. He was almost knocked out. Not only did he nearly lose his voice, he nearly lost his head. Thankfully, he was able to continue and dealt with the agonising climax of Michael Lynagh's try as professionally as always.

The awful disappointment of Michael Lynagh's immediate riposte was shattering. I will never know why we didn't simply gather the kick-off and send the ball spiralling out over the East Stand. It was one of those things. A cool head was needed in a time of frenzy. And there wasn't one available. The ball was kept alive and Lynagh killed us in the corner. Our dream of a semi-final back at Lansdowne was wiped away.

Chapter 40

MY ALL-TIME IRELAND TEAM

"This is the article that triggered the suggestion for Fred to embark on his memoir. It is a piece that came about purely by chance, or destiny, depending on your view on life. I was fated to land in a seat beside Fred Cogley, the former RTE broadcaster, a man I had seen on television through the 1970s and 1980s, a man I had never met, high in the press box of Croke Park just before Ireland mounted a late Brian O'Driscoll-inspired comeback to draw 20-all with Australia on Sunday afternoon, November 15, 2009.

I couldn't resist listening in on one or two sage-scented yarns shared between Fred and Sean Diffley. It left me with one singular thought: I would love to hear more of this.

When he turned in my direction, a convivial conversation started and expanded. There was the sense that this was a man with a treasure trove of stories stored up from a lifetime inside and outside broadcasting.

It took more than one meeting to get Fred to agree to this project. There were no promises, no expectations, no pre-agreed contract to publish, just the simple process of reviving memories, listening-and-taping over the length of a series of meetings."

Des Berry, Monday, January 16, 2012.

Evening Herald, Wednesday, December 23, 2009.

Fred Cogley is a man of many memories spread over the length of 60 years in journalism and broadcasting.

He was the voice of rugby on RTE for a generation of Irish people who revelled in the excitement of the Triple Crowns inspired by the dead-eye shooting of Ollie Campbell in 1982 and the 'give it a lash' call to action of Ireland coach Mick Doyle in 1985.

His eyes have scanned a lifetime in rugby. His lips have moulded a million words for those that could not make it to the stadiums of the world. For so long, he was our man at the match, wherever it was.

The impartiality of a commentator is something to be admired. He must hold his tongue when others would simply lash it. He must ooze objectivity when others are eaten up by the injustice of a bad decision or foul play.

Of course, there must have been many times when he would have preferred to give his opinion rather than a running commentary. He has seen many Ireland teams, good, average and worse, and he has fallen in thrall to some of the players that have graced his life, as he has theirs.

He had always seen Mike Gibson as the greatest Irish player. This opinion, once set in cement, has gradually been challenged by the consistent brilliance of Ireland's current captain, Brian O'Driscoll.

"At this point, if I had to choose between the two of them, I would go for Brian O'Driscoll as a player and as a captain for Ireland and The Lions. He is, in my estimation, Ireland's greatest ever," said Cogley.

Beside this, Cogley gives his opinion on what he sees as the greatest Ireland players, for each position, of all time.

15. TOM KIERNAN – Cork Constitution and Munster (54 caps, 1960-1973).

Honourable Mentions: Hugo McNeill, George Norton, Rodney O'Donnell, Robert Kearney.

Tommy Kiernan would come into my mind because of his fantastically long reign at full-back for Ireland.

He also captained the Lions (1968 in South Africa). Those were different days. He played at a time when the full-back was just starting to come into the line.

The role has changed so much since then. (Robert) Kearney is such a spectacular catcher-runner of the ball. Hugo McNeill was somewhere in between the both of them in terms of style. Before Kiernan, there was George Norton, another solid full-back.

I would give it to Kiernan.

14. TREVOR RINGLAND - Ballymena and Ulster (34 caps, 1981-1988).

Honourable Mentions: Tommy Bowe, Mick Lane, Tom Grace, Simon Geoghegan, Bertie O'Hanlon, Alan Duggan.

Trevor had strength and aggression in the tackle, as well as pace and strength – a great finisher. He scored some great tries, none more so than that great one against Scotland in Murrayfield in 1985.

The whole backline was involved in that movement. It began with Paul Dean on a loop move. The ball was swept out to Ringland, on the right wing. There were still 15 yards of space between him and the touchline because of how Dean had straightened the line.

Bertie O'Hanlon had other qualities in a three-quarter line that seldom moved the ball wide, foremost among them being his capacity in following up, never ever failing to nail the opposing player in possession.

Simon Geoghegan was another super player. He would have made my number one, even though he played a lot of his rugby for Ireland on the left, if he had enjoyed a few more years free of injury. He was starved of possession, but, then again, so were so many Irish wingers down the years. We had so many great players who never really had the chance to shine.

So, I go for Trevor Ringland.

13. BRIAN O'DRISCOLL – UCD and Leinster (117 caps*, 1999-).

Honourable Mentions: Noel Henderson, Brendan Mullin, Luke Fitzgerald.

I don't think you can consider anyone else coming close to him. If he is the outstanding Irish player of all time, in my opinion, over Mike Gibson, he has to be automatic at outside centre.

I actually considered Luke Fitzgerald as a centre, where he could, possibly, succeed his captain. He is so exciting to watch. He has that burst of acceleration from a standing start.

Similar to Kyle, O'Driscoll has the aura. Your eye is drawn to this guy. He is always in position to receive the ball. When he does, he has the facility, the magic, to make something happen.

When a tackle is required, he is the one to put it in (like he did to Zane Kirchner in the last seconds against South Africa). Not only is he the one to make the tackle, he is back on his feet to play the ball.

Apart from all his tries, all his attacking prowess, his complete defensive mastery, he also has, what Gibson didn't have, the capacity to captain the side without any apparent effect on his own game.

He is a leader, a captain and should have been, without any doubt, named the World Player of the Year.

12. MIKE GIBSON – Cambridge University, NIFC and Ulster (69 caps, 1964-1979).

Honourable Mentions: Paul Dean, Paddy Reid, Kevin Flynn, Michael Kiernan, Jerry Walsh, Davy Hewitt.

Scottish commentator Bill McLaren always spoke of Gibson as the greatest player of all time. He would have been close to a lot of the Scottish and great Welsh players of the 1970s. For him to say that was a huge tribute. I would go along with Bill in that Gibson was great.

He never won a Grand Slam even though he played in some of Ireland's greatest teams. There was the team of 1972, with a huge battalion of Lions, who managed wins in Paris and Twickenham only to be denied a shot at the Grand Slam when Scotland and Wales refused to travel to Dublin in that year.

Notwithstanding that, Gibson would have to be in any rugby team of legends.

11. A.J.F. O'REILLY – Old Belvedere and Leinster (29 caps, 1955-1970).

Honourable Mentions: Keith Crossan, Barney Mullan, Moss Finn.

Tony O'Reilly would have been a devastating wing in the current Ireland side. He liked to play in the centre because he felt he might see the ball now and again with an Irish backline that never got so little ball.

But, in midfield, he managed to stray off-side and so he was at his best on the wing, capitalising on any space quick possession would create. On the Lions tours he was simply legendary.

He was very athletic. He was a big man, like a Jonah Lomu of the time. He had that size and strength. He might even have been faster than Lomu. He was just very intimidating.

Even as a schoolboy at Belvedere, he was doing extraordinary things. He made sensational progression as a 19-year-old to set try-scoring records on tour with the Lions.

10. JACK KYLE – Queen's University and Ireland (46 caps, 1947-1958).

Honourable Mentions: Ollie Campbell, Tony Ward, Ronan O'Gara, Barry McGann.

As far as I am concerned, Jack Kyle was the best out-half I have seen from any country. What made him special? He had all the basic elements of an international player and a magical touch on top of that.

Ollie Campbell would have shaded Kyle as a defender. They were different sort of defensive systems from those two eras. Ollie was in your face, a straight-up tackler. Kyle was a corner-flag coverer.

The wing forward did not have to bind at the scrum. So, while his open-side flanker, Jim McCarthy say, could eyeball the opposing No. 10, it allowed Kyle the option to play like an auxiliary full-back in defence. He would appear out of nowhere to save the day with a spectacular tackle.

The New Zealanders said they were certain of one thing when they played the Lions, they never knew what Kyle would do. He had that unpredictable brilliance.

9. JOHNNY MOLONEY – St Mary's College and Leinster (27 caps, 1972-1980).

Honourable Mentions: Johnny O'Meara, Roger Young, Michael Bradley, Colin Patterson.

I'd go for Johnny Moloney. He was adaptable. He played for Ireland on the wing, as well. He was a great scrum-half, possessed great pace.

He helped Ireland to some great victories, like on his debut against France at the old Stade de Colombes in Paris in 1972. That doesn't happen every day of the week.

1. RAY McLOUGHLIN – UCD and Connacht (40 caps, 1962-1975).

Honourable Mentions: Syd Millar, Tom Clifford, Phil Orr, Marcus Horan, Nick Popplewell.

How could you forget someone like the great Phil Orr or Syd Millar? Yet, Marcus

Horan was there for the Grand Slam and for so many days before it. You would also have to say Cian Healy has huge promise.

I would go for Ray McLoughlin for his attributes as a player, his technical ability and what he accomplished with the Lions, as well as what he brought as a captain.

He started captaincy as a thing of importance. It is often forgotten how he was the first captain to take preparation seriously. He put patterns into Ireland's style of play.

2. KEN KENNEDY – London Irish (45 caps, 1965-1975).

Honourable Mentions: Keith Wood, Karl Mullen, Ronnie Dawson, Ciaran Fitzgerald.

How could you split Ken Kennedy and Keith Wood? Then again, Karl Mullen was one of the great captains before McLoughlin. He was the quiet leader. It is like debating 'who was the best heavyweight in the world?' Was it (Muhammad) Ali, (Rocky) Marciano, Joe Louis? They were different types of players.

If you go on achievement, you would go for Mullen. If you go on general ability you would probably go for Kennedy. If you go for inspirational leadership, leading from the front, you would go for Wood.

I don't know. Kennedy.

3. SEAN LYNCH – St Mary's College and Leinster (17 caps, 1971-1974).

Honourable Mentions: Gordon Wood, Ginger McLoughlin, John Hayes.

Would it be any consolation to Keith if I went for his dad, Gordon Wood? Look at Ginger McLoughlin and how he pulled the entire Irish pack across the English line for that remarkable Twickenham try of 1982. John Hayes would have to be in there for his influence over the last number of years. He has been huge in every sense of the word. He is such a big man for an Irishman.

But, although he was smaller in stature, Sean Lynch was rated by the New Zealanders as one of the most awkward prop forwards they had ever faced. He was part of that team in 1972 that could have, would have, in my opinion, won the Grand Slam.

4. WILLIE JOHN McBRIDE – Ballymena and Ulster (63 caps, 1962-1975).

Honourable Mentions: Moss Keane, Donncha O'Callaghan, Robin Thompson, Gerry Culliton.

Robin Thompson was another one to captain the Lions (1955 in South Africa). Moss Keane was an inspirational character, who always gave 100%. And then there was Gerry Culliton, who could play in the front, middle and back row.

On the other hand, Bill McBride was, and is, a legendary figure in the game. It is difficult to quantify him purely as a player. I remember, for one international, we decided to send a camera out to follow McBride's contribution, his work in the scrum, lineout, around the pitch.

He got the ball twice in the entire match. He was there. He was involved. But he handled the ball twice. I guess it could be said that, among other things, he was a great mullicker. He did the dirty work. He was a great leader of men, which he proved as captain of the Lions (1974) in South Africa.

5. PAUL O'CONNELL – Young Munster and Munster (82 caps*, 2002-).

Honourable Mentions: Donal Lenihan, Jeremy Davidson, Bill Mulcahy, Mick Molloy.

It would have to be O'Connell for his part in the Grand Slam and his Lions' captaincy. On his day, he is fantastic. What he has done with Munster. What he has done with Ireland.

Okay, he has the odd game when he is not a dominant force. But who hasn't? His work-rate is something else, as is his aerial splendour at the lineout.

6. PHILIP MATTHEWS – Ards and Ulster (38 caps, 1984-1992)

Honourable Mentions: Mick Doyle, John O'Driscoll.

Nigel Carr and Philip Matthews were probably the best double act in Irish rugby after the McKay-McCarthy pairing in the '40s. Matthews was an intelligent man, a sensation in Ireland's 1985 Triple Crown side.

In those days, to win the Triple Crown was such a huge thing. We weren't as used to success as we are now.

Matthews' all-round ability, his work at the lineout as a ball winner, his adaptability – he had the skills to play at No. 8 as well – and his competitive edge made him a real handful for anyone.

7. FERGUS SLATTERY – Blackrock College and Leinster (61 caps, 1970-1984).

Honourable Mentions: Noel Murphy, Nigel Carr, Jim McCarthy, David Wallace.

Noel Murphy was a fantastic player. He held the dubious distinction of being knocked out by a punch in his first match for Ireland and knocked out in his last match for Ireland. In between, Noel's reputation as a world-class flanker grew and he was rewarded with the captaincy of the Irish team in the '60s, which saw the emergence of McBride and Gibson, to mention but a few.

Jim McCarthy, of course, played on the 1948 Grand Slam side and would have been similar as a player to Slattery, who was very fiery, a great competitor.

Slattery had tremendous pace for a wing forward. He actually started out as a centre at Blackrock but when he moved to the flank, he never gave an inch, never took a backward step against any opponent, no matter how intimidating.

8. KEN GOODALL – City of Derry and Ulster (19 caps, 1967-1970).

Honourable Mentions: Des O'Brien, Willie Duggan, Ronnie Kavanagh, Jamie Heaslip, Noel Mannion.

These are all so different. Ken Goodall didn't have that long a career. He went to Rugby League. He was quite light for a No. 8. What set him apart was his talent as a footballer.

One abiding memory of him was galloping through a ragged Welsh defence to score at the posts at the Lansdowne Road end in 1970 to top off a famous 14-0 victory.

Willie Duggan was not the greatest trainer. The stories are many of his indifference towards preparation. He was a revelation on the Lions tours. It was there he made his reputation because they could get him really fit. He was such a hard man.

Jamie Heaslip could go on to be one of the legends of the game, but not just at the moment. Des O'Brien was very good, but not in Goodall's class, not in Duggan's class.

Note: * denotes updated cap total at the time of article going to press.

ABOUT THE CO-AUTHOR

Des Berry has been a freelance sports journalist
for 20 years, working for Independent Newspapers and *The Irish Times* in that time. He
is currently Rugby Correspondent for the
Evening Herald. This is his first book.